FINDING SAND CREEK

ALSO BY JEROME A. GREENE

Slim Buttes, 1876: An Episode of the Great Sioux War (Norman, 1982)

Yellowstone Command: Colonel Nelson A. Miles and the Great Sioux War, 1876–1877 (Lincoln, 1991)

(ed.) *Battles and Skirmishes of the Great Sioux War, 1876–1877: The Military View* (Norman, 1993)

(ed.) *Lakota and Cheyenne: Indian Views of the Great Sioux War, 1876–1877* (Norman, 1994)

Morning Star Dawn: The Powder River Expedition and the Northern Cheyennes, 1876 (Norman, 2003)

Washita: The U.S. Army and the Southern Cheyennes, 1867–1869 (Norman, 2004)

ALSO BY DOUGLAS D. SCOTT

(with Richard A. Fox, Jr.) *Archaeological Insights into the Custer Battle: An Assessment of the 1984 Field Season* (Norman, 1987)

(with Richard A. Fox, Jr., Melissa A. Connor, and Dick Harmon) *Archaeological Perspectives on the Battle of Little Bighorn* (Norman, 1989)

(with P. Willey and Melissa A. Connor) *They Died with Custer: Soldiers' Bones from the Battle of Little Bighorn* (Norman, 1998)

FINDING SAND CREEK
HISTORY, ARCHEOLOGY, AND THE 1864 MASSACRE SITE

Jerome A. Greene
and
Douglas D. Scott

Foreword by Christine Whitacre

University of Oklahoma Press : Norman

Library of Congress Cataloging-in-Publication Data

Greene, Jerome A.
    Finding Sand Creek: history, archeology, and the 1864
massacre site / Jerome A. Greene and Douglas D. Scott;
foreword by Christine Whitacre.
        p.   cm.
    Includes bibliographical references and index.
    ISBN 0-8061-3623-5 (cloth)
    ISBN-13: 978-0-8061-3801-5 (paper)
    ISBN-10: 0-8061-3801-7 (paper)
    1. Sand Creek Massacre, Colo., 1864.   2. Cheyenne
Indians—Antiquities.   3. Arapaho Indians—Antiquities.
4. Excavations (Archaeology)—Colorado—Sand Creek
Massacre National Historic Site.   5. Sand Creek Massacre
National Historic Site (Colo.)—History.   6. Sand Creek
Massacre National Historic Site (Colo.)—Antiquities.
I. Scott, Douglas D.   II. Title.

E83.863.G74 2004
978.8004'97353—dc22

                                                    2004041286

2   3   4   5   6   7   8   9   10

To the memory of
Don G. Rickey, 1925–2000,
Historian of the American West

The site of that historic [Sand Creek] affair has not been marked. If it were possible, we, as a nation, doubtless had rather the event could be forgotten.

—Walter M. Camp,
Proceedings of the Annual Meeting and Dinner
of the Order of Indian Wars of the United States
Held January Seventeenth Nineteen Hundred and Twenty

CONTENTS

List of Illustrations   xi
List of Tables   xiii
Foreword, by Christine Whitacre   xv
Preface and Acknowledgments   xxiii

Chapter 1.   The Sand Creek Massacre   3
Chapter 2.   Historical Documentation of the Location
             and Extent of the Sand Creek Massacre Site   26
Chapter 3.   Identifying the Sand Creek Massacre Site
             through Archeological Reconnaissance   63
Chapter 4.   Postarcheology Archival Conclusions
             Regarding the Location of the
             Sand Creek Massacre Site   99

Appendices
      A.   Archeological Artifact Description and Analysis   123
      B.   J. H. Haynes Cheyenne Depredation Claim   163
      C.   Cheyenne and Arapaho Annuity Requests,
           Receipts, and Lists   165

D. Lists of Abandoned Goods Found in the Camps at Pawnee Fork, Kansas (1867); Washita River, Oklahoma (1868); and Summit Springs, Colorado (1869)   177

E. List of Known Arms and Ammunition Used by the Colorado Volunteer Cavalry   183

Notes   187
Bibliography   215
Index   235

ILLUSTRATIONS

FIGURES

1. Colonel John M. Chivington   10
2. Black Kettle and other chiefs, 1864   13
3. George Bent   34
4. Aerial photographs of Sand Creek, 1936–37   38
5. Metal detecting in the South Bend of Sand Creek, 1997   65
6. Michael McFaul explains geomorphological
core-drilling work   67
7. .58-caliber round-ball-bullet cache   75
8. Crushed and flattened tin cups from the village site   75
9. Table knives, spoons, and forks found in the village site   76
10. Fragments of small tin food graters   76
11. Top and base to a tin coffeepot or boiler   77
12. Fragments of 12-pounder spherical case shot   77
13. Iron arrowheads found in 1999   78
14. Indian tools from the village site   80
15. Hide-preparation tools recovered in 1999   81
16. Steven DeVore conducting geophysical
remote-sensing work   83

17. Civil War picket pin found in the South Bend, 1997   85
18. Fragment of trade silver found in the South Bend, 1997   85
19. Plains Indian village along a creek, ca. 1870–89   110
20. Cheyenne village showing the horseshoe arrangement
    of lodges, ca. 1880–1910   111
21. Scattered placement of tipis in a Plains Indian village,
    ca. 1880–1910   112
22. Small-arms ammunition found in the village site   125
23. 12-pounder spherical case shot with Bormann fuse   133
24. Cross-section of 12-pounder spherical case shot   134
25. Brass photograph preserver and fragment of brass dress
    shoulder scale   138
26. Buttons recovered in 1999   141
27. Indian ornaments found in 1999   143
28. Tailor's thimble and New York Militia button
    recovered in 1999   144
29. Base of a Dutch oven found in the village site   148
30. Farrier's hammer and ax found in the village site   153

MAPS

1. Sand Creek vicinity   29
2. George Bent diagram of village and Sand Creek
   Massacre site, 1905–14 (University of Colorado)   36
3. George Bent diagram of village and Sand Creek
   Massacre site, 1905–14 (Oklahoma Historical Society)   37
4. Bent-Hyde regional map 1   42
5. Bent-Hyde regional map 2   43
6. Samuel W. Bonsall map, June 1868   44
7. Archivally projected site of the Sand Creek Massacre   49
8. Troop and Indian movements, November 29, 1864   57
9. Boundary of the Sand Creek Massacre site   61
10. Archivally projected site of massacre with archeological
    overlay   100
11. Land plat of the massacre site, ca. 1938   107
12. Distribution of all 1864-era artifacts found along
    Sand Creek   108
13. Possible lodge-arrangement configurations   114

TABLES

1. Sand Creek Artifacts by Functional Category   79
2. Comparison of Known Firearms Types Used by the
   Colorado Cavalry at Sand Creek to Recovered
   Ordnance Artifacts   94
3. Multidisciplinary Team Approach   118

FOREWORD

The place was well known to all the Cheyennes and Arapahos
and they used it as a camping ground for many years.

George Bent, quoted in
Life of George Bent: Written from His Letters

Look in any direction and the view stretches out uninter-
rupted, as the old adage goes, as far as the eye can see. The
site of the Sand Creek Massacre, located in Kiowa County in
southeastern Colorado, is far from the mountains that conjure
up most popular images of the state. Gently rolling prairie
grassland, the landscape is closer to that of Kansas, which bor-
ders the county on the east. Kiowa County, with an average of
less than one person per square mile, is one of Colorado's most
rural, undeveloped areas. And on a recent visit to the Sand Creek
Massacre site, I was again impressed, as I had been so many
times during the past few years, by how it was another of the

many ironies of Sand Creek that such a profoundly peaceful
place could have been the scene of such horror. Because within
this place, along a five-mile stretch of land along a creek filled
with more sand than water, one of the most brutal events in
western history took place. And even though the physical landscape is wide open, the mental one is soon overwhelmed, for
it becomes impossible not to imagine the sounds and scenes
of November 29, 1864—the images of horse-mounted soldiers
streaming in from several directions, of surprised and terrified
Cheyenne and Arapaho villagers desperately trying to save
themselves by digging shelters in the sand, and of mutilations
and deaths, and the sounds of gunshots, howitzer fire, and
screams.

Often during the two years that I was part of the National
Park Service (NPS) project team that helped locate the Sand
Creek Massacre site, I listened to the descendants of massacre
survivors speak of the voices they heard in this place. For
them, those voices were the only proof needed to confirm that
this area was, indeed, the site of the massacre. But the govern-
mental processes for national-historic-site establishment require
more-tangible, "scientific" evidence. So in 1998, through the
efforts of Senator Ben Nighthorse Campbell, Congress passed
the Sand Creek Massacre National Historic Site Study Act,
which directed the NPS to work with the Northern Cheyenne
Tribe, the Northern Arapaho Tribe, and the Southern Cheyenne
and Arapaho Tribes of Oklahoma, as well as the Colorado
Historical Society, to verify the location of the massacre. At
that time the site was a matter of great speculation. Many
believed it took place along a section of Sand Creek referred
to as the South Bend. But although archeologists had walked
across nearly every square foot of the inside corner of that
bend, they had not found the physical proof they sought,
leading some to think that the site was elsewhere. The discussion was more than academic. The lack of consensus regarding
the massacre location hindered efforts to list the site on the

National Register of Historic Places and to respond to repeated requests by Cheyennes and Arapahos to establish a memorial at the site.

That uncertainty came to an end in May 1999, when the Sand Creek Massacre Project team completed its successful search for the site. Following months of research, the project team focused its archeological efforts on a number of areas along Sand Creek. At one site within the South Bend the crews found what they were seeking. One hundred and thirty five years after the massacre, they pulled out of the soil the shattered plates, utensils, hide scrapers, awls, and personal items that once belonged to the Cheyennes and Arapahos who were camped at Sand Creek, along with fragments of the weapons used to attack and kill them.

Jerome A. Greene and Douglas D. Scott were integral to the success of this effort. By the time they began work on the Sand Creek project, Jerry and Doug, both of whom are NPS employees, had well-deserved reputations as experts in the field of the Indian wars, as evidenced by their individual and collaborative work at Little Bighorn, Washita, and elsewhere. As the project's lead historian, Jerry examined all known historical documents—maps, diaries, firsthand accounts by Indian and military witnesses, and congressional investigative reports—that could shed light on the massacre location. The project methodology also called for this research, as well as the oral histories of Sand Creek descendants, to be completed prior to the fieldwork so that the archeologists could focus on the sites most likely to yield evidence of the event. I, among others, was initially surprised when Jerry's primary recommendation was a place approximately one mile north of the area that most people believed to be the massacre site. But his reasoning would prove to be correct. Just a few weeks afterward, an archeological survey team under lead field archeologist Doug Scott uncovered over four hundred massacre-related artifacts on the site Jerry had pinpointed.

xviiiFOREWORD

Simultaneous with Jerry's efforts, Doug Scott also prepared for the upcoming survey. He interviewed local artifact collectors and, together with other team members, examined aerial photographs, the earliest dating to the 1930s, for evidence of historical trails leading to and from the massacre site. And, upon Doug's recommendation, the NPS conducted a geomorphological assessment of Sand Creek that identified, through an analysis of soil samples, those specific landforms where 1864-era artifacts potentially could be recovered. Doug's greatest contributions, however, came in the field and his subsequent analysis of what was found. His report on the condition and distribution of the artifacts and what they tell us about what happened at Sand Creek stand at the heart of this volume. Together with Jerry's contributions and those of all the project-team members, Doug's work directly contributed to the successful effort to authorize Sand Creek as a national historic site.

During the course of the Sand Creek project, many people shared with us their hopes for the proposed national historic site. Some saw it as a place of contemplation where people of all backgrounds could come to learn from the past, to know more about the Cheyennes and Arapahos who called this land home, and to honor the victims. Many envisioned it as a healing place that could promote cross-cultural understanding. But that understanding is still more a hope than a certainty, and it must be an ongoing process. Sand Creek is a landscape filled with so much history, so much meaning, and so much pain that one does not have to scratch too deeply beneath its surface to bring forth powerful emotions. And even this book, an important work of scholarship that presents in a very straightforward manner the historical and archeological evidence that helped lead to the long-term preservation of Sand Creek, is likely to stir up such responses.

The Sand Creek project team was a complex, sometimes uneasy alliance of tribal members, property owners, and government employees. As the project's team captain, I participated in numerous meetings at which the group seemed stressed to the point of fracture. But ultimately, we would come together because, fundamentally, we shared one common goal—to verify the location of the massacre so that Congress would have the information it needed to protect and preserve this special place for future generations. And as part of that effort, the group worked extremely hard to achieve agreement upon the boundaries of the Sand Creek Massacre site as delivered to Congress and as presented within this book. But although the project team reached consensus on this, many members also made it clear that they held differing beliefs as to where exactly within those boundaries are the locations of some of the key events of the Sand Creek Massacre, including the village site.

In this book Jerry and Doug, based on historical and archeological evidence, identify the site of the Cheyenne and Arapaho village that was attacked by Colonel John Chivington's troops. While many will find that evidence compelling, it is important to know that others do not, specifically Sand Creek descendants who believe that it conflicts with oral histories and traditional tribal knowledge. It also is important to understand that the methodology for the Sand Creek project called for the evaluation of four lines of evidence: historical documentation, archeological survey, tribal oral histories, and traditional tribal knowledge. As part of their many contributions to this project, over thirty Cheyenne and Arapaho descendants of massacre survivors shared stories that had been handed down through the generations. Anyone wanting to read those oral histories and learn more about the traditional tribal knowledge of the site should refer to the final NPS report on this investigation, *Sand Creek Massacre Project, Site Location Study*, as an additional reference on the subject. Future research, including additional archeological work, may resolve some of the differing interpretations. But if the discussions surrounding these points of view are fervent, they are only that way because Sand Creek is so very important to so very many people. One of my many

wishes for the Sand Creek Massacre National Historic Site is
that it will be a place where people can learn about all these
points of view, how such views are often shaped by cultural
differences, and how diverse cultures may have different interpretations of what is evident and true. Rick Frost, who served
as the Sand Creek project manager, often commented that the
boundaries of the Sand Creek Massacre site are large enough
to accommodate more than one view of history.

My most recent visit to Sand Creek was on a cloudless,
hot August morning, and we were accompanying a group of
visitors who had never been there before. Among us was
rancher Bill Dawson, who recently sold a piece of Sand Creek
land that holds not only remains of the massacre but also remnants of the line camp once used by his grandfather, a cowboy
during the days of the open range, when cattle replaced bison
on the land. Alexa Roberts, the NPS ethnographer who helped
Cheyenne and Arapaho descendants of Sand Creek record their
oral histories, and who is now the first site manager of the
Sand Creek Massacre National Historic Site, was with us too.
Also present was Rick Frost, associate director of public affairs
for the NPS Intermountain Region, who had overall responsi-
bility for the NPS project. We wished that Barbara Sutteer,
another key member of the Sand Creek project team who
served as its Indian liaison and who has since retired from the
NPS, was with us that day, as she had been on many other
occasions. As we walked to the area where many of the massacre artifacts had been uncovered, several of us commented
on how extraordinarily beautiful the site was that day and how
tall the grasses had grown now that the land was no longer
being grazed. We pointed out to the visitors the only spot of
high ground on the landscape, the bluff from which Chivington's men first saw the village. We showed them the line of
trees that marks the otherwise barely discernible Sand Creek,
including the crucial bend of the creek that makes a ninety-
degree curve, with angles pointing north and east. And while

we stood enclosed within the angles of that bend and talked about the grasses and the view and what progress was being made on opening the site to the public, my thoughts also wandered elsewhere. I thought about what a remarkable journey we all had taken to come to this place, how meaningful Sand Creek had become in all of our lives, and how very grateful I was for the opportunity to have been part of this project.

But for none of us is the effort to protect, preserve, and memorialize the Sand Creek site more important than it is for the Cheyenne and Arapaho descendants of the massacre. I am very fortunate for having been able to know and work with the tribal members of the Sand Creek Massacre Project team: Joe Big Medicine, Eugene Black Bear Jr., Laird Cometsevah, Edward Starr Jr., and Edward White Skunk of the Southern Cheyenne Tribe; William "Lee" Pedro and Alonzo Sankey of the Southern Arapaho Tribe; Anthony A. Addison Sr., William J. C'Hair, Hubert N. Friday, Burton Hutchinson, Joseph Oldman, Ben S. Ridgely, Eugene J. Ridgely Sr., Gail J. Ridgely, and Nelson P. White Sr. of the Northern Arapaho Tribe; and Steve Brady, Luke Brady, Otto Braided Hair, Conrad Fisher, Norma Gourneau, Reginald Killsnight Sr., Lee Lonebear, Mildred Red Cherries, Holda Roundstone, and Joe Walks Along of the Northern Cheyenne Tribe. While our connection to Sand Creek is recent, Sand Creek is always with them, as it will be for their descendants. It is they who hear the voices.

CHRISTINE WHITACRE

Historian, Intermountain Support Office
National Park Service

PREFACE AND
ACKNOWLEDGMENTS

This book is the product of many people's time, interest, and endeavor. It is a reflection of their contributions and deep commitment to finding the site of the Sand Creek Massacre. For some, the journey to locate the site was intensely personal and spiritual; for all, it was a meaningful experience not soon to be forgotten. And in the end, it was the dedication of all participants to the mission at hand that brought results.

The search for the Sand Creek Massacre site in 1998–99 was a multicultural as well as multidisciplinary effort. It represented a coming together of not only members of the Cheyenne and Arapaho peoples but also professionals from several disciplines, including history, ethnography, geomorphology, remote imagery, and archeology. All brought valuable perspectives and talents to the matter at hand, and the interdisciplinary contributions enabled the process to proceed smoothly and with the maximum potential for success. While most of the site-related effort involved archival investigation

and interpretation by historians and on-site archeological examination and interpretation by archeologists, the contributions
from other fields supported this work and were manifested time
and again throughout the project. The National Park Service
Sand Creek Massacre Project team consisted of National Park
Service staff, Colorado Historical Society staff, and representatives of the Southern Cheyenne and Arapaho Tribes of Oklahoma, the Northern Cheyenne Tribe, and the Northern Arapaho Tribe. As part of the site-location process, Cheyenne and
Arapaho descendants of Sand Creek Massacre participants contributed accounts that had been passed down through the generations. The National Park Service held public open houses,
encouraging local residents to come forward with information,
including possible evidence of the massacre that had been
found on their land. While historians researched maps, diaries,
reminiscences, and congressional reports for pertinent information, historic aerial photographs, the earliest dating to the
1930s, were examined for evidence of historic trails leading to
and from the massacre site. Other efforts included a geomorphological assessment of Sand Creek that identified through
soil analysis those specific landforms where 1864-era artifacts
could potentially be recovered.

Certainly the multidisciplinary approach to solving historical questions is not a new strategy and has been employed
successfully elsewhere. As a result of this enterprise, however,
the project team was able to conclusively identify the location
and extent of the Sand Creek Massacre. It must be pointed out,
however, that, while all team members acknowledge that the
massacre occurred within commonly agreed-upon boundaries,
some parties offered scenarios at variance with the National
Park Service's interpretation of the historical documents and
archeological discoveries, as will be addressed herein. The
following narrative, based largely on the National Park Service's Sand Creek Massacre site location study, published
internally in 2000,[1] is intended to exemplify the value of the

interdisciplinary approach of history and archeology in locating such historical sites as that at Sand Creek.

The authors wish to acknowledge the following individuals and institutions for their help in the initial study: Rick Frost, project director; Christine Whitacre, team captain; Barbara Sutteer, Indian liaison; Alexa Roberts, ethnographer; Lysa Wegman-French, historian; Arthur Ireland, Steven DeVore, Charles Haecker, David Hammond, Christopher Theriault, Brian Carlstrom, Matthew Wilson, Christine Landrum, Theresa Burwell, Cathy Spude, David Ruppert, Rosemary Sucec, Ed Natay, Robert Spude, James Bradford, Victoria Barela, Rhonda Romero, Catherine Colby, John Cook, Mike Snyder, William P. O'Brien, Craig Moore, Sarah Craighead, Tanya Gossett, Mark Lynott, and Thomas Thiessen, all of the National Park Service; David Halaas and Susan Collins, Colorado Historical Society, Denver; Andrew Masich, Pittsburgh, Pennsylvania; landowners Lee Ballantine, Frances and Charles B. Bowen Sr., Chuck and Sheri Bowen, Scott and Melody Bowen, Roy and Marki Bowen Laughlin, Bill and Jredia Dawson, Terry and Janet Dewitt, Marc Goodrich, Judson Goodrich, Martha Goodrich Coate, August "Pete" Kern, and Suzanne Tresko; archeology crew members in 1997 and 1999 Anne Bond, Brooks Bond, William Lees, Dick Harmon, Tom Frew, Larry Gibson, Chris Adams, Richard Fike, Julie Coleman, Douglas McChristian and the late Mary McChristian, Bob Rea, Ruthanna Jacobs, Larry Nelson, Todd Nelson, Christine Landrum, Tom Baker, Norma Irwin, Robert DeWitt; and the hardworking members of the Pikes Peak Adventure League.

Others who contributed time and/or information include Andy Senti, Denver, Colorado; Tom Meier, Boulder, Colorado; Richard N. Ellis, Durango, Colorado; Sara Wiles, Boulder, Colorado; Sarah Tuttle, Desoto Wildlife Refuge, Missouri Valley, Iowa; Gary Roberts, Tipton, Georgia; William R. Welge and Mary Jane Warde, Oklahoma City, Oklahoma; John D. McDermott, Rapid City, South Dakota; Scott Forsythe, Chicago, Illinois;

Michael McFaul, Laramie, Wyoming; Amy Holmes, Laramie, Wyoming; Melinda Ellswick, Denver, Colorado; L. Clifford Soubier, Charles Town, West Virginia; Norman Hughes, Denver, Colorado; R. Eli Paul, Overland Park, Kansas; Neil Mangum, Alpine, Texas; and Peter Bleed, Lincoln, Nebraska.

The project could not have proceeded were it not for the support, cooperation, and dedication of the Cheyenne and Arapaho Tribes of Oklahoma, the Northern Arapaho Tribe, and the Northern Cheyenne Tribe, many of whose members are descendants of the people who were at the massacre in 1864. Many of the following tribal representatives also participated in the archeological field survey: Northern Arapaho Tribe— Anthony A. Addison Sr., Eugene J. Ridgely Sr., Gail J. Ridgely, Ben S. Ridgely, Nelson P. White Sr., Hubert N. Friday, Burton Hutchinson, Joseph Oldman, William J. C'Hair, Eugene Ridgely Jr., Hubert Warren Sr., Edward Willow, Joe Waterman, and Jerry Sage; Southern Cheyenne Tribe—Laird and Colleen Cometsevah, Edward Starr Jr., Edward White Skunk, Joe Big Medicine, Arleigh Rhodes, Marybelle Lonebear Curtis, Gus Wilson, Carolyn Sandlin, Robert Tabor, Franklin Harrison, Donna Sandoval, William "Lee" Pedro, Linda DeCarlo, and Alonzo Sankey; Southern Arapaho Tribe—June Black, Stanley Sleeper, Mary Kay Sweezy, and Ida Mahaffie; and Northern Cheyenne Tribe—Joe Walks Along, Norma Gourneau, Steve Brady, Lee Lonebear, Reginald Killsnight Sr., Mildred Red Cherries, Arbutus Red Woman, Patsy Riddle, Holda Roundstone, Otto Braided Hair, Conrad Fisher, Steve Chestnut, and the late Luke Brady.

All of these people share in the success of the Sand Creek Massacre Project, and we are grateful for their help in locating the massacre site, a vital first step in properly protecting and interpreting this sacred ground.

FINDING SAND CREEK

1

THE SAND CREEK MASSACRE

At dawn on November 29, 1864, more than seven hundred U.S. volunteer soldiers commanded by Colonel John M. Chivington attacked a village of about 500 Southern Cheyenne and Arapaho Indians along Sand Creek in southeastern Colorado Territory.[1] Using small-arms and howitzer fire, the troops drove the people out of their camp. While many managed to escape the initial onslaught, others, particularly noncombatant women, children, and the elderly, fled into and up the bottom of the dry streambed. The soldiers followed, shooting at them as they struggled through the sandy earth. At a point several hundred yards above the village, the people frantically excavated pits and trenches along either side of the streambed to protect themselves. Some attempted to fight back with whatever weapons they had managed to retrieve from the camp, and at several places along Sand Creek, the soldiers shot into them from opposite banks and presently brought forward the howitzers to blast them from their scant defenses. Over the

course of seven hours, the troops succeeded in killing at least
150 Cheyennes and Arapahos, mostly the old, the young, and
the weak. During the afternoon and the following day, the soldiers wandered over the field, committing atrocities on the
dead, before departing the scene on December 1 to resume
campaigning.

Since the day it happened, the Sand Creek Massacre has
maintained its station as one of the most emotionally charged
and controversial events in American history, a seemingly
senseless frontier tragedy reflective of its time and place. The
background of Sand Creek lay in a whirlwind of events and
issues registered by the ongoing Civil War in the East and West,
the overreactions by whites on the frontier to the 1862–63
Dakota uprising in Minnesota and its aftermath, the status of
the various bands of Southern Cheyenne and Arapaho Indians
vis-à-vis each other as well as other plains tribes, the constant
undercurrent of threatened Confederate incursions, and the
existing state of politics in Colorado along with the self-aggran-
dizing machinations of individual politicians in that territory.
Perhaps most importantly, the seeds of Sand Creek lay in the
presence of two historically discordant cultures within a geographical area that both societies coveted for disparate reasons,
a situation designed to ensure conflict.

General Background

Throughout the first years of the Civil War, Colorado officials
brooded over possible secessionist tendencies of the territory's
populace, and apprehensions arose over Confederate influences
in Texas, the Indian Territory, and New Mexico potentially
spilling across the boundaries to disrupt Colorado's relations
with its native inhabitants. In Colorado Territory, reports of the
Minnesota Indian conflict fostered an atmosphere of fear and
suspicion that, however unjustified, contributed to the war with
the Cheyenne and Arapaho Indians in 1864–65. During 1862

and 1863, most regional depredations involved, not warriors from these tribes, but Shoshones and Utes, whose repeated raids on emigrant and mail routes south and west of Fort Laramie (in present southeastern Wyoming) disrupted traffic and threatened the course of settlement. Aggressive campaigning in 1863 by columns of California and Kansas troops, including the massacre of a village of Shoshones at Bear River in present Idaho by a force commanded by Colonel Patrick E. Connor, abruptly ended these tribes' forays. Meanwhile, on the plains east of the Rocky Mountains, Indian troubles were mostly confined to bands of Kiowas, Kiowa-Apaches, Arapahos, and occasional Comanches, who stopped wagon trains bound over the Santa Fe Trail; elsewhere, the Lakotas and Pawnees maintained traditional conflicts with each other, encounters with only incidental effect on regional white settlement.[2]

CHEYENNES AND ARAPAHOS

Of all the plains tribes, the Cheyennes and Arapahos appear to have been the least offensive to white settlers at this particular time. Both tribes had been in the region for decades. The Cheyennes, Algonquian-speaking people whose agriculturalist forebears migrated from the area of the western Great Lakes, had occupied the buffalo prairies east of the Missouri River by the late seventeenth century. With the acquisition of horses, their migration continued, and over the next few decades, the Cheyennes ventured beyond the Black Hills as far north as the Yellowstone River and south to below the Platte. By the first part of the nineteenth century, the tribe had separated into northern and southern bodies that still maintained strong band and family relationships. In the conflicts that followed over competition for lands and game resources, the Cheyennes became noted fighters who forged strong intertribal alliances with the Lakotas and the Arapahos. The Arapahos, Algonquian speakers possibly from the area of northern Minnesota, had located west of the Missouri River by at least the late 1700s and probably very much earlier, and by the early nineteenth century they were variously established in what is now Montana, Wyoming, South Dakota, Nebraska, and Colorado. Their alliance with the Cheyennes extended back to the Cheyennes' entrance onto the eastern prairies, when both were semisedimentary peoples, and was grounded in mutual enmity (at that time) toward the Lakotas' growing regional domination as well as intertribal trade considerations. (Like the Cheyennes, in time the Arapahos gravitated into northern and southern regional divisions, with the southern group eventually coalescing in the area that included south-central Colorado.) Despite occasional Cheyenne-Arapaho rifts, mutual warfare with surrounding groups during the early 1800s solidified their bond and presently included the Lakotas; together, the three tribes variously fought warriors of the Kiowas and Crows, and in the central plains Arapaho and Cheyenne warriors drove the Kiowas and Comanches south of the Arkansas River. A relatively small tribe, the Arapahos were driven by circumstances to become resourceful in the face of intertribal conflicts and the potential adversity wrought by the presence of Anglo-Americans.[3]

TREATY OF FORT WISE

In 1851 the Cheyennes and Arapahos subscribed to the Treaty of Fort Laramie, which acknowledged their occupation of land lying between the Platte River on the north and the Arkansas River on the south, running from the area of the Smoky Hill River west to the Rocky Mountains. By the late 1850s, the southern divisions of both tribes ranged through central Kansas and eastern Colorado as they pursued their hunting and warring routine with enemy tribes and, for the most part, ignored the gradual inroads of whites into their country. In 1857 the Southern Cheyennes experienced a confrontation with troops at Solomon's Fork, Kansas, and their subsequent attitude toward whites had become one of tolerance and avoidance.[4] During the Colorado gold rush and the concomitant movement by whites into and through the territory, most of the Cheyennes and Arapahos remained tranquil, and peace factions headed by Black Kettle and White Antelope of the Cheyennes and Little Raven of the Arapahos sought to maintain this. But the tide of emigration associated with the gold rush, particularly along the Platte and Arkansas valleys, led government authorities to impose new strictures on the people.[5]

In 1861 these chiefs touched pen to the Treaty of Fort Wise, a document that surrendered most of the land previously prescribed in the Fort Laramie Treaty and granted them instead a triangular-shaped tract along and north of the upper Arkansas River in eastern Colorado, where they would henceforth receive government annuities and learn to till the soil. The accord, however, did not include the consent of all Cheyennes and Arapahos living in the Platte country, and those leaders who signed drew enduring resentment from the northerners who were resisting such changes. Many of the affected people, including the band of Southern Cheyenne Dog Soldiers who repudiated the concept of any territorially confining pact, continued their age-old pursuits in the buffalo country and refused to move onto the new reservation. Similarly, the Kiowas and Comanches to the south remained disinclined to participate in the treaty.[6]

The immediate circumstances leading to Sand Creek grew out of the Treaty of Fort Wise and the desire of Colorado territorial governor John Evans to seek total adherence to it by all of the Cheyennes and Arapahos.[7] Within the atmosphere prevailing in the wake of the Minnesota outbreak, Evans, an ambitious visionary, became committed to eliminating all Indians from the plains so that travel and settlement could proceed safely and without interruption; he was also interested in seeing the transcontinental railroad reach Denver and wanted eastern Colorado free of tribesmen to facilitate that development. Adding to this, Evans and others feared that the tribes might somehow be influenced by the Confederate cause, to include being drawn into a plan to cut communications between the East and California by seizing posts in the Platte and Arkansas valleys. Concentrated on the Upper Arkansas Reservation, the Indians not only might be better controlled but also would be altogether cleared from roads used by miners and settlers. To this end, Evans invited the tribal leadership to attend a council scheduled for September 1863 on the plains east of Denver.

The Cheyennes and Arapahos were clearly not interested, however, and none appeared to negotiate; most regarded the treaty as a swindle and refused to subject themselves to living on the new reserve. Moreover, they believed the area devoid of buffalo, whereas the plains of central Kansas still afforded plentiful herds. Coincidentally, at Fort Larned, Kansas, a Cheyenne man was killed in an incident that fueled considerable controversy among the Indians and hardened their resolve against more treaties. Governor Evans took the refusal to assemble as a sign that the tribes were planning war; he used the rebuff, along with rumored incitation of area tribes by northern Sioux, to promote the notion to Federal officials that hostilities were imminent. Although Evans may have sincerely believed that his territory was in grave danger, it has been suggested that he lobbied to create a situation that would permit him to forcibly remove the tribesmen from all settled areas of Colorado.[8]

EVANS, CHIVINGTON, AND THE PLAINS WAR OF 1864

Evans's accomplice in the evolving scenario was Colonel John M. Chivington, a former Methodist minister who had garnered significant victories against Confederate troops at Apache Canyon and Glorieta Pass in New Mexico. Nicknamed "The Fighting Parson," Chivington governed the Military District of Colorado within the Department of the Missouri, whose

commanders were often preoccupied with operations else-
where, thus affording the colonel an opportunity to play out
his military and political fortunes on the Colorado frontier.[9]
In January 1864, reorganization of the military hierarchy placed
Chivington's district under Major General Samuel R. Curtis's
Department of Kansas, a jurisdiction that remained considerably immersed in campaigns against Confederates in eastern
Kansas and the Indian Territory.[10] As the war proceeded in the
East, however, both Chivington and Evans grew alarmed at
seeing territorial troops increasingly diverted to help fight
Confederate forces in Missouri and Kansas. The governor lob-
bied for their return and requested that regulars be sent to
guard the crucial supply and communication links along the
Platte and Arkansas valleys. Facing widespread manpower
deficits in the East, Washington initially rejected his appeals.[11]

Chivington endorsed Evans's notion that the Indians in his
territory were ready for war, even though evidence indicates
that, despite the transgressions of a few warriors, the tribesmen
believed they were at peace. In April 1864, however, when live-
stock, possibly strayed from ranches in the Denver and South
Platte River areas, turned up in the hands of Cheyenne Dog
Soldiers, Evans and Chivington interpreted it as provocation
for the inception of conflict. In response, troops of the First
Colorado Cavalry skirmished with those Indians at Fremont's
Orchard along the South Platte River. Acting on Chivington's
orders to "kill Cheyennes wherever and whenever found," soldiers during the following month assaulted numerous inno-
cent Cheyenne camps, driving out the people and destroying
their property, and in one instance killed a peace chief named
Starving Bear, who had earlier headed a delegation that met
with President Abraham Lincoln in Washington. In retaliation,
parties of warriors mounted raids along the roads in Kansas,
especially between Forts Riley and Larned, but refrained from
all-out conflict. Attempting to stem the trouble, Curtis's inspector general advised against further Chivington-like forays and

Fig. 1. Colonel John M. Chivington. Courtesy Western History Department, Denver Public Library.

instead counseled conciliation with the Cheyennes and protection of the travel routes. He complained that the Colorado men did "not know one tribe from another and . . . will kill anything in the shape of an Indian."

But it was too late. Following the murders of several more of their people, the Cheyennes escalated their raiding, and their camps soon swelled with stolen goods. Marauding warriors from among the Arapahos, Kiowas, and Lakotas, usually without the endorsement of their chiefs, opened attacks on white enterprises along the trails bordering the Platte, Smoky Hill, and Arkansas Rivers in Nebraska and Kansas, killing more than thirty people and capturing several women and children. In Colorado warriors attacked and murdered an entire family, the Hungates, at Box Elder Creek, only thirty miles from Denver. Public display of the victims' bodies, coupled with fearful pronouncements from Governor Evans's office, drove most citizens from isolated ranches and communities to seek protection in Denver. In one panicked missive to the War Department, Governor Evans called for ten thousand troops. "Unless they can be sent at once," he intoned, "we will be cut off and destroyed." Although the Cheyennes received blame for the Hungate tragedy, Arapahos later confessed to the deed.[12]

Responding to the crisis, in July and August 1864 General Curtis directed several columns of troops to scour the country west, north, and south of Fort Larned. While the campaign brought meager results, it succeeded in opening the route west along the Arkansas because of increased garrisons at the Kansas and Colorado posts. Curtis now strengthened his administration of the area by establishing a single district, the District of the Upper Arkansas, commanded by Major General James G. Blunt, to replace those that had previously monitored Indian conditions. Similar administrative changes were made in Nebraska. There, in August, Cheyennes attacked homes along the Little Blue River, killing fifteen settlers and carrying off others. In response Curtis mounted a strong campaign with Nebraska and Kansas troops to search through western Kansas, but the soldiers found no Indians. Similarly, in September Blunt led an expedition out of Fort Larned, eventually heading north seeking Cheyennes reported in the area. On September 25 two companies of Colorado troops under Major Scott J. Anthony encountered a large village of Cheyennes and Arapahos at Walnut Creek and engaged them, fighting desperately until Blunt arrived with support. The command pursued the Indians for two days, then withdrew from the field.[13]

PEACE INITIATIVES

Following these operations, Blunt and Curtis became distracted from the Indian situation by a sudden Confederate incursion into Missouri that demanded their immediate attention. The diversion permitted Colonel Chivington to step forward, just at a time when the Cheyennes, Arapahos, and other tribes began slackening the war effort in preparation for the winter season. Buffalo hunting now superseded all else, and Cheyenne leaders like Black Kettle, who had previously urged peace, regained influence.[14] Black Kettle learned of a proclamation issued by Governor Evans calling upon all "Friendly Indians of the Plains" to divorce themselves from the warring factions and to isolate their camps near military posts to ensure their protection. Those who did not thus surrender would henceforth be considered hostile. In late August the chief notified Major Edward W. Wynkoop, commander at Fort Lyon, along the Arkansas River near present Lamar, Colorado, of his desire for peace.[15] Following up, the major led his command from the First Colorado Cavalry out to meet Black Kettle and the Arapaho leader, Left Hand, at the big timbers of the Smoky Hill River near Fort Wallace, Kansas.[16] At that council the Cheyennes and Arapahos turned over several captive whites and consented to meet with Evans and Chivington in

Fig. 2. Black Kettle (center seated) and other chiefs at Camp Weld near Denver, 1864. Courtesy Western History Department, Denver Public Library.

Denver to reach an accord. Then Black Kettle and the other leaders followed Wynkoop back to Fort Lyon.

When Black Kettle and six headmen arrived in Denver, the city was in a turmoil because of the conditions wrought by the Indian conflict. Incoming supplies of food and merchandise had been stopped by the warfare, and the citizenry was still shaken by the Hungate murders. Furthermore, in August the governor had published a proclamation, contradicting his earlier one, that called upon citizens to kill all Indians and seize their property, effectively extending an invitation for wholesale bloodshed and thievery. Evans had meantime received from federal authorities permission to raise a regiment of one-hundred-day U.S. volunteers, to be designated the Third Colorado Cavalry, and Chivington was preparing it for field service. All of these developments made Evans's earlier pronouncements ring hollow, especially with many of the territory's citizens clamoring for vengeance. Moreover, the governor needed to back up his earlier war predictions with Washington officials and clear up questions regarding the status of Indian lands in Colorado. If the tribes went unpunished now, he believed it would likely only encourage them to renew the warfare next year.[17]

At the council at Camp Weld near Denver on September 28, 1864, Evans spoke evasively to the chiefs, informing Black Kettle that, although his people might still separate themselves from their warring kin, they must make their peace with the military authorities, in essence turning the situation over to Chivington. Anxious for peace, Black Kettle and his entourage acceded to all conditions, and Chivington told them that they could report to Fort Lyon once they had laid down their arms. But the Camp Weld meeting was fraught with "deadly ambiguities." The Indians departed convinced that since they had already been to the post they had made peace, though neither Evans nor Chivington admitted that such was the case. Furthermore, a telegram from General Curtis admonished, "I want no peace until the Indians suffer more . . . [and only upon] my

directions." Evans notified Washington authorities of the continued hostility of the tribesmen and of the need to deal with
them by force of arms, noting that "the winter . . . is the most
favorable time for their chastisement." Yet, in consequence of
the Camp Weld meeting, Black Kettle prepared his people to
accept the conditions and surrender themselves as prisoners
of war.[18]

First to arrive in late October at Fort Lyon were 113 lodges
of Arapahos under Little Raven and Left Hand. Because as prisoners the Arapahos could not hunt, Major Wynkoop issued
rations to the destitute people while assuring them of their
safety. But this action directly countered General Curtis's policy of punishing the tribes, and when word of the major's char-
ity reached district headquarters at Fort Riley, tempers flared.
Wynkoop was summarily called there to explain his actions.
Major Anthony, of Chivington's First Colorado Cavalry, replaced
him at Fort Lyon. On arrival at Fort Lyon in early November,
Anthony refused the Arapahos further provisions and tem-
porarily disarmed them. When Black Kettle reached the fort,
he reported that his lodges were pitched some forty miles away
at Sand Creek, a location that Anthony approved because he
had no rations to feed the Cheyennes. The major told them that
he was seeking authority to feed them at Fort Lyon. Wynkoop,
who the Indians trusted, had given them assurances of Anthony's
integrity, and the Cheyenne leaders had accepted these conditions prior to Wynkoop's departure from Fort Lyon on November 26. Advised to join Black Kettle's people at Sand Creek,
only the Arapaho leader Left Hand complied and started his
few lodges in that direction; Little Raven took his followers far
away down the Arkansas.

MILITARY PREPARATIONS

Meanwhile, Colonel Chivington orchestrated events in Denver that would climax in the confrontation with the Cheyennes

and Arapahos at Sand Creek. Following a failed statehood vote, in which he was defeated as a candidate for Congress, Chivington directed his efforts to readying the new regiment, locally castigated as the "Bloodless Third" because its members had yet to kill a single Indian, which was fast approaching the end of its men's one-hundred-day enlistments. Composed of but partly trained officers and undisciplined men from the local community, the Third Colorado Cavalry had been organized by Colonel George L. Shoup, who had previously served under Chivington.[19] Earlier that fall, Chivington had envisioned attacking bands of Cheyennes reported in the Republican River country, but by November (and perhaps secretly all along) he targeted Black Kettle and his people; his every movement appeared calculated to that end, for the tribesmen technically were not at peace and were awaiting Curtis's consent before moving to Fort Lyon. In October, amid this tense atmosphere, Colonel Chivington armed his command and, with Shoup commanding the regiment, started companies to assemble at Bijou Basin, sixty miles southeast of Denver.[20]

On November 14 Chivington himself marched out of Denver with companies of the Third and First Colorado Cavalry regiments headed toward the Arkansas River. The weather turned foul, and the movement was beset with drifting snows that delayed units from rendezvousing at Camp Fillmore, near Pueblo. On the twenty-third Chivington inspected his united command, then all proceeded east along the Arkansas. The troops reached Fort Lyon at midday, November 28. Chivington had traveled quickly and quietly, and his approach surprised the garrison. To keep his presence and movements secret, the colonel placed a cordon of pickets around the fort and refused to allow anybody to leave. At Fort Lyon, Major Anthony greeted Chivington and, apprised of his mission to find and destroy Black Kettle's camp as a prelude to striking the Smoky Hill villages, gave his wholehearted support to the extent of providing additional troops and offering guidance to the village.

Some officers protested that Black Kettle's people were de facto prisoners of the government, awaiting only General Curtis's permission before they should arrive at the post, and that to strike them would violate promises made earlier by Wynkoop as well as by Anthony. Chivington responded that it was "right and honorable to use any means under God's heaven to kill Indians that would kill women and children, and 'damn any man that was in sympathy with Indians.'"[21]

At around 8:00 P.M. on the twenty-eighth, Chivington led his column out of Fort Lyon and moved parallel to an old Indian trail that headed northeast. Scarcely any snow lay on the ground. His command consisted of Shoup's Third Colorado Cavalry and about one half of the First Colorado Cavalry, divided under Major Anthony and First Lieutenant Luther Wilson, in all about 725 men bundled in heavy overcoats. Mules pulled along four howitzers and their ammunition and equipment. Some thirty-seven miles away on the northeast side of Sand Creek stood Black Kettle's village of approximately one hundred lodges housing about five hundred people. Other Cheyenne leaders in the camp were Sand Hill, White Antelope, Bear Tongue, One Eye, and War Bonnet, and the few tipis of Arapahos with Left Hand stood detached a short distance away.[22] Although some men were present, many had gone hunting, leaving mostly women, children, and the elderly in the village. Through the night of November 28–29, all were oblivious to the closing proximity of the soldiers.[23]

THE MASSACRE

Chivington's force kept a lively pace through the cold, moonless night, so that the first streaks of dawn on November 29 revealed the white tipis of the Cheyennes a few miles off to the northwest. Advancing closer, the soldiers gained a ridge overlooking Sand Creek from which they could clearly discern the camp. Pony herds ranged on either side of the stream, and

Chivington dispatched units to capture and corral the animals before the Indians might use them. As the tribesmen slowly awakened, the troops descended into the dry streambed and moved northwest along it, with the howitzers in tow. About a half mile from the village, Chivington halted the men so that they could remove their overcoats and other luggage. He exhorted them at the prospect before them, then sent them forward toward the camp, whose occupants had gradually become aroused at the noise of the approaching horsemen. Nearing the lower end of the village, the soldiers deployed their force along both sides of the stream. As the startled Indians ran out of their homes, howitzers hurled exploding shells that turned the people away to congregate near the westernmost lodges while their leaders tried to communicate with the attackers. Then shooting erupted everywhere. The leader White Antelope ran forward, arms raised and waving for attention, but a soldier's bullet cut him down. Black Kettle, proponent for peace and guardian of his people, reportedly raised an American flag and a white flag on a pole near his lodge to announce his status, but it was ignored in the heat of action.

Chivington's command kept up their small-arms fire from positions northeast and southeast of the camp. Caught in a crossfire, the warriors responded by attempting to shield the women, children, and elderly who ran to the back of the lodges. Most of the howitzer rounds fell short of their mark, though some burst over the village. As the soldiers advanced on horseback along either side of the creek, they maintained their shooting, and those on the north (east) bank of the stream passed through the fringe of the camp. The mass of people began to flee in all directions for safety. Many ran into and up the creek bottom, which appeared to afford a natural protective corridor leading away from the assault. Riding on either side of the Indians, however, the cavalrymen indiscriminately fired hundreds of rounds into the fleeing tribesmen and began to inflict large numbers of casualties among them. Meantime, other Indians bolting the village at the opening of the attack had managed to obtain horses and were running generally north and southwest over the open terrain as they tried to elude squads of pursuing Coloradoans. Many of them were chased down and killed by the flying troops.

But it was the mass of people in the streambed that drew the attention of most of the soldiers. As they reached a point variously estimated to be from two hundred yards to a half mile above the village, these people—composed mostly of non-combatants—sought to find shelter in hastily dug pits and trenches in the creek bed, most excavated by hand at the base of the dry stream's banks. The Sand Creek bottom was several hundred yards wide at this point, and the people sought shelter along either side, digging hiding places and throwing the sand and dirt outward to form protective barriers. Having pursued the Cheyennes and Arapahos to this location, the troops dismounted on the edges of the stream and approached cautiously. Some began firing at Indians sheltered in the pits beneath the opposite side, while others crawled forward and discharged their weapons blindly over the top of the bank. Thus trapped, the people fought back desperately with what few weapons they possessed. Shortly, however, the howitzers arrived from downstream, took positions on either side of the Sand Creek bottom, and began delivering exploding shells into the pits. This bombardment, coupled with the steady fire of the cavalry small arms, was too much for the Indians, and by the time the affair was over at around 2:00 P.M., at least 150 Cheyennes and Arapahos lay dead, most of them killed during the slaughter in the defensive pits above the village or in the streambed as they ran from the camp to elude the soldiers. Chivington lost nine men killed and thirty-eight wounded in the encounter. Throughout the balance of the day, parties of cavalrymen roamed the area for miles around finishing off any survivors they could find. That night, nonetheless, many of those wounded during the carnage managed to get away from

the pits and join other village escapees who, over the next several days, journeyed northeast to the Cheyenne camps along the
Smoky Hill River. Surprisingly, despite the suddenness and
ferocity of the Sand Creek assault, the majority of villagers,
including many who were severely wounded, somehow escaped
the soldiers and survived.

Those who did not survive became the objects of widespread mutilation at the hands of the soldiers, particularly of
members of the "Bloodless Third." Over the next day, these
largely untrained and undisciplined troops, including some
officers, roamed the site of the destruction, scalping and otherwise desecrating the dead, thereby compounding the butchery
of the event. The soldiers then plundered and burned the village, destroying its contents. The captured pony herd traveled
south with Chivington as he continued his campaign, and the
dead and wounded soldiers were removed to Fort Lyon. Chivington had earlier planned to mete similar treatment upon the
Smoky Hill assemblage but instead turned toward the Arapaho
village that Major Anthony had earlier sent away from Fort
Lyon. These tribesmen had fled by the time the troops reached
the mouth of Sand Creek at the Arkansas River. The Third
Colorado then moved upstream to Fort Lyon before heading
back to Denver, where they were greeted on December 22 by
a throng of cheering citizens ecstatic over the "victory" of
Sand Creek. Scalps from the Indian victims were ceremoni-
ously exhibited at a local theater as the soldiers recounted their
participation. As if the true number of deaths were not enough,
Chivington boasted of having killed between five hundred and
six hundred Indians in his attack.[24]

OUTCRY AND AFTERMATH

In the aftermath of Sand Creek, as word gradually spread about
the brutality of the onslaught, questions arose about Chiving-

ton's version of events. The truth shocked and sickened most Americans. In 1865 Sand Creek became the focus of three federal investigations, one military and the others congressional, looking into justification for and details of the action. Senator James R. Doolittle (R-Wisconsin), chairman of the Senate Committee on Indian Affairs, directed an inquiry following receipt of information about the event that "made one's blood chill and freeze with horror." In the West, General Curtis was ordered to find out what had occurred at Sand Creek. The examinations resolved that Chivington and his troops had conducted a premeditated campaign that resulted in the needless massacre of the Cheyennes and Arapahos and that the subsequent atrocities were an abject disgrace. By then, however, the colonel and his men were out of the service and could not be prosecuted for their actions, and only Chivington's political future suffered. The Joint Committee on the Conduct of the War concluded in its assessment of Chivington that "he deliberately planned and executed a foul and dastardly massacre which would have disgraced the veriest savage among those who were the victims of his cruelty." The committee also resolved that Governor Evans "was fully aware that the Indians massacred so brutally at Sand Creek, were then, and had been, actuated by the most friendly feelings towards the whites."[25] Ultimately, Evans paid the price for his involvement in events prior to the massacre and was dismissed as governor. In time the Cheyenne and Arapaho victims of Sand Creek received scant restitution through the Treaty of the Little Arkansas, concluded in 1865, which purported to compensate them for suffering and property losses, a provision as yet unfulfilled. The treaty repudiated Chivington's massacre and promised to bestow lands on chiefs and survivors of Sand Creek whose parents or husbands had fallen at the Coloradoans' hands, as well as redress for white citizens who had been affected by the warfare.[26]

Significance of Sand Creek

The Sand Creek Massacre is historically significant for several reasons. In terms of lives lost, both the Cheyennes and Arapahos experienced familial and societal disruptions that have since spanned generations. For both peoples, the site of the massacre is sacred ground, consecrated by the blood of lost forebears and venerated today by descendants and friends of those who died as well as of those who survived. While the event thus affected both tribes, it most directly carried devastating physical, social, political, and material consequences among the relatively small (about three thousand) Cheyenne population and indisputably changed the course of their tribal history. Beyond the basic human loss, the deaths of numerous chiefs in the massacre, occurring at a time when the Cheyennes were already experiencing fragmentation in their system with the evolution of the Dog Soldier Band, ultimately had long-range influences on the structural bonds within Cheyenne society. The Council of Forty-Four, the central entity of Cheyenne government, was crippled with the losses of White Antelope, One Eye, Yellow Wolf, Big Man, Bear Man, War Bonnet, Spotted Crow, and Bear Robe, besides those of the headmen of three warrior societies.[27] In addition, the losses in material fixtures, including homes, clothing, furnishings, and even artwork, during the destruction of Black Kettle's village were immense, with immediate and future ramifications within the tribal community. Among the fifty or so Arapahos at Sand Creek, seemingly few survived, and their chief, Left Hand, was mortally wounded in the massacre. Other effects among the Arapahos were similar to those among the Cheyennes, and the Arapaho bands in the Arkansas country were divided ever after.[28]

A major result of the Sand Creek Massacre was its effect on the course of Indian-white relations, notably the implementation of federal Indian policy over ensuing decades. Although largely instigated independently by federalized territorial forces operating under the license of Colorado authorities, Sand Creek and its aftermath produced an atmosphere of pervasive and nervous distrust between the U.S. government—principally the army, as the instrument of national policy—and the plains tribes that complicated their associations and compounded negotiations on virtually every matter. In a single destructive strike, the Colorado troops had eliminated all of the Cheyenne chiefs who had favored peace; those leaders who survived Sand Creek thereafter became staunch advocates of resistance. News of the treachery spread rapidly among the tribes. As one official warned regarding an upcoming meeting with Indians when troops might be operating in the vicinity, "An angel from Heaven would not convince them but what another 'Chivington Massacre' was intended." The months following Sand Creek witnessed an eruption of warfare throughout the central plains, with Cheyenne, Lakota, and Arapaho warriors attacking the emigration routes along the North Platte, South Platte, Republican, and Arkansas valleys. To the north, Sand Creek added further fuel to the invasion of Indian lands already underway there via the Bozeman Trail, producing several army expeditions against the tribes as well as an unsuccessful attempt to militarily occupy the region. On the southern plains, troops attempted to subdue the tribes and overawe them with similar campaigns. In 1865, 1867, and 1868, tenuous treaties arranged between the government and the plains Indians sought to isolate them on designated tracts removed from the principal arteries westward. But peace remained elusive, and the conflicts of the 1870s, including the Great Sioux War of 1876–77, had their origins at least partly in the Sand Creek Massacre and its long-term unsettling effects among the plains tribesmen.[29]

The event played a related role in the Indian reform movement, as partly manifested in the subsequent congressional investigations, and initially produced an outcry against the military that continued throughout the period of the post–Civil War Indian conflicts. The effect was to place the army in

the position of trying to prevent noncombatant casualties during its Indian campaigns, a concept that was not always possible given the realities of the military tactics of Indian warfare,
which included surprise dawn attacks on villages whose occupants were often asleep. Traditional impressions to the con-
trary, because of public indignation over Sand Creek and the
antimilitary bias it produced, both Generals William T. Sherman
and Philip H. Sheridan, whose administrative domains included
the plains region, sought to keep noncombatant losses low in
the late-nineteenth-century campaigns, an objective that was
not always achieved. In addition, partly because of the federal
inquiries that followed it, Sand Creek directly influenced congressional thinking about the role of the army in Indian policy;
it not only heightened antimilitary bias among Indian reform-
ers but also blunted then-current efforts to transfer control of
Indian affairs from the Interior Department to the War Department. Moreover, Sand Creek became an important symbol in
the movement for Indian reform and, from 1865 through the
1880s, was repeatedly highlighted as proof of the essential
inhumanity of federal policy. In more recent times, it has been
used by Indians and the modern Indian reform movement as
proof of the genocidal intent of U.S. Indian policy.[30]

Sand Creek was one of several clearly indisputable human
catastrophes that influenced the course of Indian-white relations on the frontier during the last half of the nineteenth century, the others being the Bear River Massacre of Shoshone
Indians on January 29, 1863 (cited above), in which at least 250
tribesmen perished; the Marias River Massacre of January 23,
1870, wherein troops assailed a camp of Piegan Indians in
northwestern Montana Territory, leaving 173 people dead; and
the Wounded Knee Massacre of December 29, 1890, resulting
from an escalating confrontation between soldiers and Lakota
Indians on the Pine Ridge Reservation in South Dakota, in
which Indian fatalities numbered at least 250.[31] In the first two
cases, the massacres ended extended periods of conflict with

those small bands and doubtless exhibited some of the same cultural manifestations among those peoples as among the Cheyennes and Arapahos after Sand Creek. Wounded Knee occurred after the Lakotas had been forcibly settled on reservations. Yet because of the influences of the pervasive Cheyenne and Arapaho societies throughout the Great Plains region, the cultural, political, and military repercussions from Sand Creek truly lingered for a generation, affecting intercultural relationships in matters of peace, war, and daily existence that in many respects have continued to the present. Thus, in its immediate, direct, and long-range effects upon the Cheyenne and Arapaho societies and the plains Indian community generally, as well as in its immediate and subsequent bearing on the progression of federal Indian and military policy respecting the plains tribes, the Sand Creek Massacre was an event of outstanding significance as reflected within the broad national patterns of American history.

2

Historical Documentation of the Location and Extent of the Sand Creek Massacre Site

In 1998 Congress passed P.L. 105-243, the Sand Creek Massacre Site Study Act of 1998, which required the National Park Service, in consultation with the State of Colorado, the Cheyenne and Arapaho Tribes of Oklahoma, the Northern Cheyenne Tribe, and the Northern Arapaho Tribe, to undertake "to identify the location and extent of the massacre area" prior to initiating a special-resource study to determine the suitability and feasibility of making the site a unit of the National Park System. The project encompassed an integrated multidisciplinary approach to include archival research conducted by historians, the collection of oral histories by ethnographers, traditional tribal investigations by Sand Creek Massacre survivor descendants and tribal leaders, and examination by geomorphologists and remote-imagery specialists followed by onsite archeological exploration by archeologists.

The area where the massacre occurred, and where the site of that event was to be searched for and ultimately discovered, is in Kiowa County, in southeastern Colorado, about thirty miles north of the modern community of Lamar and the same approximate distance west of the Kansas state line. In early November 1864 one village of mostly Southern Cheyennes, numbering at least one hundred lodges but including several of Arapahos and totaling as many as 500 people, all professing peace and headed by Chief Black Kettle, approached Fort Lyon along the Arkansas River (where the city of Lamar stands today). On approval from the post commander, the Indians located some forty miles away at Sand Creek, northeast of the fort. There, at dawn on November 29, 1864, a large force of soldiers—some 725 men composed of the Third Colorado Cavalry (one-hundred-day volunteers) plus five companies of the First Colorado Cavalry, accompanied by four 12-pounder mountain howitzers, all under the command of Colonel John M. Chivington of the First Colorado—struck Black Kettle's village. The assault came essentially from the south and east, with small-arms and howitzer fire driving most of the occupants out of the lodges to scramble up the creek bottom away from the attackers, although many others fled west, southwest, and northwest across the prairie. The cavalrymen followed, some advancing along each side of Sand Creek and firing their weapons indiscriminately at the fleeing people, many of whom were women and children. Other troops fanned out to chase after the people trying to get away over the undulating landscape bordering the stream. Somewhere, perhaps at several places in the low-bluffed recesses of the creek bottom stretching north-west of the village, the troops cornered and fired at pockets of the terrified villagers as they entrenched themselves for pro-tection in hastily dug sand pits and attempted to fight back. Presently, the Coloradoans brought up at least two and perhaps more of the howitzers, directed them at the sand pits, and unleashed several rounds of spherical-case ordnance that exploded among the Indians, bringing injury and death to scores of them, largely noncombatant women, children, and the elderly. By all accounts, the slaughter that ensued from dawn until the afternoon caused the deaths of at least 150 (and likely many more) villagers, while Chivington's casualties totaled but nine men killed and thirty-eight wounded. Following the massacre, many of the Indian dead were mutilated by the soldiers. After the encounter, Chivington ordered his men to burn the village and destroy its property; two days later he led his troops down Sand Creek to the Arkansas River to resume campaigning. Cheyenne and Arapaho survivors made their way northeast during the ensuing days to camps of their kinsmen along the forks of the Smoky Hill River.[1]

Accounts of the massacre by participants are generally quite specific in describing various elements of the action; they are much less specific in describing the precise location and extent along Sand Creek where the massacre took place. (Although local residents and community and regional organizations placed a marker along Sand Creek in Kiowa County in 1950 [NW 1/4, Section 25, Township 17 South, Range 46 West, Sixth Principal Meridian], the designation of the massacre site seems to have been based largely upon the beliefs of then-local citizens. The designation has since become clouded by time, disparate opinions by a variety of informed and uninformed people, and the lack of scientifically retrieved significant artifactual evidence to validate it. A State of Colorado–funded project administered by Fort Lewis State College to find the site in 1995–98 was inconclusive.)[2] Participant testimony seemed most important for aiding the archival search regarding the potential extent of the massacre site, especially in the knowledge that the event included at least two major contributing locations that, though interrelated, occurred on separate and distinct areas of the site. They are the village area, embracing a logically open, flat, or somewhat terraced tract on the north (east) side of Sand Creek sufficient to accommodate as many as one hundred lodges, and a location to the west where the streambed of the creek turns northwest and becomes confined by slightly rising bluffs on

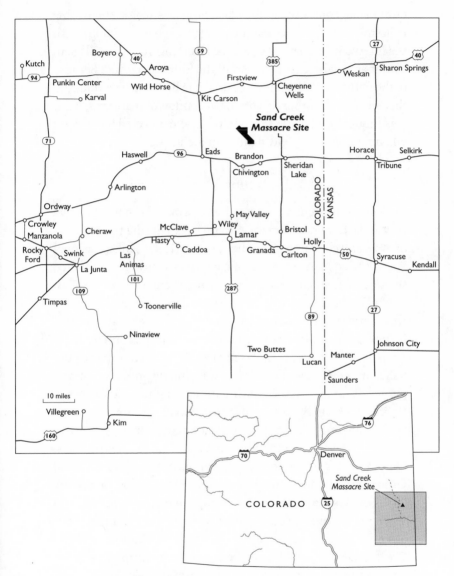

Map 1. The Sand Creek vicinity.

either side, constituting the place or places where the fleeing
tribesmen sought cover in sand pits or trenches and (along with
the intervening length of streambed running from the village to
the pit area) where a major part of the killing occurred. Because
of the nature of their respective uses, the first as village and conflict site and the other as a principal conflict or massacre site, it
was thought that these separate yet interconnected focus areas
when found might yield significant archeological data.

METHODOLOGY

Research into archival sources for information about the location and extent of the massacre site began during the summer
of 1998 and continued into the spring of 1999. Three National
Park Service historians and one contract historian conducted
the research, aided as necessary by representatives of the Colorado Historical Society, the various Cheyenne and Arapaho
tribes, the tribally recognized Sand Creek descendants organizations, the Boulder History Museum, and appropriate landowners. Methodology consisted of an initial review of the published literature about Sand Creek, including primary material
published in assorted government documents. This was followed by extensive research into archival resources existing
within and outside of the State of Colorado, notably historical
maps, manuscript and published diaries, soldier testimonies,
contemporary and later newspaper accounts, General Land
Office surveys, homesteading records, U.S. Geological Survey
(USGS) maps, army officers' scouting reports, post records, and
veterans' tabloids. Every attempt was made to locate and consider Cheyenne and Arapaho participant accounts of the Sand
Creek massacre. In all instances the inquiry focused on references to the location and extent of the Sand Creek Massacre site
or upon data from which some aspect of the desired information
might be interpreted. Pertinent data that were considered to be

of use in locating the site and its extent were then extracted from the source material for evaluation for accuracy and comparison with other data, such as aerial photographs and USGS maps of the Sand Creek area. Three interim reports on the status of the archival research, incorporating discussions and compilations of data bearing on the objective, were produced in September 1998 and in January and April 1999. It is important to note that the following presentation is based upon those materials deemed to bear most significantly on the subject of the *location* and *extent* of the massacre site and selected from among the many archival sources assembled since the project began.[3]

FINDINGS REGARDING THE LOCATION OF THE SITE OF THE SAND CREEK MASSACRE

The archival search for information to identify the site of the Sand Creek Massacre resulted in an accumulation and examination of written reports, diaries, and reminiscences of individuals who were present at the event; historical maps, particularly those contemporary with the period of the massacre as well as those based upon reminiscence; historical aerial photographic documentation; and the compilation and examination of various land records relating to the course of Sand Creek and possible changes in its configuration through the years. Employing these assorted documents, the search for the massacre site concentrated on the evaluation of evidence relating directly to the location and configuration of Sand Creek proper, together with certain of its affluents; the distance traveled by Chivington's troops in advancing for their attack; the trail or route of approach of the troops from Fort Lyon; the postmassacre bivouac site of Chivington's command; and historical maps bearing directly on the place and event.

Sand Creek

Sand Creek takes its head in east-central Colorado near the
community of Peyton and runs northeast approximately 50
miles to near the town of Limon, where it abruptly turns
southeast and continues southeast and south for approximately 125 miles until it joins the Arkansas River a few
miles east of present Lamar. In the course of its southeast-
wardly progression, the creek makes a number of notable
bends, two of which, because of their relative distance from
Fort Lyon, were considered important geographic indicators
as to the possible location of the massacre site. The bends
lie approximately 8 miles apart and for purposes of this
report are designated the North Bend and the South Bend.
The South Bend corresponds to the location of the historical-site marker placed in 1950 and has been the traditionally
embraced site of the massacre. A major tributary that factors significantly in the determination of the location of the
site is Rush Creek, which enters Sand Creek from the northwest approximately 20 miles above the latter stream's confluence with the Arkansas and about 5 miles south of the
present community of Chivington. (Research into General
Land Office records of the Sand Creek area and comparisons
to modern USGS maps led to concerns that the course of the
stream had possibly changed during the years since 1864,
particularly in the area of the South Bend. Results of geomorphological testing conducted in December 1998, however, suggest that there is little evidence to indicate past
major channel shifting on this part of Sand Creek.[4] Moreover,
computerized comparisons of 1890–91 USGS maps with modern USGS maps indicate numerous and gross errors in topography and stream alignment as registered on the early maps,
doubtless caused by the less-rigorous surveying practices of
the time.)

Distance from Fort Lyon

Contemporary accounts of the massacre generally describe the site as being between 25 and 45 miles north or northeast of Fort Lyon (at the Arkansas River), the departure point of Chivington's force on the night of November 28, 1864, and situated about 38 miles west of the mouth of Sand Creek.[5] The preponderance of the accounts states that the site where Chivington attacked the Indians was 40 miles from Fort Lyon. Several specify the site as being on or near the "Big Bend of Sandy Creek" and the "South Bend of Big Sandy," an area consistent with one or another of the aforementioned bends.[6] Straight-line distance from Fort Lyon to the North Bend is 37.7 miles, while that to the South Bend is 34.7 miles,[7] both short of the preponderant 40-mile distance given in the historical records; the course over the military trail from the post to the Indian village would likely have been several miles longer, considering normal meanderings of the route over the existing landscape.[8]

Trail from Fort Lyon to the Village

George Bent (1843–1918) was a mixed-blood son of William Bent, who, with his brother, Charles, had established Bent's Fort along the Arkansas in the late 1820s, and Owl Woman, his Southern Cheyenne wife. Reflective of this background, George Bent successfully coexisted in both white and Cheyenne worlds during his early years. In a reminiscent account of Sand Creek, Bent, who was in the village at the time of Chivington's attack and survived, indicated that the village stood on the north bank of Sand Creek at the point where an "Indian trail made by lodge poles" crossed the stream. Bent later recalled that "a lodge trail ran from near Fort Lyon in a northeasterly direction to the head of the Smoky Hill [River], and we were encamped where this trail crossed Sand Creek."[9] Bent made two sketch diagrams of the village area, both of which clearly

Fig. 3. George Bent. Courtesy Western History Department, Denver Public Library.

show lines indicating Chivington's approach, possibly along or near the Indian trail, which is not otherwise indicated on either diagram. Despite the fact that Bent, aided by other Cheyenne participants, produced his schematic representations of the village layout more than forty years later, they contain a remarkably high level of detail, doubtless because of his and his assistants' direct knowledge.[10] But Bent's diagrams show "Chivingtons Trail" proceeding from the south, intersecting the streambed at a right angle, and entering the village, a configuration at variance with the immediate and reminiscent accounts of soldier participants who maintained that they entered the dry Sand Creek bottom and marched along it for a considerable distance before opening their attack from the northeast and southeast.

The lodge-pole trail running from near Fort Lyon was probably the same route passed over by Black Kettle and his delegation when they moved back to Sand Creek following their visit with Major Scott Anthony just days before the massacre. It reportedly crossed that stream, possibly bisecting the village area, and continued northeast to the Smoky Hill River. Examination of 1930s Soil Conservation Service photographs of the area comprising Sections 24 and 25, Township 17 South, Range 46 West, indicates the presence of several trail remnants crossing Sand Creek both east and west of the present historical-site marker that might indicate the location of the lodge-pole trail.[11]

At least two soldiers reported that their column followed an Indian trail during the advance to the village site.[12] One man recalled that, on leaving the post on the evening of November 28, Chivington's command followed "well worn trails that marked the line of Indian travel."[13] The military trail from Fort Lyon seems thus to have paralleled, and perhaps at times overlaid, the lodge pole trail for most of its distance to the village and then might have guided Chivington's direct approach to the camp. A few veteran-soldier accounts mention that the troops rode through a pond of water en route north on the trail.[14]

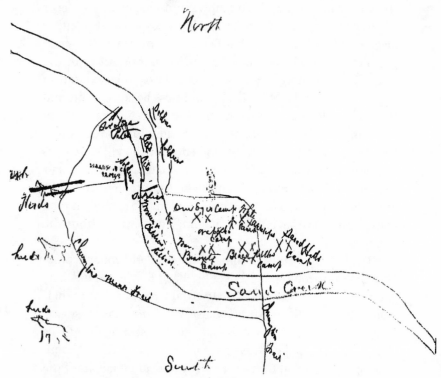

Map 2. George Bent diagram of the village and Sand Creek Massacre site, prepared sometime during 1905–14, the earliest known of his two renderings. Depicted within the village are "One Eye's Camp," "White Antelope's Band," "Arapaho Camp," "Sand Hills [sic] Camp," "Black Kettles [sic] Camp," and "War Bonnet's Camp." Also portrayed are the sand pits, the Indian horse herds, "Chivington's trail," troop placements, and the area in the streambed where women and children were killed. Folder 1, George Bent–George Hyde Papers, courtesy Western History Collections, University of Colorado Libraries, Boulder.

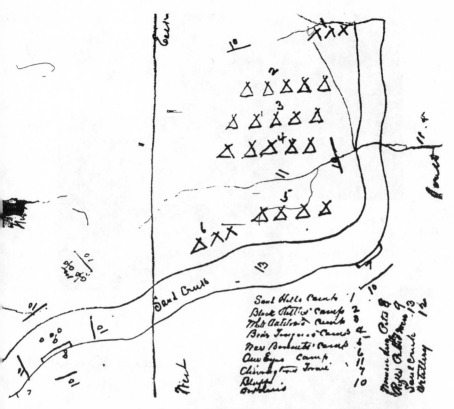

Map 3. George Bent diagram of the village and Sand Creek Massacre, prepared sometime during 1905–14, though likely after the other drawing. Numbers on the diagram correspond to the legend: 1–6 depict the camps within the village, including that of Black Kettle (2); 7 is the "bluff"; 8 denotes the sand pit dug by women, while 9 depicts those dug by men; 10 portrays the placement of soldiers; 11 shows Chivington's trail; 12 depicts howitzer placement; and 13 represents Sand Creek. Cheyenne/Arapaho Agency File, "Warfare," 1864–85, Indian Archives Division, Oklahoma Historical Society, Oklahoma City. Microfilm Roll 24.

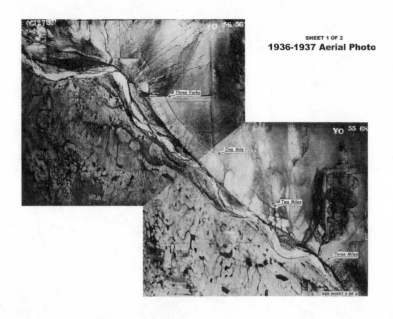

1936-1937 Aerial Photo

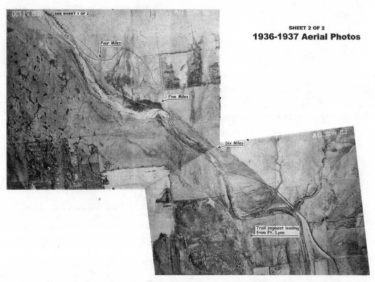

1936-1937 Aerial Photos

Fig. 4. Aerial photographs of Sand Creek, 1936–37, showing mileage markers from "Three Forks." Courtesy National Archives.

Several shallow rain basins or ponds are present today at a distance of approximately eleven miles north of the site of Fort
Lyon. Aerial photographs taken in 1997 confirm the presence
of these ponds as well as of a remnant trail consistent with the
military route leading north from the area of Bent's New Fort,
which adjoined Fort Lyon on the east, and that passed directly
through a natural water-filled basin.[15]

Postmassacre Camp of Chivington's Command

Several participant accounts indicate that, after spending two
days and two nights at the scene of the massacre, Chivington
moved his command south and bivouacked along Sand Creek.
Sergeant Lucian Palmer of Company C, First Colorado Cavalry, testified specifically, "we camped in Sand Creek, 12 miles
from the battle-ground, the night of the 1st of December."
Diarist Henry Blake, Company D, Third Colorado Cavalry,
reported that on December 1 the command "camped 13 miles
below on Sand Creek." And Private Hal Sayre noted in his
diary that the troops "took the back track and camped tonight
[December 1] on dry creek [Sand Creek] 15 miles south of battle field." Yet another diarist, John Lewis Dailey, reported
camping that night fifteen miles from the massacre site "on a
watery tributary," while Morse Coffin, Company D, Third
Colorado, stated that the command moved "about fifteen
miles toward Fort Lyon, where we camped for the night."[16]
These figures align well with the approximate distance north
from the confluence of Rush and Sand Creeks and would place
the massacre site in the area of the South Bend. On December
2 Chivington sent his dead and wounded back to Fort Lyon,
undoubtedly over the trail his troops had used during their
march out the night of November 28–29. The colonel accompanied the remainder of his men down Sand Creek in a southeasterly direction toward the Arkansas River as they resumed
campaigning.

Maps

A large number of published and manuscript historical maps were consulted for geographical information about streams, trails, roads, land use, ownership, and other data that might help locate the massacre site. While most of these contained limited useful information for the specific purposes of this project, they were cumulatively valuable for the regional knowledge they imparted. But only one manuscript map contained significant information that pertained directly to the location of the Sand Creek Massacre site, as discussed below.

The George Bent–George Hyde Regional Maps

Besides the two diagrams he provided during about 1905–14 representing the configuration of the Cheyenne-Arapaho village along Sand Creek at the time of the massacre, George Bent helped render two maps showing the broader region of eastern Colorado Territory on which he designated the location of Black Kettle's village. These maps were initially prepared by historian George E. Hyde, who was gathering narrative material for a biography of Bent. Hyde evidently traced the charts from existing 1890–91 USGS topographical maps and then mailed them to Bent with instructions to mark place names on them. Although his grasp of the geography and topography of the land traversed by the Cheyennes and Arapahos in their peregrinations was generally superb, Bent, possibly because of gross inaccuracies in the available topographic map that Hyde sent him, was apparently unsure of the precise location of the Sand Creek Massacre site. On one (map 1) he indicated that Black Kettle's camp stood along the stream at its big north bend, some eight or nine miles above the present historical marker; on the other (map 2) he placed the scene of the massacre well below the confluence of Rush Creek with Sand Creek, at least thirty miles from his other projection and some twenty-five miles below the present marker. The lack of certainty evident in Bent's two regional maps thus discounted their value in discerning the exact location of the massacre.[17] Moreover, because Bent's two diagrams of the village at the time of the massacre did not specify exactly where along Sand Creek it stood, and his placements of the village on the regional maps were at odds with one another, his diagrams were also of little value in locating the massacre site. Thus, despite the likely valuable intrinsic features regarding the layout of the Indian village (though these are by no means precisely the same in each drawing), the Bent diagrams were further clouded by their relationship to the Bent-Hyde regional maps.

The Bonsall Map and Aerial Confirmation

The signal manuscript map found to date that definitively establishes a site for the Sand Creek Massacre is that drawn by Second Lieutenant Samuel W. Bonsall, Third U.S. Infantry, stationed at Fort Lyon. The map, discovered in 1992 in the Chicago Branch Center of the National Archives, is closely contemporary with the action in that Bonsall prepared it in June 1868, at or near the time of his march and within four years of the massacre. Prepared in accordance with *United States Army Regulations* in the form of a strip map and journal documenting the route of his detachment of eleven infantry soldiers from Fort Lyon to Cheyenne Wells as they escorted Lieutenant General William T. Sherman east following a tour of frontier sites, Bonsall's map is graphically detailed with regard to landmarks and place names and includes time and mileage readings between marches.[18] Without question, it is the most important document yet located to convincingly posit the site, which is designated thereon as "Chivingtons Massacre."[19]

The ascendance of the Bonsall map in the project led to a corresponding pursuit of information about Bonsall himself as well as that of some circumstances of the purpose and activities of his detachment's trek between Fort Lyon and Cheyenne

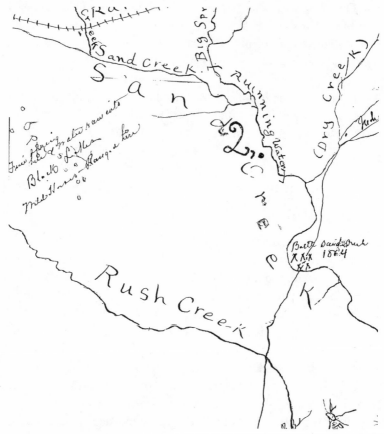

Map 4. Bent-Hyde regional map 1. Folder 10, George Bent–George Hyde Papers, courtesy Western History Collections, University of Colorado Libraries, Boulder.

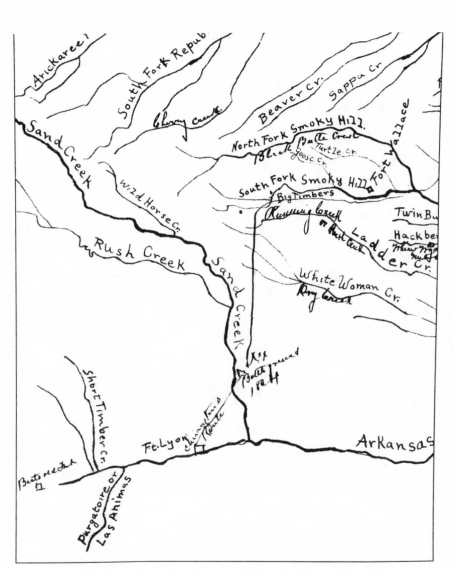

Map 5. Bent-Hyde regional map 2. Folder 10, George Bent–George Hyde Papers, courtesy Western History Collections, University of Colorado Libraries, Boulder.

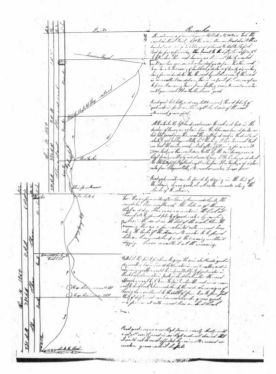

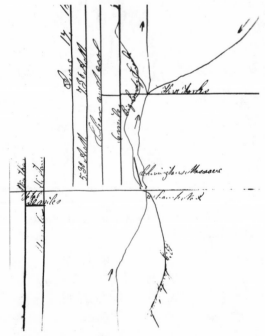

Map 6. Samuel W. Bonsall map, June 1868. The enlarged inset shows "Chivingtons Massacre" site in relation to "Three Forks." Courtesy National Archives, Great Lakes Branch.

Wells. Samuel Bonsall was from Bloomington, Indiana, and four months after the outbreak of the Civil War, at age twenty-two, he enlisted in the Eighteenth Indiana Volunteer Infantry Regiment. Commissioned a second lieutenant within five months, he won promotion to first lieutenant in July 1863. Bonsall resigned from his regiment in September 1864 but within three months joined the Sixth U.S. Veteran Volunteers as a captain. He was known during the war as "a brave and competent officer and gentleman" and a veteran of "a half dozen pitched battles." Mustered out in April 1866, in May he joined the Third U.S. Infantry as a second lieutenant. He served as regimental adjutant from February to October 1867 and advanced to first lieutenant in July 1868. Like many officers on frontier duty, Bonsall fought a drinking problem. In August 1872, on the advice of his commanding officer, he resigned from the army and returned to Indiana. Efforts to regain his commission, which included direct appeals to General Sherman and President Ulysses S. Grant, proved unsuccessful, and Bonsall never returned to the army.[20]

Direct evidence of the purpose of the lieutenant's movement appears in Fort Lyon Special Orders No. 66, which dictated: "1st Lieut. S. W. Bonsall 3[d] U.S. Infantry will take one Non commissioned Officer and ten (10) men . . . and report to Lieut Genl W. T. Sherman, Commanding Military Division of the Missouri, as escort to Fort Wallace, Kas. After performing this duty he will return to this Post without delay. The detachment will take eight (8) days rations. The Quartermasters Department will furnish the necessary transportation, two (2) wagons and four extra mules."[21] Sherman had been at Fort Union, New Mexico Territory, on June 11, 1868, and had proceeded from there to Trinidad, Colorado, and Fort Lyon. Although Bonsall was authorized to accompany the general to Fort Wallace, in fact the escort lasted only until they reached the stage line at Cheyenne Wells. Sherman described his journey thus: "At Fort Lyon, I crossed over to the Smoky Hill Line reaching it at

Cheyenne Wells, whence I came by stage to Fort Wallace, and the end of the Kansas Branch of the Pacific Railroad."[22] From there Sherman entrained east to Fort Leavenworth to meet Major General Philip H. Sheridan, commander of the Military Department of the Missouri at Fort Leavenworth and in whose department Sherman's tour took place, and then proceeded to his own headquarters in St. Louis.[23]

A reminiscent account by Luke Cahill, a noncommissioned officer who served in the Third Infantry between 1866 and 1869 and was posted at Fort Lyon in 1868, discusses the mission, which included a tour by Sherman of the scene of the Sand Creek carnage. According to Cahill, Bonsall commanded the detachment, which reached the battleground "about two p.m." Furthermore, wrote Cahill, "After dinner, General Sherman requested that all the escort hunt all over the battleground and pick up everything of value. He wanted to take the relics back to Washington. We found many things, such as Indian baby skulls; many skulls of men and women; arrows, some perfect, many broken; spears, scalps, knives, cooking utensils and many other things too numerous to mention. We laid over one day and collected nearly a wagon load."[24]

Further information indicates that Bonsall developed a continuing knowledge of the massacre site and that his visit there with Sherman was not but a fleeting occurrence. In 1866 an officer of the Army Medical Museum had asked that skeletal specimens of tribesmen killed in the course of army-Indian encounters in the West be shipped to the museum for examination and to ascertain the effects of gunshot trauma inflicted at the time of death. The request resulted in the collection and forwarding of numerous remains, including some from Sand Creek that were picked up at the site between 1867 and 1870. According to records in the National Anthropological Archives of the Smithsonian Institution, at least two skulls (one identified for unknown reasons as that of a Kiowa Indian) were collected by Lieutenant Bonsall at the massacre site, probably in

1870.[25] Together with the Cahill manuscript, these references are important benchmarks for placing Bonsall at the massacre site on at least two known occasions, thus establishing for him credibility for his presumed knowledge of the location of "Chivingtons Massacre" as reflected on his map of June 1868.

In the following discussion of the Bonsall map, distances in parentheses reflect modern straight-line measurements and are provided as comparisons for Bonsall's own mileage figures, which were derived either from army odometer readings or reasoned estimates of distance traversed.[26] Because Bonsall's figures are rounded off, it is assumed that the distances reflected on his map represent the latter, that is, judgments of the approximate distance than of precise odometer-registered figures. Internal evidence indicates that, although this route to Cheyennes Wells had not been extensively used before, by June 1868 it was becoming increasingly used as a military road. Bonsall's map shows that his detachment left Fort Lyon at 5:30 A.M. on June 16 and moved generally northeast and north from Fort Lyon, probably along the same route used by Colonel Chivington less than three and a half years earlier. About two hours later, at a point 11 miles out, Bonsall's detachment encountered a "Large basin [with] no outlet," shortly followed by another of identical description. In his accompanying journal, the lieutenant notes that the "basins would hold water in wet weather, and in very rainy weather would be impassable." Analysis of aerial photos taken of the area in 1954 confirms the course of the trail through these features exactly as depicted on Bonsall's map.[27] His party continued on the trail through both basins (one of which was possibly the lake, or pond, encountered by Chivington's men on the night of November 28–29, 1864) for another 8 miles before making a temporary camp just above the junction of Rush Creek with Sand Creek, called "Greenwoods Camp" on the map but referenced in the journal as "Camp No. 1." Here, at 11:00 A.M., they halted for "five hours to graze the animals."[28] Apparently at around 4:00 P.M., the detachment proceeded north for another two hours, covering a distance of 11 miles, though perhaps more like 12 miles (13.1 miles), from the Rush Creek confluence to the point where the trail crossed Sand Creek.[29] Bonsall relates that en route his men "found plenty of good water by sinking a box in the sand in the bed of the creek." The lieutenant made his bivouac, designated "Camp No. 2" on his map, on the east side of the road and on the west (south) side of Sand Creek. By his estimate he had traveled about 30 or 31 miles (34.7 miles) from Fort Lyon.

At a point on his map just beyond the ford of Sand Creek, the lieutenant drew a bold line representing a distance of about two miles in length along the north (east) side of the stream and denoted it as the site of "Chivingtons Massacre." It is obvious from the site's delineation that it was already a well-known landscape feature. Furthermore, its pronounced representation on Bonsall's map without doubt signified its importance along the route because of General Sherman's presence and declared interest in it, resulting in the collection there of human remains and artifactual specimens. The detachment camped at the ford from 6:00 P.M. of June 16 until 5:30 A.M. of June 17, when it moved on. Importantly, the Bonsall map indicates the location of the Sand Creek Massacre site by placing it in relative position to the river bend, the road from Fort Lyon, and the road's crossing of Sand Creek. Bonsall's distances conform within tolerance of modern calculations to place the massacre site near, yet above, the South Bend of Sand Creek and probably within parts of modern Sections 10, 11, 13, 14, 15, 22, 23, 24, and 25, Township 17 South, Range 46 West, and Sections 19 and 30, Township 17 South, Range 45 West. The historical-site marker placed in 1950 stands in NW 1/4, Section 25, Township 17 South, Range 46 West.[30]

On June 17 Bonsall's detachment moved on past the massacre site. Six or seven miles north of their previous night's camp, they reached a point designated on the map as "Three Forks,"

Map 7. Archivally projected site of the Sand Creek Massacre.

where the route split into three roads. Bonsall's journal entry suggests that neither he nor his command were familiar with this part of the route. "At Three Forks the left hand road crosses the creek and leads in the direction of Denver. An ox train from the Arkansas bound for Denver had lately passed over this road. The right hand road is the direct and shortest road to Cheyenne Wells, but thinking it bore too much East we took the center road, which after following for a mile was lost. We then went due North by the compass, over a high prarie [sic], with a gradual ascent, very little broken, and struck the Old Butterfield Stage Road eight miles from Three Forks, and sixteen miles from Cheyenne Wells."

The importance of identifying Three Forks lay in its relative distance, approximately six miles, from the trail crossing at Sand Creek, where Bonsall's detachment spent the night of June 16–17 just below (south of) the designated massacre site, and its distance of approximately four miles north of the designated massacre site itself. Soil Conservation Service aerial photographs taken in the 1930s—some seventy years after the event—precisely confirm Three Forks as delineated on Bonsall's map (see figure 4, p. 38); moreover, what appears to be the road along the north (east) side of Sand Creek over which the Bonsall party traveled in 1868 is clearly shown. By following southeast along the road from Three Forks for the distance of over six miles that Bonsall shows, the likely site of the Sand Creek ford is reached about six and one-third actual miles away. Bonsall's map indicates that the area of the massacre began approximately one-quarter to one-third of a mile above the ford and stretched along the stream for a distance of about two miles.[31]

The Bonsall party returned from Cheyenne Wells on June 19, having sent General Sherman east by stage to the railhead of the Kansas Pacific line. The infantrymen returned to Three Forks by an alternate route that saved them a few miles. From there they followed their earlier trail past the scene of "Chivingtons Massacre," probably camping at the same places, and on back to Fort Lyon, which they likely reached late on June 20. Bonsall's map does not reflect for the return trip the same information about distances marched and times of arrival at particular places. In comparing information on the map with that contained in the Cahill account, there appear to be discrepancies regarding the time of arrival at the massacre site on June 16 (Cahill states "around two o'clock p.m."; Bonsall, 6:00 P.M.)

and the amount of time spent there (Cahill states that the men "laid over one day," whereas Bonsall indicates that they spent only one night there.) Cahill was correct in stating that "it took one day from the battleground to the railroad," though he should have said "stage line" rather than "railroad." Yet Cahill's is a reminiscent account prepared as many as fifty years after the fact, while Bonsall's journal and map constitute a documentary record officially rendered at the time. Regardless, in its content and simplicity of presentation, the Bonsall map embraces the most directly compelling contemporary information yet found about the location of the Sand Creek Massacre site.

FINDINGS REGARDING THE EXTENT OF THE SITE OF THE SAND CREEK MASSACRE

Extent as used here defines spatial limits that are inclusive of the broad sweep of an entire immediate historical event. Regarding the Sand Creek Massacre, *extent* refers to the areal expanse of terrain, or range, over which occurred Chivington's attack on the village, the subsequent slaughter in the streambed and in the sand pits above the village, and all related troop and Indian movements and actions, to include the general area of approach of the troops when in closing proximity to the village and the general areas of rising terrain bordering either side of the creek where the Indian pony herds grazed and over which many of the tribesmen fled to escape the onslaught or were pursued by soldiers. Most documentary material located in the course of this research appears in the testimony and recollections of people, both Indian and white, who were there on November 29, 1864. Information contained in these sources offers clues to the extent of the site, most commonly in the form of precise or approximate distances registered between points. Thus, the major component properties defining the extent of the Sand Creek Massacre site consist of the area where Black Kettle's village stood; the area or areas where major killing took place in defensive sand pits excavated upstream from the village; and the intervening and immediately adjoining terrain where associated actions took place.

The Village Site

Virtually all sources that consider the position of the village mention that it stood on the north (east) side of Sand Creek, and one soldier testified that its edge was within fifty yards of the creek.[32] George Bent's two diagrams of Black Kettle's village (see maps 2 and 3) show its relative position on the north (east) side of Sand Creek at the time of the massacre, but these depictions lack proper scale and, seemingly, proportion.[33] The Cheyenne Little Bear, according to Bent, noted that the village lay below a bend in Sand Creek to the north.[34] Bent allowed that the site had been used by the tribes for many years previous and that in the village, "each band was camped by itself with its lodges grouped together and separated by a little open space from the camps of the other bands."[35] Estimates on the linear extent of the principal village, which contained approximately one hundred lodges of the various bands, indicate that it occupied an area of about a quarter to a half mile or more in length.[36] There is no known corresponding figure reflecting the approximate width of the camp. Also in the area (some sources indicate one-half to three-quarters of a mile from the main camp) stood a small group of perhaps as many as eight lodges said to belong to the Arapahos.[37] The presence of a spring near the village was essential because of the Indians' need to access a steady and reliable fresh-water source; at this location at this particular time of year, Sand Creek itself yielded some, though relatively little, water, and much of this was likely used for the horses and for other camp-related purposes. The area lies in what is termed a perennial stretch, a length of somewhat consistent groundwater percolation as opposed to flows generated by storms. This was undoubtedly the primary reason for the site's traditional use, yet according to participant testimony at the time of the massacre, the streambed was practically dry.[38] Cheyenne oral history has indicated the presence of a spring near the village site, and a 1997 overflight confirmed the presence of one in the area that could have been accessed by the people. Moreover, the most current topographic quadrangle map indicates this spring as well as other intermittent streams entering Sand Creek from the north in the area of interest.[39] Given the limit imposed by Lieutenant Bonsall's map, which places his trail ford of Sand Creek immediately below, or south of, the massacre site, and Bent's description from Little Bear, who was in the village and who remembered that the stream turned north within one hundred yards of the northernmost lodges of the village (together with other cumulative knowledge regarding area land use during and after the massacre, as discussed in appropriate sections below), the site of the village was postulated to be in the NW 1/4 of Section 24, Township 17 South, Range 46 West, and possibly extending onto the SW 1/4 of Section 13, Township 17 South, Range 46 West (see map 7). Furthermore, either of Bent's village diagrams correspond reasonably well with this area in terms of directional alignments, the stream's approximate contours relative to that on the modern USGS map, and the comparable distance between the village and the area of the sand pits.[40]

The Sand Pits

Estimates of the distance between the village and the area of the sand-pit defenses (including, from the records, the area to which the howitzers were drawn and emplaced) to the northwest differ widely in the various participant accounts of the encounter, ranging from a low of three hundred yards to a high of just over two miles but with most coalescing at around a quarter mile to one mile.[41] Chivington reported that the pits, or trenches as he called them, "were found at various points extending along the banks of the creek for several miles from the camp."[42] It is important to note that some participants who registered greater distances described them from the point of inception of the attack below the village, or perhaps from the lower part of the village, and sometimes included movements upstream beyond the point where the howitzers fired into the sand pits to places where lesser action occurred.[43]

Considering the fact that many of the people fleeing the village led or carried children and elderly noncombatants through the sandy streambed and also had to throw up hurried defenses below the banks, the distance between the camp and the sand pits would appear to have been smaller than greater. The majority of accounts describe the streambed at the point where the sandpits were dug as measuring about two hundred yards or more in width, though at least one placed the width at a quarter mile.[44] Despite some variances, the preponderance of statements indicates that the banks of Sand Creek in this area measured anywhere from six to fifteen feet high.[45] While most of the accounts agree that the Indians took refuge in the pits along both sides of the creek, some specify that the major defensive activity occurred along the west (south) bank.[46] And George Bent's two diagrams of the village and massacre site show a length of women-dug pits along the base of the west bank, while three or more rifle pits occupied by warriors appear in the center of the streambed. Based on the above factors, coupled with knowledge of the existence of sandbanks of varying height in the area, it was conjectured that the site of the sand pits lay in the SE 1/4, Section 13, and in Section 14, Township 17 South, Range 46 West, approximately a half mile or less above the suggested village site (see map 7).[47]

Two braces of howitzers took part in the action at the sand pits. After a few salvoes discharged during the opening of the attack, the howitzers, two of which belonged to the First Colorado and two to the Third, were brought up the creek and, from positions on opposite sides, fired into the areas of the occupied sand pits, apparently from several different vantages and at alternate times.[48] On one of his diagrams, Bent placed two of the guns on the north (east) side of Sand Creek, a short distance from the bank and opposite of, yet slightly below (south of), the location of the pits.[49] Although unspecified, the angles of fire of the pieces had to have been such as to prevent any direct firing into the troops on the banks who were pouring small-arms fire into the defenses.[50] As for the construction of the sand pits, one soldier participant described them as being "deep enough for men to lie down and conceal themselves, and load their guns in; some of them I should think were deeper than three feet."[51] Chivington said that the "excavated trenches" measured "two or three feet deep."[52] And a veteran soldier recalled: "along the base of the bank they had dug a trench four feet deep, throwing the dirt forward, which made a formidable breastwork. . . . Along the top of the bank they had dug rifle pits about 50 feet apart, which would shield four or five men each."[53] At least two other statements support the notion of the Indians entrenching along the tops of the bluffs.[54]

Other Factors of Extent

Besides the unquestionable core areas represented in the village site and the major concentration of sand pits, other elements contributing to determine the extent of the massacre site would include the location of the small Arapaho camp; the pony herd areas; the area of the approach of the army columns, together with the expanse they occupied while ascending Sand Creek to the area of the sand pits; the points of the initial howitzer emplacements; the area of other offensive and defensive actions farther upstream along the creek as well as over the surrounding countryside; the hospital area; and the bivouac area of Chivington's troops over the two nights following the massacre. At least one official report and two participant accounts (one a reminiscent statement rendered some forty-three years

later) specify the location of a lesser camp of as many as eight
lodges apparently detached from and one-half to three-quarters
of a mile below the main village and presumably on the north
side of the stream.[55] One of George Bent's diagrams locates the
major Indian pony herds on land away from the south (west)
bank of Sand Creek opposite the village (see map 2). According
to Bent, some of these animals had been driven off during the
night by Chivington's Mexican scouts. Those remaining apparently ranged some distance south and east of the camp, for First
Colorado troops encountered them during their approach that
morning at least one mile to the east. Estimates of the number
of ponies and mules captured range from 450 to 600. The animals were corralled by the herders, apparently in the area of the
South Bend of Sand Creek, "a mile or so south of the village"
and likely on the tract north of the present marker.[56]

As for the area of the army's approach to the village, the
documents agree that Chivington's command marched into
the area from the south and reached the proximity of the camp
coming generally from the southeast. The troops likely first
viewed the Indian encampment from an eminence some three
to five miles away,[57] then continued rapidly forward until they
reached a hill from which the village could be seen from one
to two miles distance.[58] The command descended to the broad
creek bottom. At a point approaching the village, the command
split, with First Lieutenant Luther Wilson's battalion moving
across to the north (east) side of the creek to a point northeast
of the village, while Major Anthony advanced to a point on the
south (west) bank southeast of the camp. Colonel George L.
Shoup's Third Colorado Cavalry followed and proceeded to a
point perhaps a half mile from the village, where the soldiers
halted to dispense with unwieldy luggage and prepare for the
attack.[59] Following that, they struck out through the deep sand
toward the encampment, gravitated to the right, and ultimately
came in on the rear of Wilson's troops on the north bank. Both
Wilson's and Anthony's units were approximately one hundred

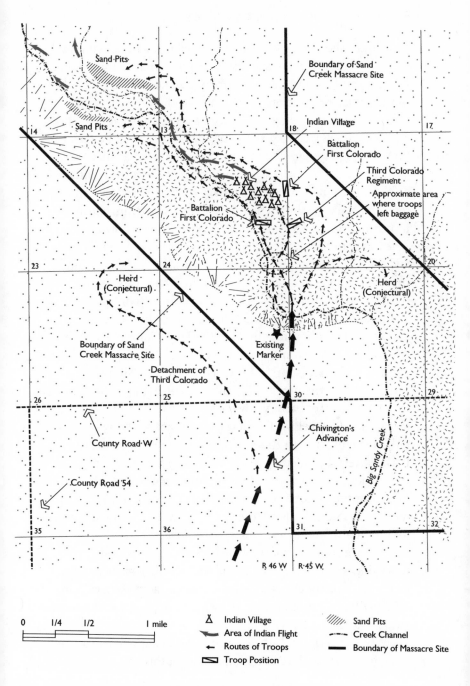

Map 8. Troop and Indian movements, November 29, 1864.

Within the map:

Sand Pits

Boundary of Sand Creek Massacre Site

Sand Pits

Indian Village

14 13 18 17

Battalion First Colorado

Third Colorado Regiment

Approximate area where troops left baggage

Battalion First Colorado

23 24 20

Herd (Conjectural)

Herd (Conjectural)

Boundary of Sand Creek Massacre Site

Existing Marker

Detachment of Third Colorado

26 25 30 29

Chivington's Advance

County Road W

County Road 54

Big Sandy Creek

35 36 31 32

R 46 W R 45 W

0 1/4 1/2 1 mile

△ Indian Village   ▨ Sand Pits
🡒 Area of Indian Flight   -·-·-· Creek Channel
← Routes of Troops   ━━━ Boundary of Massacre Site
▱ Troop Position

yards from the lodges when they opened fire with small arms on the village and its occupants.[60] As the action unfolded and the villagers fled upstream, the troops pursued them, generally in their relative positions but "in no regular order," on either side of Sand Creek, shooting in a crossfire pattern at the Indians. It was reported that the pursuing bodies of soldiers were "two or three hundred yards apart" during this advance.[61]

In the opening attack, at least some of the four howitzers discharged rounds toward the village that dispersed the tribesmen and perhaps sparked their initial flight upstream and away from the soldiers. Although the precise location of the guns when they fired is not yet known, the recollections of officers and soldiers indicate that they remained some distance behind, though in the general proximity of their respective units, as the troops closed on the encampment. Some contemporary statements allowed that "the artillery [was] in the bed of the creek." Accounts of members of the First Colorado Cavalry relate that Chivington ordered their battery to fire from a high point slightly left (south) of the "Fort Lyon battalion" on the south bank of the creek.[62] Meantime, the guns of the Third Colorado Cavalry battery advanced so far on the north bank, though still well below the village, that Major Anthony's troops pulled themselves to their left as a precautionary measure. Both batteries evidently discharged ordnance, but only the rounds delivered from the Third's battery seemingly took effect in or near the village.[63] Given the effective range of eight hundred yards and the maximum range of twelve hundred yards for mountain howitzers firing spherical case at five degrees of elevation, a zone of expectancy where artillery-related artifactual evidence (friction primers and such) could logically appear might reasonably be established within a radius of five hundred to fifteen hundred yards as scaled from points within the suspected area of the village.[64]

While the principal attack and massacre continued for seven or eight hours, collateral action occurred throughout a wide swath of the surrounding country as some of the tribesmen attempted to flee and scrambled for safety in all directions. Some headed southwest across Sand Creek in their flight and were pursued by soldiers; others fled northeast of the village, where detachments of cavalrymen ran them down until dark.[65] Following the initial attack and the confrontation in the sand pits, squads of cavalry scoured the countryside seeking escapees, and Major Anthony reported, "the dead Indians are strewn over about six miles."[66] Nonetheless, many of the men, women, and children who had been in the village and the sand pits managed somehow to elude the pursuit, especially after night fell, and ultimately journeyed northeast some fifty miles to find succor among friends and relatives camped in the Smoky Hill River country.

According to at least one reminiscent account, during the action at the pits, Chivington sent word back to troops at the village to save several of the largest tipis for sheltering his wounded men, who were being transported there by ambulance wagon. The tipis were cleared out to accommodate these men, and the field hospital was thus established close in the vicinity of the abandoned Cheyenne camp at the approximate time that some of the Coloradoans began destroying its contents.[67] Regarding the area where the troops bivouacked following the massacre, it seems that most of the command likewise occupied a tract immediately adjacent to the village. Chivington reported that he "encamped within sight of the field," and other soldiers noted that the camp was "in the upper end of the Indian village" and that it took "the form of a hollow square." A place in the vicinity of the camp possessing fairly level terrain and available water would likely have proved attractive for Chivington's seven-hundred-plus-man force.[68]

Taking into account the above factors relating to the extent of the massacre site, the area incorporating the village and the principal concentration of sand pits upstream from it comprised a linear area of perhaps one and one-half miles, an estimate that conformed closely with the approximately two-mile length registered by Lieutenant Bonsall. Adding to this the area of immediate approach and of the initiation of action by the troops below the village would extend the linear area south- east by approximately two miles, while fighting along the stream above and northwest of the sand pits likely took place for another couple of miles or so, presenting a possible overall length of extent of five and a half miles (see map 9). More dif- ficult to ascertain because of the even greater lack of clarity of events is the corresponding breadth of the area of action on either side of Sand Creek, an expanse that would encompass the area of the herds, the gun emplacements, and the auxiliary movements of Indians and soldiers over the landscape away from the central massacre site. Because the streambed meas- ured as many as two hundred yards across in places, and troops ascending either side from the village to the sand pits were perhaps as many as three hundred yards apart, a width for the linear corridor of at least one-half mile is suggested, though one and one-half miles might more appropriately incorporate areas where some of the associated actions addressed above occurred. Of course, in its broadest sense, the wide-ranging activities of the troops and Indians beyond the village and streambed took place at undetermined distances away from the primary action. When asked in formal inquiry his judgment of the full extent of the massacre site, Captain Silas Soule of the First Colorado Cavalry succinctly replied, "about four or five miles up the creek, and one or two each side."[69] From all appearances, he was close on the mark.

ARCHIVAL STUDY CONCLUSION

The archival record leaves little doubt that the Sand Creek Massacre took place in the area of the South Bend of Sand Creek, though not precisely at the bend. Rather, the evidence gleaned from the Bonsall map, the two Bent diagrams, and a

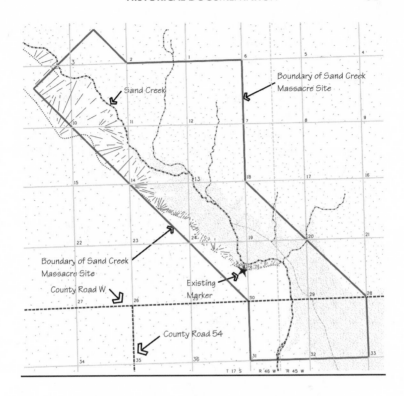

LEGEND

☐ Sand Creek Massacre Site Boundary

0 1/4 1/2   1 mile

Scale of Distances

SAND / 80,009
IR 77 1-00

Map 9. National Park Service boundary of the Sand Creek Massacre site.

host of participant testimony and other documents led to the conclusion that the major property encompassing the village lay upstream, probably in present Sections 24 and 13. As well, while the exact site of the sand pits, the other major resource property where so many people were killed, is presently not conclusively known, a projection based on archival materials tentatively indicates that this encounter occurred in Sections 13 and 14.[70] To recapitulate, based on available records and literature, the area of the location and extent of the immediate massacre site, to include the likely areas of all associated features and actions, measures approximately five and one-half miles long by one and one-half miles wide in a swath running diagonally northwest to southeast and enclosing throughout that distance the linear course of Sand Creek. Included within this boundary are parts of Sections 10, 11, 13, 14, 15, 22, 23, 24, and 25, Township 17 South, Range 46 West, and parts of Sections 19 and 30, Township 17 South, Range 45 West (see map 7). Inside this broad, encompassing swath of land, the stark tragedy of Sand Creek played out in all its horror.

3

IDENTIFYING THE
SAND CREEK MASSACRE SITE
THROUGH ARCHEOLOGICAL
RECONNAISSANCE

Archeological investigations have long been a part of the tool kit used by researchers of historic sites. Today scholars see the disciplines as complementary, where each develops independent lines of evidence that are melded into a comprehensive and inclusive interpretation of past events. The Sand Creek Massacre Location Study is, in many ways, the epitome of such a multidisciplinary endeavor. In this case the 1997 archeological study raised a number of questions that could only be effectively addressed by further historical research. The reanalysis of the historic record and the discovery of additional historical documents led to a new view regarding the location of the village site and the sand pits. With the revised locational information in hand, new hypotheses were generated to be addressed using archaeological methods and theory.

1997 ARCHEOLOGICAL INVESTIGATIONS

The location study's archeological component began as part of
the Fort Lewis College effort headed by Dr. Richard Ellis. In
1995 Fort Lewis College was awarded a grant from the State of
Colorado to study and locate the Sand Creek Massacre site.
Ellis developed a research design that called for the skills of
archeologists, historians, geologists, map experts, aerial photog-
raphers, and Cheyenne and Arapaho representatives to work
together to establish the location of the site.

Utilizing the George Bent diagrams of the village as a primary resource, Ellis's team defined two land areas that match
the features present on the sketches. The two bends in Sand
Creek that appeared to most closely match Bent were the traditionally identified site, located on land owned by William F.
"Bill" Dawson, and a second and more northerly bend, owned
by William Rhoades and referred to as the North Bend.[1] Initial
archeological fieldwork was conducted in late September and
early October 1997 and used a combination of metal detector
and visual-inventory techniques.

The 1997 metal detector survey located a relatively small
quantity of artifacts. A total of only fifteen items were collected
during the field investigations, and only six of those, located in
the South Bend, dated as early as 1864. The archeological report
of the 1997 investigations drew few definitive conclusions
regarding the location of the Sand Creek Massacre site from
the physical evidence. The North Bend was excluded since
only post-1866 artifacts were found there. The1864-era artifacts found in the South Bend were too few in number and type
to say if they represented the November 1864 event or some
other activity occurring in the early 1860s. The report closed
with several recommendations for future research. Among the
conclusions was the recognition that the land areas inventoried might have been the wrong locations and that more historical research should be undertaken to place the site more

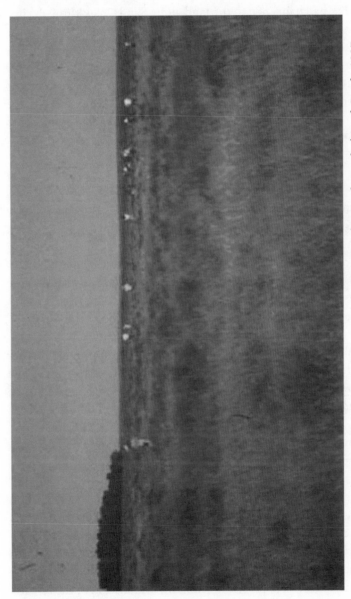

Fig. 5. Pikes Peak Adventure League members metal detecting in the South Bend of Sand Creek, 1997.

accurately on the landscape. Also, it raised the question as to
what had happened to the land along Sand Creek through time
and if the creek had shifted or flooded so often as to cause the
site of the massacre either to be buried below the depth range
of metal detectors or to have been destroyed by the abrasive
action of floodwaters. A recommendation was made to have a
geomorphologist, a specialist in landform changes, study the
site and determine how much change if any, had occurred to
the landforms in Sand Creek over the last 135 years.

Geomorphology as an Investigative Tool

One of the first priorities of the National Park Service study
was contracting for a geomorphological study of Sand Creek
and its terrace system. Michael McFaul of La Ramie Soil Services conducted the work for the park service by boring three-
inch-diameter holes with a truck-mounted soil-coring device
at various points along Sand Creek. These soil cores, or columns,
were compared to the known and dated geology and soil depositional sequences for the area. Organic materials were also
collected and used for radiocarbon dating to provide further
refinement to the dating of the soil deposition sequence. The
geomorphological study concluded that there appeared to be
little or no soil buildup or aggradation of soil on the terraces
for several hundreds of years, and some of the valley floor may
have only minimal aggradation due to flooding or wind-blown
deposits.[2] The sediment cores also revealed less subsurface
disturbance than expected, with less sediment aggradation
than previously thought. Some areas immediately adjacent to
the streambed and within the floodplain may contain deposits
that are deep enough to prevent the effective use of metal
detectors, but only in that narrow and currently active stream
channel. The geomorphological research indicated that the
general lack of appreciable sediment aggradation in the last 135
years made the choice of metal detectors a nearly ideal inventory

Fig. 6. Michael McFaul explains the geomorphological core-drilling work to tribal representatives.

tool, thus indicating that the 1997 archeological metal detecting inventory of the South Bend was accurate and the lack of artifactual finds was not due to deep burial of the site nor its loss to erosion.[3] It became clear that the alternative theory that Ellis's team had not inventoried the appropriate location was the more plausible explanation for not finding more evidence of the massacre.

EARLY RELIC COLLECTING ACTIVITIES AT SAND CREEK

Another aspect of the National Park Service multidisciplinary research effort was the documentation of earlier artifact-collecting efforts begun by Ellis's team. Along with documentary research, aerial-photograph interpretation, and tribal-research efforts, local artifact collectors were contacted to determine if they had either relics or knowledge of the Sand Creek Massacre site.

Local tradition and historical documentation indicate that the Sand Creek site was subject to relic collecting over many years. The extent to which these collecting efforts affected the site cannot be fully assessed, given the current state of knowledge, but it appears that some collecting began immediately after the massacre. In 1932 the Colorado Historical Society accepted a collection purportedly from the site, noting, "The Society has received a gift from Mrs. Blanche Squires Lester (Mrs. Barton G. Lester), comprising a number of valuable Indian relics which were gathered at the Sand Creek battlefield in December 1864, by her father, George C. Squires, formerly of Boulder, Colorado." George Squires was a member of Company D, Third Colorado Cavalry, which remained at the Indian village until the morning of December 1, 1864.[4]

As noted earlier, Lieutenant General William T. Sherman, in the company of Lieutenant Bonsall, visited Sand Creek in June 1868 during a tour of frontier military sites. The party is reported to have collected relics and human remains from the area, which were supposedly sent to Washington, D.C.[5] The human remains were repatriated to the tribes some years ago, and unfortunately all traces of the other relics have disappeared. An early Kiowa County homesteader, Henry Fluke, who lived about three and a half miles south of the Dawson property, is reported by Colorado historian Wilbur Stone to have collected cannonballs, arrows, and other evidence of the fight in the early 1900s.[6]

Visits with the family of a well-known local collector, the late Preston "Dick" Root, produced additional oral history about Sand Creek Massacre relics. Root apparently visited and collected at the Sand Creek site many times during the 1930s and 1950s, scouring the field each time there was a significant dust storm that caused various portions of the site to be exposed; he was the owner of a small store in Chivington and is reported to have closed shop to go artifact hunting after any dust-bowl-era windstorm. His family reported that he collected many items from the battlefield, including bags of round balls (bullets) and arrowheads. They also mentioned that the Sand Creek collection was sold about twenty years ago to a man in Nebraska who intended to establish a private museum, but the buyer died before his museum opened, and the collection was subsequently dispersed. Family members identified the general area of Root's finds as about one to two miles northwest of the Sand Creek commemorative marker on the Dawson property.[7] Another local collector also reported collecting relics of the Sand Creek Massacre some distance north of the commemorative marker.[8]

Between July 1989 and October 1993, metal detector hobbyist Fred Werner made five trips to Sand Creek for the purpose of relic collecting the massacre site. He detected, in a nonsystematic way, portions of the bluffs and creek bottom on the Dawson property. Werner reported that neither he nor his traveling companions found any battle-related relics during their wandering up and down Sand Creek.[9]

In 1992 William Schneider metal detected and conducted some geophysical scans of portions of the Dawson and Bowen properties.[10] He found four items on the bluffs located on the west side of Sand Creek in Sections 25 and 26, Township 16 South, Range 47 West. He also recovered two fired musket-size percussion caps, two dropped (unfired) .58-caliber Minié balls, and a segment of the threaded fuse ring of a 12-pounder mountain howitzer shell or case shot reportedly just south of the North Bend.

Chuck and Sheri Bowen, son and daughter-in-law of landowner Charles B. Bowen, began metal detecting their land along Sand Creek in March 1998 in an attempt to find the Sand Creek Massacre village and sand pits. The authors viewed their collections on several occasions in 1999 and again in 2002. The Bowens have collected thousands of artifacts from their lands, principally in Sections 14 and 10, Township 17 South, Range 46 West. Some of their items are late nineteenth century and early twentieth century in origin. That part of the collection is dominated by post-1880 tin cans, mass-produced cut nails, farm machinery, and bullets and cartridge cases postdating the 1864 event and quite likely associated with the short-lived settlement of Upper Water Valley, or New Chicago, that once existed in Section 14. Artifacts observed were .45-, .44-, .38-caliber and other later cartridge cases and bullets as well as blacksmithing tools and farm machinery parts indicating later site occupation.

But the Bowens have recently recovered hundreds of period small-arms ordnance (.50-caliber Maynard bullets, .52-caliber Sharps bullets, .54-caliber balls fired in Model 1841 rifled muskets, .54-caliber Starr bullets, .58-caliber Minié balls, and others) and 12-pounder mountain howitzer shell or spherical case-shot fragments in Section 14 along the creek terraces. The 1864-era artifacts in their collection include, among other items, iron arrowheads; iron cone tinklers; brass bracelets; at least one 12-pounder shell fragment; at least three 12-pounder case shot, including fuse rings; three Bormann time fuses (two set for two seconds and one for five seconds of flight); hundreds of case-shot balls; percussion caps; an iron chain consistent with a Civil War canteen stopper chain; sprue from casting lead bullets; some melted and burned metal of undetermined origin; a broken coffee grinder; a crushed brass kettle; broken cast-iron kettles; a broken Dutch oven; iron hoes; an ax head; a hide scraper made from an old flintlock gun barrel; and a brass cavalry spur.

Given that the relic-collecting oral traditions place the site some distance north of the commemorative marker and that the 1997 systematic archeological inventory essentially questioned the validity of the South Bend of Sand Creek (the site immediately below the marker) as the site of the camp location, it became clear that the 1999 archeological field investigation needed an expanded search area. With the majority of the lines of evidence converging and pointing to the village being located nearly a mile north of the traditional site in the South Bend, the archeological team developed a strategy for conducting the inventory to locate physical evidentiary remains of the village and the attack by the Colorado volunteers.

1999 NATIONAL PARK SERVICE
ARCHEOLOGICAL INVESTIGATIONS

The 1999 archeological field investigations again relied on metal detecting as the best available technique to find buried metal objects relating to the village and the attack. The use of metal detectors as a tool for systematic inventory is well documented in the field of historic archeology and especially on Indian wars battlefields.[11] The archeological team developed a research design that identified the methods and techniques to be employed in the next phase of the field investigations. As with the first phase, the Colorado Historical Society and the various tribal representatives became full participants in its review and final development. A contingency for what protocols would be followed should any human remains be found was developed and approved by all concerned, though that process was not

needed since no human remains were found during the field
investigations. The research design specified that the inventory
phase would employ electronic metal detectors, visual survey
methods, and piece-plot recording techniques as part of the
standard archeological field-recording procedures. The purpose
of these investigations was to locate and identify any archeological sites, features, or artifacts in the study area. The primary
research goals were to determine if any physical evidence
existed in the study boundary that could be associated with the
site of the Cheyenne and Arapaho village attacked by Chivington on November 29, 1864.

The inventory phase included three sequential operations:
survey, recovery, and recording. During survey, or inventory,
artifact finds were located and marked by either metal detecting the ground surface or by visual inventory. The survey team
lined up and walked designated transects, or sweeps, until an
area was completed. The recovery crew followed and carefully
uncovered subsurface finds, leaving them in place. The recording team then plotted individual artifact locations using a total
station transit and electronic field book to collect location
information on each object or feature found, assigned field-
specimen numbers, and collected the specimens.

The 1999 effort covered ground not investigated in 1997.
The team used a systematic approach, working outward from
the areas searched in 1997 toward the target area one mile north
of the South Bend. The metal detector team began its systematic transects on the south and west side of that bend. Working in a line, the team swept from the south side of Sand Creek
back and forth, in an east-to-west direction, between the monument commemorating the massacre and an eastern property
fence line until the terraces were inventoried. Many finds of
twentieth-century fencing, baling wire, and other detritus associated with modern agricultural practices were made, but no
artifacts that dated to the nineteenth century. The team then
moved up the west side of Sand Creek to the north end of the

1997 inventory area. Metal detector transects were laid out north and south, covering the terrace above the Sand Creek floodplain. About thirty-five hundred feet north of the South Bend, 1864-era artifacts appeared in the holes dug at the metal detected target locales. These artifacts were in a band some three hundred feet wide and about twelve hundred feet long north to south. Among the finds were .54-caliber Starr carbine bullets, .52-caliber Sharps bullets, a .32-caliber bullet, an iron arrowhead, and two fragments of 12-pounder spherical case shot.

This concentration of artifacts was an exciting find, but what did it mean? Archeological investigations are based on the use of the scientific method as expounded in the field of the physical sciences. Hypotheses or questions are generated to be answered by the acquisition of data. As new data are found and recorded, the hypotheses are tested and accepted or rejected. New data, especially unexpected discoveries, require new questions to be developed and tested. This is a constantly evolving process, to which the finds along the west side of Sand Creek were subjected. The artifacts were clearly of the types that dated to the 1860s. And the ordnance items were the same types—the Starr, Colt, and 12-pounder spherical case shot—known to have been used by the Colorado volunteers.[12] Thus their presence allowed the team to accept the notion that these pieces were somehow involved in the events of November 29, 1864. To establish what their roles may have been, new hypotheses were generated and tested against the data. The two most obvious questions were either if the artifacts and their depositional context were related to the flight for survival of the villagers or if each represented gunfire that had overshot its mark and embedded itself in this area as it reached the end of its maximum trajectory.

The team reasoned that if these artifacts were the remains of shots fired at the fleeing tribesmen, more would likely be found to the north along the course of the creek and possibly to the west as well. The inventory team swept farther west with no additional finds, and little was found to the north until the property boundary separating the Dawson lands from that of the Bowen's was encountered. There a few bullets were found. The floodplain of the west side of Sand Creek was also swept with no finds in that area.

The lack of other ordnance artifacts to the north, south, and west, indicated that the flight-for-survival hypothesis was lacking. While it could not be rejected outright, the lack of supporting evidence suggested that an alternative explanation was more likely. The overshot theory was the next to be investigated. If the finds did represent ammunition falling to ground at the end of its trajectory and there were no 1860-era artifacts to the west, south, or north, then the next place to look was the area east (on the north side) of Sand Creek.

The team crossed the streambed and began the metal detector sweeps along the eastern margins of Sand Creek. Within minutes, 1860-era artifacts were being uncovered in quantity. Among those items were cast-iron kettle parts, utensils, tools, iron arrowheads, a cache of horseshoe nails, and a pile of .58-caliber round balls numbering over 170. These bullets were lying on an old soil surface known as a paleosol at a depth of about eight inches. This collection was likely in a bag or pouch when lost, and it lay undisturbed on a ground surface that had not seen the light of day for around 130 years. These bullets and other artifacts lay at a depth in the soil exactly as predicted by the geomorphological study.

The metal detector team continued sweeping the floodplain and the terraces on the east side of Sand Creek in a systematic reconnaissance. An area covering over thirteen hundred feet by five hundred feet of the first terrace east of the creek yielded over three hundred artifacts related to the encampment of the Cheyenne and Arapahos and Chivington's attack on the village. The artifacts found here included fragments of cast-iron kettles, skillets, tin cups, tin cans, horseshoes, horseshoe nails, plates, bowls, knives, fork, spoons, barrel hoops, a coffee grinder, a coffee pot, iron arrowheads, bullets, and cannonball fragments.

Fig. 7. The .58-caliber round-ball-bullet cache as it was excavated.

Fig. 8. Crushed and flattened tin cups from the village site.

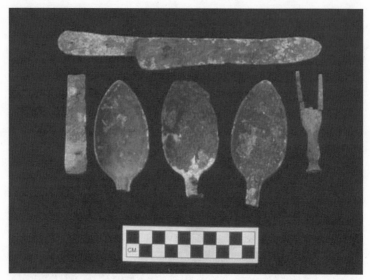

Fig. 9. Table knives, spoons, and forks found in the village site. The shafts of the spoons, one knife handle, and the fork, including the tines, have been deliberately broken.

Fig. 10. Fragments of small tin food graters, commonly called radish graters.

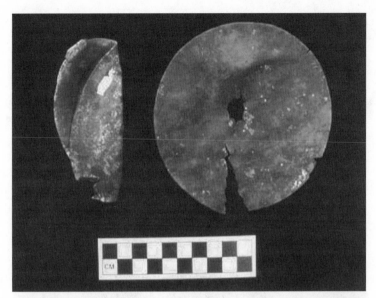

Fig. 11. The top and base to a tin coffeepot or boiler. Note the hole in the center of the base, caused by either a bullet or a pickax.

Fig. 12. Fragments of 12-pounder spherical case shot.

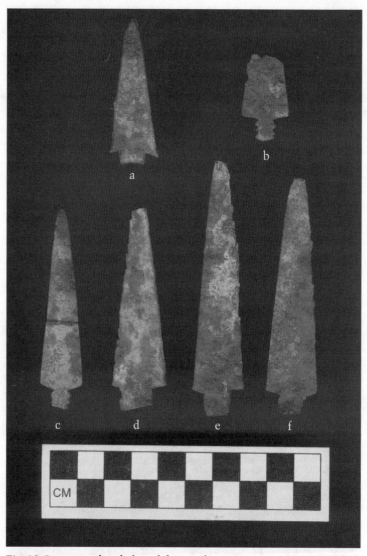

Fig. 13. Iron arrowheads found during the 1999 investigations: a., d.–f. unfinished arrowheads (note the unfinished cut edges on e. and f.); b. a base of a camp-made arrowhead; c. a commercially made arrowhead.

TABLE 1

Sand Creek Artifacts by Functional Category

Firearms and Munitions
.30-caliber
.32-caliber
.36-caliber
.44-caliber
.44-caliber Henry
.50-caliber bullets and
    cartridge case
.52-caliber bullets
.54-caliber bullets
.56–56-caliber Spencer cartridge
    case
.58-caliber bullets and centerfire
    cartridge case
Cannon-related case-shot
    fragments
Lead fragments
Percussion caps and cap tins
Trade gun or musket part
Arrowheads

Military Equipment
Shoulder-scale fragment
General-service buttons
Canteen stopper ring
Picket pin

Personal Items
Suspender grip
Buttons
Boot nails
Photograph preserver
Trade-silver fragment and
    ornament
Bells
Shear or scissor
Thimble
Tinkling cones

Camp Equipage and Utensils
Tin cups
Tin pans
Tin plates
Tin bowls

Tin coffeeboilers/pots
Tin buckets
Tin grater
Coffee grinder/mill
Cast-iron kettles
Cast-iron pots
Cast-iron skillet
Iron basting spoon
Iron table spoon
Iron table fork
Iron table knife
Iron butcher knife
Meat skewer
Tin cans
Sardine can
Potted-meat can
Condensed-milk can
Trunk lock
Kerosene lamp part
Gas-jet lighting device

Tools
Axe
Awls
Files
Hammer
Flesher/scrapers
Wedge

Horse Equipage
Spur
Saddle plate
Bridle parts
Tack buckles
Horseshoes
Horseshoe nails
Wagon hardware

Fasteners
Cut nails
Wire nails
Brass tack
Strap iron
Barrel hoops

The concentration also included artifacts that are usually considered unique to Indian sites of the nineteenth century. Besides the arrowheads, some of which were in an unfinished condition, were a variety of iron objects modified for Indian uses. These included knives altered to awls, iron wire altered to awls, fleshers or hide scrapers, strap iron altered by filed serrations as hide-preparation devices, and several iron objects altered by filing

Fig. 14. Indian tools from the village site: a. iron scraper or flesher bit; b. scissors-blade fragment with the W-shaped notch; c. a knife tip altered by filing a W-shaped cutting surface; d. strap iron with two W-shaped notches; e. strap iron with a serrated edge, an awl tip, and a W-shaped notch; f. a triangular file.

Fig. 15. Hide-preparation tools recovered in 1999: a. flat iron scraper or flesher fragment; b., c. strap iron altered to a hide scraper or cutting tool by filing serrations; d. iron scraper or flesher bit.

to serve a cutting or scraping purpose, possibly to groove arrowshafts. The complete listing of the artifacts recovered and the attendant analysis is included as Appendix A.

Geophysical Investigations

Another level of inventory was also carried out in conjunction with the metal detecting work. A geophysical remote-sensing assessment was conducted on a portion of the presumed village site that had one of the highest concentrations of artifacts. Remote sensing relies on nonintrusive geophysical instrumentation to look beneath the soil surface in an attempt to locate anomalies or buried features. Four contiguous sixty-foot-square blocks were laid out, and archeologist Steven DeVore ran his remote-sensing scans across the grids with three separate devices. Two utilized the principal of electromagnetism, an EM 38 and an EM 61, and the third was a magnetometer, specifically a Fluxgate gradiometer. The EM 61 and the magnetometer were successful in locating several small anomalies that are likely more-deeply buried metal objects. No evidence of hearths or tipi circles was seen in the remote-sensing scans.[13]

ARCHEOLOGICAL DATA ANALYSIS

With the field data collected, the next step was to clean, catalog, and analyze the artifacts and their associated depositional information. The analysis identified the artifacts by function and compared them with other similar artifacts to determine their date of origin and deposition. The location of each find had been precisely mapped and that information recorded. The locational context of each object and how it related to every other object was also analyzed. The primary research issue to be answered with the archeological data was whether or not the artifacts recovered represented the remains of Black Kettle's village. The artifacts, their distribution on the landscape, and the context in which they were recovered would provide the answer. The pertinent questions were: does the artifact assemblage date to 1864; do the artifacts represent an Indian camp; and is there physical evidence to support the proposition that this site was attacked?

The artifact analysis and description clearly show that the majority of items indeed date to the mid–nineteenth century

Fig. 16. Steven DeVore conducting geophysical remote-sensing work on the village site.

for origin and use. While no individual piece can be said to have been made and exclusively used in 1864, the composite assemblage is consistent with items manufactured and used at that time period. The majority of artifacts easily fall within the range of use for 1864.

There is also limited evidence that the prehistoric inhabitants of southeast Colorado used the general area of Sand Creek. The few prehistoric items found during the investigations are consistent with the relics recovered by the many collectors who have searched the area over several decades and clearly demonstrate nearly ten thousand years of intermittent human occupation of the landscape.

At the other end of the spectrum are the camp debris and other evidence of the late-nineteenth-century Euro-American settlement of the area. This began in earnest during the 1880s. There is physical evidence of that occupation and land use scattered over the area investigated. Tin cans from meals, wire from the construction and mending of fences, and late-nineteenth-century stove parts may reflect the remains of a camp associated with the construction of an irrigation canal or simply a cattlemen's roundup camp. This post-1864 occupation evidence continues up to the present, with bits and pieces of ranching and farming debris and exemplified by the automobile parts and modern cans and nails found on site.

Regardless of this evidence of a span of occupation from prehistoric to modern times, there is ample separation in the clusters of artifacts, in a chronological sense. Although not abundant, the first evidence of human occupation of the Sand Creek drainage is prehistoric. Second, and clearly separated from the first by millennia, is the mid-nineteenth-century-artifact assemblage that is consistent with an 1864 battle-related date. Finally, and again clearly separated from the mid-nineteenth-century assemblage, though only by twenty or more years, is the late-nineteenth-century cluster. This last artifact group has a continuum that reaches to the modern era. Thus the artifact collection contains a major assemblage that consistently dates to the 1864 event horizon.

Artifacts of the 1864 period have been variously found along the Sand Creek drainage, beginning with the South Bend and continuing northerly to the Bowen Middle Bend, a small curve in the stream between the more prominent North and South Bends. There are two significant concentrations of artifacts in that three-and-a-half-mile stretch, one is on the eastern side of the creek near the center of Section 24, Township 17 South, Range 46 West, and the other, found by Chuck and Sheri Bowen, is on their property in Section 14.

The South Bend was inventoried in 1997. That area yielded a few 1864-period artifacts, and William Dawson subsequently recovered several others. These items include two round rifle balls, a .69-caliber musket Minié ball, a bullet fired in a .44-caliber Colt revolver, a military picket pin, a part of a military shoulder scale, two military buttons, two axes, a fragment of trade silver, and a brass arrowhead. A possible military saddle ring and a .54-caliber Minié ball were also recovered in 1997, but they were over a quarter mile north of the South Bend. The

Fig. 17. A Civil War picket pin as found in the South Bend, 1997.

Fig. 18. A fragment of trade silver found in the South Bend, 1997.

1864-period artifacts indicate that some activity or activities occurred in this bend of Sand Creek in about 1864, but they are so scattered and dispersed that they do not constitute evidence of the campsite.

Several possible explanations can be advanced to explain the presence of these items. One is that the Indian pieces were lost when other camps were abandoned at other dates, including the real possibility that this locale was once the site of a Black Kettle village, but that the camp was moved sometime prior to November 29, 1864, for sanitary purposes, to improve grazing for the animals, the exhaustion of available resources at the site, or for other reasons. It is also possible that the military items were lost as a result of Chivington's men stashing their extraneous equipment before the attack on the village or because some of the Coloradoans camped at this locale after the attack.

The Bowen Middle Bend has yielded only a few 1864-era artifacts to the investigations. But Chuck and Sheri Bowen have collected literally hundreds of artifacts from another slight curve in the stream now called the Bowen South Bend. Some date to the post-1880 era and probably represent the now-nonextant community of New Chicago. This later, rather intense occupation has partially obscured the evidence of the earlier occupation period. Nevertheless, the Bowens have found significant number of items that may constitute the site of the separated Northern Arapaho camp and very possibly evidence of the sand pits. The village evidence appears concentrated on the terrace on the east bank of the creek. The sand-pit evidence was found in the form of bullets and 12-pounder spherical-case and shell fragments concentrated on the western bank of Sand Creek. Other combat-related materials lay scattered along either side of the stream in Sections 10, 14, and 15, Township 17 South, Range 46 West. They were widely scattered and there was no other definitive evidence of a concentration of camp debris of the 1864 period. Yet the scattered period artifacts indicated that these lands played a role in the massacre and the flight for survival by the Cheyenne and Arapaho.

The largest concentration of 1864-era artifacts to date was found on the northeastern side of Sand Creek near the center of Section 24, Township 17 South, Range 46 West. The artifact cluster, situated on an terrace above Sand Creek, measured about 1,350 feet long, trending southeasterly to northwesterly, and about 500 feet wide and was considered to be the main campsite occupied by Black Kettle and the Cheyenne.

There is also an area on the eastern margin of the concentration that contains a number of more modern objects, such as sanitary tin cans, fencing wire, wire nails, and other twentieth-century items. These were intermingled with and obscured the 1864-era objects in that area of the site. This group of artifacts probably relates to ranching activities that occurred during the Euro-American settlement of the area. Roundups were one reason that stove parts and tin cans may be present, and the items may be related to the construction of a nearby irrigation canal. The old archeological saw that good camping spots are continually reused seems proven once again. But despite the intrusive modern material, there is no doubt that the majority of finds concentrated on this eastern terrace of Sand Creek were consistent with Indian occupation in the 1860s.

The presence of Indian campsites with artifacts dating to about 1864 begs the question, is this the Cheyenne and Arapaho village occupied by Black Kettle? Short of finding an item with a known 1864-camp-resident-name glyph scratched on it, other lines of evidence must be used to make the identification. There is a wealth of comparative data from Cheyenne and Arapaho annuity requests, annuity lists, and other correspondence that provide a set of comparative data.[14]

One such source is a depredation claim by J. H. Haynes, an 1864 government contractor to the Upper Arkansas Agency (included as Appendix B). His contract specified that he would construct buildings at the agency and at related irrigation features. During November 1864, he lost his working stock and tools to Cheyenne and Arapaho raiders. On December 17, 1865, he filed the first of many claims for reimbursement for losses valued at $18,864.62. It would be 1868 before his claim was settled, and then only for only $2,500. Among his losses were a variety of blacksmithing tools, carpenter tools, felling axes, shovels, and hoes.[15] These items would leave archeological remains at a site.

The Cheyennes and Arapahos were also parties to several treaties with the federal government, obligating authorities to supply the tribes with a variety of goods. These annuity payments were made beginning in the 1850s and continued until well after 1864.

The annuity lists, requests, and correspondence were researched, transcribed, and compiled (see Appendix C) and clearly demonstrate that most of the artifact types found during the archeological investigations and by the Bowens were the same types as listed for issue to the Cheyennes and Arapahos. Tin cups, bowls, plates, coffee grinders, coffee pots, kettles, pans, knives, forks, spoons, fleshers, axes, butcher knives, horse tack, guns, lead, and bullets are consistently listed in these records. These are the durable goods provided, the items that can be expected to survive in the archeological record, and indeed such pieces were found during the field investigations. There are many more items of a perishable nature, such as flour, sugar, salt, dresses, and such, that would leave only minor or negligible traces over time.

The lists for the Cheyennes and Arapahos are only the tip to a very large material-culture "iceberg." Similar annuity lists for the Kiowas and Comanches also exist.[16] A very extensive record of goods for sale or trade to Indians on the upper Missouri River at Fort Union, Dakota Territory, in the 1855 period has also been assembled and studied.[17] These show that many of the same material items were readily available and a part of the trade, gifts, and sales to many different tribes on the Great

Plains during the middle of the nineteenth century, in particular during the years immediately before and after 1864.

Ideally, there should be an inventory of goods captured and
destroyed by the Colorado cavalrymen at Sand Creek compiled
after the attack on the village. But, given the units' laxity of
military protocol on any number of fronts, perhaps it is not
surprising that no such record has surfaced during the documentary research. The closest thing is a brief statement by cav-
alryman Morse Coffin describing the aftermath of the attack,
wherein "the other [tipis], together with the many tons of
Indian supplies which the village contained, were piled and
burned. There must have been tons of dried buffalo meat, and
large and numerous packages of coffee, sugar, dried cherries,
saddles, bridles, and lariats, robes, and skins, numerous new
axes, [and] many well-filled medicine bags."[18]

Without the ideal list from Sand Creek, such sources from
comparable attacks must also be consulted. Appendix D lists
Cheyenne, Arapaho, and Lakota camp goods captured and
destroyed in three separate events; all involved some of the same
people who were in the village at Sand Creek on that cold
November morning. The first is from a Cheyenne and Lakota
village destroyed along Pawnee Fork in April 1867 near Fort
Larned, Kansas. This village had tons of material goods left
behind when the wary Indians fled an overwhelming force of
soldiers led by Major General Winfield Scott Hancock and Lieutenant Colonel George Armstrong Custer. This inventory represents the actual contents of a village where the captured material was broken up, piled, burned, and destroyed. These items
are clearly comparable to those found in the Sand Creek archeological investigations.

The second list is that of the Washita attack, which took
place on November 27, 1868, near present-day Cheyenne, Oklahoma, only a little more than a year after the abandonment of
the village at Pawnee Fork. Some of the same Cheyennes participated in both events. The document identifies the goods

captured and destroyed by the Seventh Cavalry after they routed the Washita villagers and contains twenty-two types of materials. In comparing the Washita list to the Pawnee Fork list, which itemizes fifty types of goods, one notes significant differences. There are fourteen types of goods found at Washita that are not on the earlier list: horses, saddles, coats, rifles, revolvers, bullets, lead, bullet molds, gunpowder, bows, arrows, shields, blankets, and tobacco.

The third list represents items recovered at the encounter that took place on the eastern Colorado plains at Summit Springs in 1869. There the army victors of the surprise attack on Cheyenne Dog Soldiers identified forty-two material types abandoned and destroyed when they captured the village. There are nineteen types present at Summit Springs that do not have a comparable item from the Pawnee Fork village: horses, rifles, revolvers, bullets, bullet molds, lead, gunpowder, percussion caps, bows, arrows, shields, war bonnets, moccasins, dresses, coats, glass bottles, hammers, meat, and gold coins.

Comparisons between the Washita and Summit Springs captured goods show only a few types not on the other list. The difference between the Washita and Summit Springs village contents and that for the Pawnee Fork site is striking. Yet there is a difference in the manner in which the villages' contents were captured that must be taken into account. Hancock and Custer captured a deliberately abandoned village, while the Washita and Summit Springs villages were captured after surprise attacks. The Cheyennes and Sioux in the Pawnee Fork village had time to take what they needed and wanted, leaving behind many less important or less portable items. Notably absent from the Pawnee Fork inventory are weapons and equipment for hunting and warfare—almost all of the items abandoned at Pawnee Fork were domestic items. If one removes the weapons and associated equipment and regalia from the Washita and Summit Springs lists, then there exists a striking similarity between the encampments' remaining domestic goods.

After removing the weaponry and related materials from the Washita list, there are only four items that do not correspond between it and the Pawnee Fork site: coats, blankets, tobacco, and horses. These differences can be explained by the fact that the Pawnee Fork villagers used their horses to flee Hancock's command. Nor is it surprising they would take blankets and coats, for it was April and the weather was still cool. Tobacco, if present at Pawnee Fork, is almost self-explanatory.

Using the same method in removing the weaponry and related materials and comparing the Summit Springs contents to the Pawnee Fork site, the differences are reduced to only eight items: horses, meat, glass bottles, moccasins, dresses, coats, hammers, and gold. The same reasoning can be applied as to why these were not present at Pawnee Fork. The differences are simply a matter of what was abandoned as opposed to what was lost in acts of war.

The only other comparable village site to be archeologically investigated is Pawnee Fork. The recovered artifacts were compared to the items recovered from the Sand Creek site. There are arrowheads, kettles, tin cans, knives, gun parts, bullets, and many other objects that are of the same type and period as those recovered at Sand Creek.[19] The similarities between the two sites are striking. Factoring out the firearms and ordnance materials from the Sand Creek sample and comparing it to the Pawnee Creek assemblage shows a high degree of correlation in the types of Euro-American goods present in both camps.

The Sand Creek sample is nearly all metal, which reflects the fact that the inventory method employed metal detectors to find the artifacts. The presence of nonmetallic items in the Pawnee Fork assemblage is probably more reflective of the testing and excavation strategy used there rather than of a true difference between the two archeological assemblages.

The two artifact assemblages have firearms-related artifacts in both as well as clothing items such as buttons and other fasteners. Each also has some military items (other than firearms) present in the form of buttons. The camp-equipage class demonstrates a good degree of correlation in the presence of coffee mills, knives, tin wares, cast-iron wares, and other utensils. Horse equipage of similar types is also present in both camps. The differences between the two archeological assemblages are seen as less important than the similarities due to the variant investigation and recovery methods.

Perhaps the most striking similarity between the two collections is their broken and fragmented condition. In neither artifact assemblage is there a reasonably intact item, apart from bullets or buttons. All of the larger items, particularly camp equipage and horse gear, are broken, fragmented, or crushed. In both cases this damage appears to be deliberate and not the result of random cattle tramping or natural freeze-thaw cycles. The extensive damage the artifacts suffered is likely the result of intentional injury. In both cases the military commanders ordered the villages burned and their contents destroyed. The damage seen in the artifacts is the physical expression of those orders, to render the goods unserviceable to the Indians. By crushing and breaking the items needed by the Cheyenne and Sioux, the army succeeded in impoverishing the people and forcing them to seek aid from other sources.

It is abundantly clear from comparisons with the available annuity lists, inventories of captured and destroyed goods, and the one other archeologically studied Cheyenne camp (at Pawnee Fork) that the concentration of artifacts found at Sand Creek in Sections 14 and 24 are consistent with an Indian village of the 1860s era. The weight of comparable evidence shows that it is very likely that the Sand Creek assemblage is an 1864-era Cheyenne community.

The final issue to be addressed is whether or not there is evidence in the archeological record that this is the village attacked by the Coloradoan cavalry. The archeological record contains strong evidence that is consistent with the conclusion that this area is the site of Black Kettle's village and the slightly separate Arapaho camp attacked by Chivington's forces. Present in the locations are two lines of evidence that this village was attacked and destroyed. First is the evidence of arms and munitions. The village site yielded bullets for various calibers and types of firearms, including the .52-caliber Sharps rifle or carbine, .54-caliber Starr carbine, .54-caliber musket, .58-caliber musket, .36-caliber revolver, and .44-caliber revolver. These weapon types and calibers were used during the American Civil War and can be readily dated and identified. Appendix E lists the known ordnance used by the First and Third Colorado Cavalry during late 1864. The concordance of the archeological munitions finds and the lists of weapons in the volunteers' hands is quite remarkable—they match exceedingly well.

In addition, there has been some limited archeological investigation of one of the Colorado volunteer campsites in eastern Colorado at Russellville. Among the artifacts recovered there are numerous bullets of the types known to fit the handguns and shoulder arms of the First and Third Cavalry.[20] The Russellville archeological collection and the Sand Creek collection also show a very high degree of concordance.

Perhaps the single most important artifact type that can definitively identify this village as the one attacked by Chivington are cannonball fragments. The Colorado volunteers employed four 12-pounder mountain howitzers during their attack. The cannon fired three types of ammunition—shell, spherical case, and canister. Ordnance tables of the Civil War period prescribe one shell, six case, and one canister round for each howitzer's ammunition chest.[21] Four 12-pounder spherical case fragments were found during the archeological investigations. Chuck and Sheri Bowen have recovered at least three other case-shot fragments and one 12-pounder shell fragment on their lands, and one other is known to be in a private collection.

These cannonball fragments are nearly unequivocal evidence in their own right that this is the site of the Sand Creek Massacre.

The firearms artifact distribution also adds to the story. There are three concentrations of firearms artifacts as well as several widely dispersed bullets. The first consisted of bullets, both fired and unfired, found in the village site. Almost all calibers associated with the Colorado volunteer units were present. The unfired rounds quite probably represent cartridges dropped or lost by the soldiers as they moved around the camp. Some were probably dropped in the heat of the attack, others may have simply fallen from open cartridge boxes as the soldiers moved about. Another possibility is that some of the unfired rounds represent soldiers throwing away bullets after using the powder to start fires either during the time they camped in the abandoned village or while trying to burn and destroy the Indians' abandoned materials.

TABLE 2

Comparison of Known Firearms Types
Used by the Colorado Cavalry at Sand Creek
to Recovered Ordnance Artifacts

Known Caliber and Types	Represented Archeologically?
12-pounder mountain howitzer	Yes
.71-caliber muskets	Yes
.69-caliber muskets	No
.58-caliber muskets and .58-caliber rifled muskets	Yes
.56-caliber Colt's revolving rifles	No
.54-caliber rifles	Yes
.54-caliber Starr carbines	Yes
.52-caliber Sharps carbines	Yes
.44-calbier Colt revolver	Yes
.44-calbier Starr revolvers	Yes
.36-caliber Colt Navy revolvers	Yes
.36-caliber Whitney revolvers (used standard .36-caliber bullet)	Yes

A 12-pounder howitzer case fragment was also found in the village. It provides mute testimony to the fact that the artillery shelled the camp.

The second concentration of firearms artifacts was found on the west side of Sand Creek and about one thousand feet directly opposite the village. These items were found along a line about twelve hundred feet long. Sharps and Starr bullets were uncovered as were two 12-pounder case fragments. These probably represent rounds that overshot their intended targets in the camp or were simply ricochets from the firing on the camp. Another possibility is that the bullets and cannonball fragments represent rounds fired at fleeing Cheyenne and Arapaho tribesmen. The narrow linear distribution, however, more likely reflects overshot or ricochet rounds falling to earth once their maximum range was reached. This artifact distribution probably reflects firing along nearly the entire length of the village and as such is another strong indicator that the site was attacked and fired upon.

The third concentration of bullets and cannonball fragments is on the Bowen land in Section 14. There, on the western side of the creek, the Bowens have found 12-pounder case shot, shell, and three Bormann time fuses. Bullets, most in calibers used by the First and Third Colorado Cavalry, also abound. Dispersed among those bits of lead and iron that represent the hail of fire poured into this area were a few simple tools, two hoe blades, an ax head, and a hide scraper made from an old gun barrel. These items could be what the Cheyennes and Arapahos used to dig the expedient shelter pits, the sand pits. Although no formal and detailed description or analysis has been conducted on the Bowen collection, there is little question that it is a significant assemblage of detritus of war. Strikingly, the Bowens have found little in the way of bullets or evidence of Indian weapons in their searches of their property. But a detailed study of their collection would either alter that perception somewhat or reinforce it.

The other widely dispersed firearms artifacts were found east of the village, ranging from nine hundred to eighteen hundred feet, and north of it, ranging from a few hundred feet to well over two and a half miles. Among the bullets closest to the camps are also mingled bits of village items, such as coffee grinders, that may reflect attempts to salvage a treasured item at the time the Cheyennes and Arapahos fled the attack on their homes. The distribution of these fired bullets and the two privately collected cannonball fragments clearly show the line of the flight for survival taken by the villagers and the pursuit conducted by the Colorado troops.

The firearms data is particularly striking in two respects: the absence of bullets or other weaponry evidence of resistance either in the camps or related to the defense of the sand pits. Bullets representing weapon types that can be reasonably associated with the Cheyennes and Arapahos are singularly absent from the artifact collection from the campsites and in the areas surrounding the presumed location of the sand pits on the Bowen property. The absence of definitive artifacts of resistance is consistent with Indian oral tradition that the attack came as a complete surprise. Evidence of combat or armed resistance is not great but more compelling, as seen in the firearms artifacts found along the flight-for-survival route. The flight for survival and the defense of the sand pits are two important elements in the Sand Creek story. The artifacts related to the former indicate there was some, albeit limited, armed resistance by those fleeing the village (though more study of the Bowen collection should be undertaken to test this assumption).

The final bit of evidence that identifies this area as Black Kettle's village is the condition of the artifacts found in the camps. Every spoon, the fork, all tin cups, and the plates, bowls, and containers—buckets, pots, and kettles—have been crushed and flattened; even the tin cans are crushed. The cast-iron pieces—kettles, pots, and the skillet—are broken. The patterns of crushing and breakage point to the intentional destruction of the items so as to make them unserviceable to their owners.

This methodical and deliberate destruction is also duplicated in the Pawnee Fork camp assemblage of 1867. The historical records of both Sand Creek and Pawnee Fork demonstrate that the wealth of material in the camps was burned and destroyed. The archeological record sustains this in a very clear and dramatic manner.

The archeological data, including the artifact distributions and the artifacts themselves, overwhelmingly point to the approximate center of Section 24, Township 17 South, Range 46 West, as being Black Kettle's camp of November 1864, and the Bowens' land in Section 14 as the site of a separate northern camp on the east side and the sand pits on the west side of the creek. There are three main lines of archeological evidence that lead to this conclusion.

1. The majority of artifacts are types that were in use in 1864 and are comparable to goods given or acquired by the Cheyennes and Arapahos in the years immediately preceding and following the massacre.
2. Internal evidence shows that the camp material was intentionally destroyed.
3. The arms and ammunition evidence demonstrates that combat occurred at this site, and the armament artifacts are consistent with those carried by the First and Third Colorado Cavalry, the units that that perpetrated the massacre.

In summary, a number of reasonable conclusions can be drawn from the archeological record. There is little doubt that the South Bend was a site in the attack. Chivington certainly crossed this area, perhaps having his command leave behind unnecessary or burdensome equipment. The picket pin, military buttons, and the bullets found there may be evidence of this. The presence of Indian items in the South Bend suggests that Indians had camped on that site at one time during the mid-nineteenth century.

Black Kettle's village was located twelve hundred to fifteen hundred yards north of the South Bend of Sand Creek. The site is situated on a terrace on the eastern side of the creek. The camp-debris distribution indicates that the general village structure was somewhat linear in alignment, following the contour of the terrace, which trends northeast to southwest. The actual placement of individual tipis or band-group tipis is not known, but overall village orientation appears to have been longer than it was wide, the main camp being about 1,350 feet long and perhaps 500 feet wide. The eastern margin of the village is partially obscured by late-nineteenth-century canal building and ranching activities. A northern campsite has been found by the Bowens but requires further analysis and documentation to confirm the assumption that it is the Northern Arapaho camp. The terrace was apparently a good camping spot for at least two cultures. There is archeological evidence for the flight from the village, particularly to the north and east.

Personal and camp items were apparently salvaged and carried away by the Indians in their headlong flight away from the attacking Coloradoans. Some of the items were dropped and became the artifacts that were subsequently recovered during the archeological investigations or found by the landowners and others. The distribution of bullets and cannonball fragments on the Bowen South and Middle Bends indicates that the flight and fight continued in a northerly direction for at least two miles and perhaps more.

The preponderance of evidence, both historical and archeological, demonstrates that Black Kettle's village was located in Sections 24 and 14, Township 17 South, Range 46 West. The presence of typical Indian camp items in the archeological record, the physical evidence of armaments pointing to a one-sided attack on the village, and the strong evidence of the intentional destruction of the abandoned material all aid in validating the site as the location of the Sand Creek Massacre.

4

POSTARCHEOLOGY ARCHIVAL CONCLUSIONS REGARDING THE LOCATION OF THE SAND CREEK MASSACRE SITE

Knowledge gained of the location of Black Kettle's village at Sand Creek during the archeological reconnaissance of May 1999 invited a reevaluation of certain elements of the documentation that initially helped define the area likely to hold material evidence of the campsite. The major concentration of village-related-artifact discoveries lay about a quarter mile southeast of the area that historical documentation indicated to be the site. The projected site was based primarily on Lieutenant Samuel Bonsall's 1868 map and on collateral information contained in the immediate testimony of officers and men who were present at the massacre as well as in reminiscent Cheyenne statements given during ensuing years. Taken together with the documentary materials, the archeological findings also help refine the scenario about how the events of the Sand Creek Massacre unfolded. The following observations are offered for the purpose of augmenting and solidifying the knowledge gleaned from the documentary record in light of

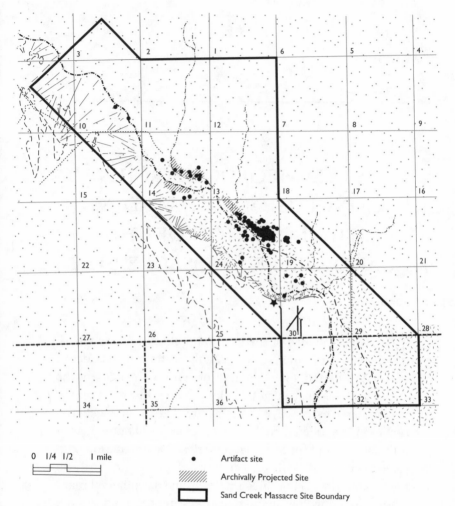

0 1/4 1/2   1 mile

•   Artifact site

▨   Archivally Projected Site

▭   Sand Creek Massacre Site Boundary

Map 10. Archivally projected site of massacre with archeological overlay.

the archeological findings and, thus, of providing further defi-
nition for the designated location of the massacre site.

THE BONSALL MAP AND THE GEORGE BENT DIAGRAMS

As a primary means of identifying the location and extent of
the Sand Creek Massacre, the Bonsall map of June 1868 and the
data derived from it proved of inestimable value. First, the chart
complied with period army regulations in terms of exactness
and of noting "every point of practical importance" on the
route—including the location on the ground of "Chivingtons
Massacre." Second, it was executed within four years of the
massacre and is thus contemporary with the event; when
Bonsall's detachment moved over the historic ground, it still
brimmed with direct evidence of the slaughter, both in terms
of material items and human remains. Further, the field commanded special attention because of General Sherman's presence and singular interest in it. Information from this map,
compared and correlated with data from other sources on modern aerial-survey photos, made possible the projection and ulti-
mate archeological determination of the location and extent
of the massacre site. The cumulative evidence from the Bonsall
map indicates that the village, and thus the beginning of the
massacre, took place not in the "V" of the South Bend, but
seven-tenths of a mile to the north at the point where the South
Bend begins its curve northwest. There is no doubt that the
Bonsall map, because of its immediacy to the event as well as
its routinely bureaucratic origins, constitutes an honest representation that genuinely registers the site of the massacre.
It proved to be a document of extraordinary significance.

For many years, conclusions about the location of the massacre site have rested with interpretations of the two George
Bent diagrams, which suggest that the Indian village—and thus
the beginning of the action—occurred in the pronounced "V"
of the South Bend some seven-tenths of a mile south of where

Bonsall's map specifies. Indeed, a rigid, face-value, nonanalytical interpretation of Bent's unscaled diagrams might allow their comfortable alignment with a topographic map of the South Bend. The Bent works, which closely approximate each other (but which also contain some significant differences if one studies them), were seemingly prepared between 1905 and 1914, from forty to fifty years after the massacre (see maps 2 and 3).[1] The diagrams appear to be schematic representations based upon the recall of Bent himself and Cheyenne survivors of Sand Creek. Although they contain invaluable information about who was there and the relative positioning of camp groups and features, they are not graphically precise depictions rendered on the site immediately after the event. Indeed, as earlier indicated, the titleless drawings are not referenced on either of the Bent-Hyde regional maps, so it is not known with certainty the place along Sand Creek that the diagrams are intended to represent, though it has been assumed that they depict the South Bend. It is important to note that the recollections of Bent and his associates placed the village near a bend, and the archeology—albeit based on interpretations afforded by the Bonsall map—has confirmed that the camp indeed stood in the proximity of a bend. But if Bent's diagrams affirm that the village stood directly in the South Bend "V" as they depict, they erroneously portray Chivington's trail as entering the village immediately from the south, a representation that could not have happened according to the immediate testimony of soldiers and officers who were present, much of it taken within weeks or months of the event and which suggests considerable activity and movement by the troops *after* having reached the creek bottom and *before* opening their attack.[2] Yet if Bent's diagrams are instead viewed as unscaled drawings with disproportionate features intended to illustrate the basic layout of the village and the events at Sand Creek, then their variances with other information are accountable and explain why the creek, village, and sand-pit defenses appear to be contiguous or closely so throughout. Indeed, if Bent's portrayal was meant rather to suggest that the village stood in the area of the South Bend, the archeologically disclosed village site then conforms with his diagrams.

Under such an interpretation, the troops indeed approached the camp from the south, following the Fort Lyon–Smoky Hill Trail, and crested the hill where the present marker stands, from which point they viewed the village a mile away to the north before descending to the Sand Creek bottom and following the streambed due north toward the area of the village site.[3] Again, because of the spatial limitations imposed in Bent's diagrams, the site of the sand pits appears practically to adjoin the west end of the village. In his reminiscent account, however, Bent states that the sand pits were "about two miles up the creek," above the village, thus suggesting that his diagrams—even in his own mind—were not rendered to scale. Most likely, considering the approximately two-mile extent of the massacre site as indicated on the Bonsall map as well as the testimony of participants, the area of the sand pits appears to begin approximately three-quarters of a mile above the area of the archeologically discovered village and extends for perhaps one-quarter mile to one-half mile along the creek in Sections 13 and 14, Township 17 South, Range 46 West. In addition to the archeological findings in that area, the width of the creek bottom in Section 14 conforms with the estimates of two hundred to five hundred yards given by participants.[4]

TOPOGRAPHICAL CONSIDERATIONS

There are landform constraints, particularly in the extent of available space and in the closing presence of the low bluffs adjoining the south side of the creek bottom, that would also reduce the likelihood that the village stood in the immediate area of the South Bend. Formal testimony by military participants indicates that after moving up the Sand Creek bottom perhaps as far as a half mile, the troops deployed by battalions in columns of fours in ascending Sand Creek. Those on the north (east) bank moved into a position to approach the village from the northeast, while those on the south (west) side of the village prepared to fire into the lodges from the southeast.[5] Considering the topography of the immediate South Bend area, in particular the rising ground and enclosing bluffs on the south side of Sand Creek, the presence there of a large number of lodges would have inhibited a column of several hundred cavalrymen from maneuvering in the manner described. In fact, only in the northeast quarter of Section 25, on approach to the area of the archeologically discovered village site, would an expanse of terrain sufficient to accommodate these tactical dispositions begin to appear.[6]

Furthermore, if the village stood directly in the "V" of the South Bend, the action (based upon the testimony of military participants) ostensibly would have to have been initiated downstream to the south, yet presumably above the radical southward turn of Sand Creek three-quarters of a mile east of the marker site, an extremely constricted expanse for the known operations. Moreover, considering the hour of the attack, the troops would have to have been off the trail and operating over uncertain terrain in the darkness. Existing testimony provides no support for this theory of the strike, nor is there documentary reference to the troops coming up the streambed and around a sharp bend to the west in initiating their assault.

Beyond the fact that the trail from Fort Lyon intersected Sand Creek in the immediate area of the historical marker, the hill where the marker reposes is additionally significant as being the highest point adjoining Sand Creek on its south (west) side. There is no similar prominent landform throughout the three-quarter-mile distance east to the abrupt southward bend.[7] If the troops trailing north along Sand Creek had deviated from the Fort Lyon Trail and approached via a route east of the marker's site, it would have to have been within that three-quarter-mile stretch, an area devoid of particularly high ground. Given the location of the archeologically discovered village site, there is nowhere else besides this hill that the First and Third Colorado troops, in the manner specified in the testimony, could have reached a prominence from which they could view the distant village, then drop into the bottom and advance to within a half mile of it (where the Third discarded their dunnage) and otherwise deploy for their attack. The configuration of landforms thus does not support an alternative approach to the village when considered in conjunction with the immediate testimony of massacre participants.

REEXAMINATION OF LOCAL SOURCES

In view of the archeology establishing the village site on the north (east) side of Sand Creek near the center of Section 24 and the more isolated camp in Section 14, several local sources earlier considered have assumed more significance regarding the location of the massacre site. Specifically, they relate to the position of the village and its relationship to the location of the headgates of the Chivington Irrigation Canal, which stood in the southeast quarter of Section 24. For example, a 1940 account by a man who accompanied John Chivington's visit to the site in 1887 stated that the massacre took place "at a point where the creek broadens out . . . and near which the Chivington irrigation canal has been taken out [constructed]."[8] Further, in 1910–12, a settler named A. J. Ingram filed on land adjoining Sand Creek. He wrote: "This is the same place that Col. Chivington attacked the Indians and the Sand Creek Massacre took place in 1864. I was here when the Chivington Irrigation Company was organized, and the headgates for the canal was [sic] partly on my place [in Section 24]."[9] In addition, a plat of the area drawn in 1938, though traced from a crude drawing made earlier by a settler name John Baumbach, showed what is designated "Chivington's Battle Field" located above, or north of, the headgates of the irrigation ditch.[10] What all of this suggests is that the village site, with all its debris, was located immediately adjacent to where the headgates of the Chivington canal were later erected in Section 24. As well, at least three references (one of them hearsay) to artifact-collecting activities in this area indicated that the major collecting spot was located one to two miles north of the historical marker, a position correlating well with the archeologically determined village site.[11]

Sand Creek Village Location and Hypothetical Organization

Historical documentation places five hundred people in the camp, distributed among one hundred lodges. The major, or most intense, Sand Creek artifact concentration as discovered through archeology is distributed over the landscape in an area of 1,350 by 500 feet, or about a quarter mile long by one-tenth of a mile wide. A more generalized artifact distribution, excluding isolated individual finds, covers an space of over a mile in length. Are either of these areas large enough to hold the recollected number of lodges, or could the camp have extended farther north, south, and/or east?

Unfortunately, none of the participants left a detailed description of the camp or its organization. The closest approximations available are the Bent diagrams. Those two works show only generalized occupation areas. It is necessary to look to historic and ethnographic resources on Cheyenne and Arapaho village organization to gain some additional insight into the possibilities for the manner in which the Sand Creek camp was organized.

Fortunately, there are a number of historic photographs of Cheyenne and Plains Indian camps taken in the early third quarter of the nineteenth century that provide some visual representation of camp organization, and there are anthropological

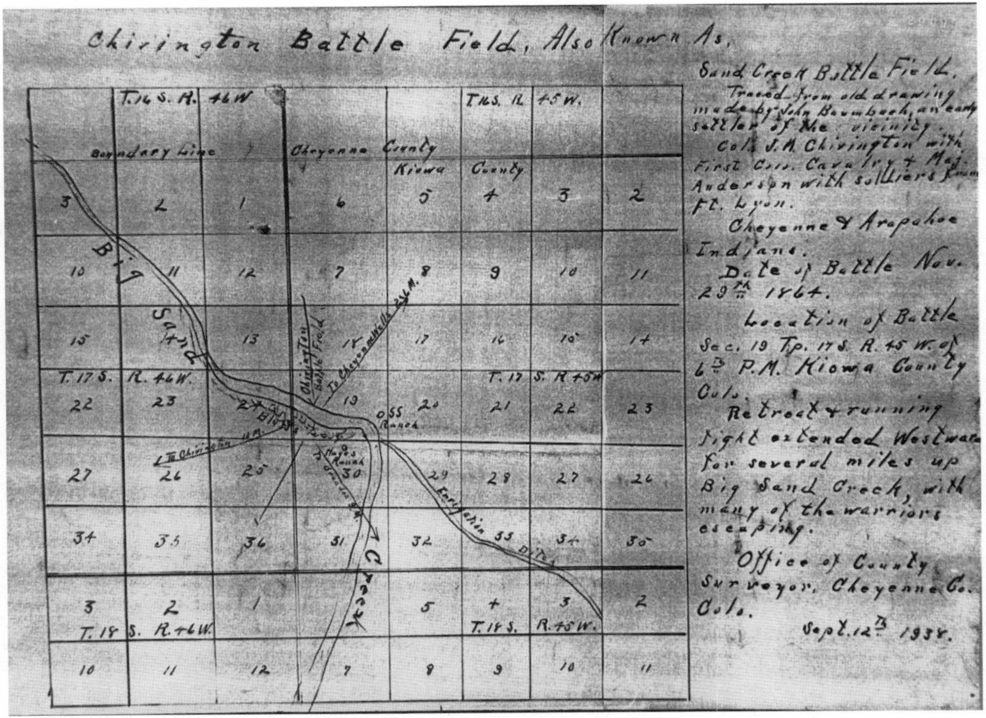

Map 11. A land plat (based on a drawing of John Baumbach) showing the location of the massacre site (presumably the village area) in relation to the Chivington Irrigation Canal, ca. 1938. The memorandum accompanying this map notes that the section numbers are incorrect, probably because of a faulty early "wagon wheel" survey, but that "for all practical needs [respecting juxtaposition of the massacre site and the canal], . . . [the plat] is correct." Item G4313, K451, 1864, B3, courtesy Colorado Historical Society.

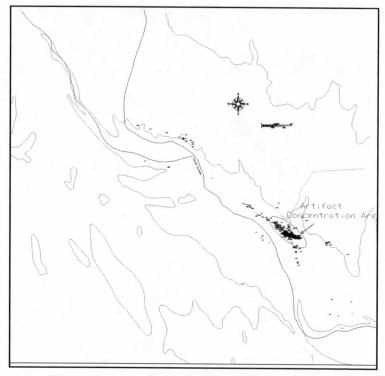

Map 12. Distribution of all 1864-era artifacts found along Sand Creek.

models of camp organization that the Sand Creek artifact distribution can be compared against.[12] The generalized model of
a tipi camp layout for different Plains Indian groups demonstrates that, while individual tribes had idealized arrange-
ments, these were rarely achieved due to the vagaries and constraints of landforms. Villages were arranged in many different
ways. Circular camps were often reserved for special ceremonies such as a sun dance. Other layouts regularly used were
semicircular, or horseshoe shaped; linear; and even scattered.
Randomly placed tipis occurred most often in temporary sites
where no ceremonies were expected to be performed. Camping along rivers and streams was common during the winter

months, when there was little threat of flooding. Spring, summer, and fall camps tended to be on higher terraces above water courses in order to seek protection from flash floods and to allow for greater protection from surprise attack, due to the greater visibility gained with increased elevation.

The idealized Cheyenne camp, exclusive of the sun dance and other major ceremonial gatherings, was semicircular, or horseshoe shaped. This was especially used when a ceremonial tipi was placed at the eastern opening of the arrangement. While large groups might employ the horseshoe shape, it was more often used by extended-family or band groups. In larger gatherings of tribesmen, there might be several of these band-group horseshoe-shaped units clustered to form the larger camp. Such a scene is depicted in several historic photographs of Cheyenne camps on both the southern and northern plains.

A tipi in the mid-nineteenth century was approximately twenty feet in diameter. Each represented an extended-family unit dwelling among the Cheyenne and Arapaho. Typically, an extended-family unit would consist of five to twelve persons— on occasion as many as eighteen—who might occupy a single tipi. The available photographic evidence shows that the individual lodges were often spaced fifteen to twenty feet from one another among those pitched in extended-family and band groups regardless of specific camp layout, linear, semicircular, or other. Thus the distance from the center of one tipi to the next would be approximately forty feet.

Using the conservative figure of five occupants per tent with a forty-foot spacing from tent center to tent center, a camp containing five hundred people and arranged in a linear fashion would require one hundred tipis taking up approximately four thousand linear feet, or about three-quarters of a mile.

It is unlikely that the Sand Creek camp was arranged in such a strictly linear fashion. But there are a number of other organizational possibilities. Two plausible scenarios can be developed based on the depictions of the camp drawn by George

Fig. 19. Nineteenth-century photograph of a Plains Indian village along a creek, ca. 1870–89. Courtesy Western History Department (X33920), Denver Public Library.

Fig. 20. A Cheyenne village showing the horseshoe, or open-U, arrangement of lodges, ca. 1880–1910. Courtesy Western History Department (X32009), Denver Public Library.

Fig. 21. A randomly scattered placement of tipis in a Plains Indian village, ca. 1880–1910. Courtesy Western History Department (X32049), Denver Public Library.

Bent. Both are clusters of tipis that assume Bent's drawings represent two or more lodge clusters. Using the idealized ethnographic camp-layout model—one of horseshoe-shaped band
units comprising at least ten tipis—the space required by one
hundred dwellings, with an idealized 40-foot spacing between
individual lodges, would be ten camp circles occupying about
2,000 feet by 160 feet total, if arranged in a linear fashion. The
second scenario places the camp circles in a more random
manner, one more consistent with the representative group-
ings rendered by George Bent. In this scenario some camp
units would be anchored on the stream and others placed farther away, creating a wider camp distribution but with sub-
stantially less length, the ten camp circles taking up an area of
only about 1,000 by 500 feet. All arrangement scenarios fit
within the broad artifact-distribution area as documented
archeologically, and the postulated random-tipi camp distribution fits well within the densest artifact concentration.

Oral Histories and Traditional Tribal Methods

As part of the study process, researchers solicited oral histories
from among the Northern Arapaho, Northern Cheyenne, Southern Arapaho, and Southern Cheyenne descendants of Sand
Creek Massacre survivors, looking to obtain information that
might assist in the location of the massacre site. More than
thirty descendants provided oral histories or prepared statements about family knowledge of the attack.[13] Their trans-
generational accounts evoke the pain of the attack as well as
the loss of their ancestors and how the tragedy still resonates
among their societies. Information derived from the interviews
regarding the location of the Indian village varied considerably.
Three informants stated that it stood in the South Bend "V,"
one stated that it extended from the South Bend to the area
where the archeological discoveries were made, one placed it
in Estes Park, another in Kit Carson, and a third in Fort Collins;

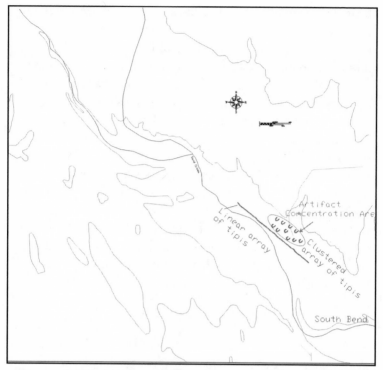

Map 13. Possible lodge-arrangement configurations showing how one hundred dwellings might fit into the Sand Creek landscape.

the remaining informants did not specify a location for the village in their statements. Even though the oral histories offered few specifics regarding the site location, they did provide general topographical information regarding landforms and watercourses, including the presence of a spring near the village, that were consistent with the area of the projected site as archeologically disclosed.[14]

Traditional tribal methods of site location also occurred during the project research. These generally took the form of sensing spiritual presences and/or of hearing the voices of women and children and horses and other animals or of seeing a domed light while on the site of the massacre. Several individuals

recounted experiences while in the area of the village and massacre site, most of them involving hearing women's and children's voices and the sounds of horses. Sightings there of sacred
animals, such as badgers and eagles, have also given important
cultural meaning to the location. Of the experiences described
during the course of the Sand Creek Massacre Project, one person placed the village and massacre site in the "V" of the South
Bend, while another placed it farther north in an area compati-
ble with the projected village site. During the archeological
reconnaissance in 1999, Northern Arapaho elders offered prayers
in the direction of the projected village area to assure that artifacts would be found there. Following the archeological discoveries, a Cheyenne pipe ceremony took place at this location,
additionally providing ceremonial blessing to the sacred ground.

In 1978 the Cheyenne Arrow Keeper, Red Hat, made Cheyenne Earth in the South Bend, thereby formally consecrating the
site of the massacre at that point. In Cheyenne society the
Arrow Keeper occupies a supremely responsible religious position as keeper of the *Maahotse*, or Four Sacred Arrows, that
stand at the heart of tribal religious belief, embodying the future
welfare of the people and representing a cornerstone of Cheyenne origin and culture. As such, Red Hat's designation of the
South Bend site is not only important but also perhaps of tran-
scendent significance in the Cheyennes' determination of where
the village stood and where the massacre began.[15]

An example derived from oral history and traditional
methods that also includes interpretation of Bent's diagrams
and an analysis of the archeologically discovered village site is
that offered by Laird Cometsevah, a chief of the Southern
Cheyennes. Cometsevah believes that the village stood in the
South Bend "V" and that the archeologically discovered site
represents two separate survival pits among the sand-pits area
that the village occupants fled to during Chivington's attack.
Under this scenario, the Coloradoans approached the east end
of the village in the South Bend from the south, one column

splitting and driving the Indians west and northwest in their flight while another rode west atop the bluff south of Sand Creek to the west end of the village before turning north in their pursuit of the tribesmen.[16] These alternative locations were acknowledged by the project members, and they are questions that remain to be addressed with additional documentary research, archeological investigations, and the gathering and evaluation of oral histories. Employing the multidisciplinary and scientific method in this study allows for the recognition of alternative hypotheses, though it also calls for the use of preponderance of evidence to reach a conclusion. Our interpretation of all the evidence points to the village site being north of the South Bend of Sand Creek, though we acknowledge that other points of view do exist and can be tested and retested in the future.

Conclusion

The disposition of the site of the archeologically defined village site, together with its immediate environs, suggests a refined scenario in which the attacking soldiers initially approached the camp from the south but began their enveloping maneuvers probably within a quarter to a half mile of descending the overlook and fording the creek (see map 8). Lieutenant Luther Wilson's battalion seems to have crossed the creek first; part of it then struck out after the Indians' herd located from a half mile to one mile east of the village while part approached the lodges from the northeast and/or east. Major Scott Anthony's battalion, part of which had previously rounded up horses, evidently followed Wilson's initial approach and descent from the bluff and continued north and slightly west to assume a position on the southeast of the camp by the time Wilson had completed his own movement. Once in position, both units opened fire on the village, which evidently by that time was partly deserted. Colonel George Shoup and the Third Colorado (with Colonel Chivington in attendance) approached after Anthony and Wilson had taken position. In a subsequent maneuver, Anthony's troops forded the creek (probably in the vicinity of the stock pond in the southeast quarter of Section 24) to its south (west) side to begin their attack against the tribesmen fleeing upstream in the bed of Sand Creek.[17] Simultaneously, Wilson, Shoup, and the remaining troops likewise pursued the Indians on the north (east) side of the stream all the way to the sand pits, where the greatest portion of the massacre took place.

Multidisciplinary Team Approach to Studies of the Past

A valuable lesson of the Sand Creek study goes well beyond the ability of the individual participants and even the value of contributions from specific disciplines to identify the site. Perhaps one of the lasting contributions is the value of the multidisciplinary team approach to solving a problem of the past. The National Park Service, as have many other groups, has effectively used the team approach on many occasions, but when the Sand Creek location study was given to the service, project managers immediately saw the absolute necessity of a this approach to solve the problem, given the disparity of opinion as to the site's location.

The Sand Creek team managers sought the advice of many people in several disciplines to develop the research team's membership in a way that would meet the needs of the special-resource-study goals. The team members were sometimes developed in depth from various disciplines such as history and archeology, with each member having specific goals to accomplish. Table 3 summarizes the disciplines composing the team and the role and function of each in the study effort.

TABLE 3
Multidisciplinary Team Approach

Team Members	Role and Responsibility
Historians	Reassess records and maps
Ethnographer and tribal members	Collect oral histories
Remote sensing	Aerial photographic analysis and geophysical ground studies
Geomorphology	Soil studies to determine landform changes
Archeology	Visual and metal detector inventory

Historians were identified who were to study the existing documentation, reassess historical records, and evaluate cartographic resources related to the location of the village on Sand Creek. Ethnographers and tribal members were given the task of gathering oral histories on the massacre from living descendents of both victims and survivors. Tribal representatives were involved in all stages of the research effort, their advice sought on every aspect, from the scope of the project design to reviews of the final product and at every point in between.

Expertise was clearly required in the analysis of historical and recent aerial photography, especially after the value of the Bonsall map became apparent. These experts examined a variety of repositories seeking the earliest possible aerial photography of the area. Computer scanning of imagery became imperative to the remote-sensing analysis.

While the historical reassessment and the remote-sensing work were underway, so were geomorpological studies. This field of soil science, which documents the changes in landform over time, was another critical element of the special-resource study. Knowing whether the landforms had changed little, been eroded away, or covered by the accumulation of soil during the dust bowl was critical to understanding the potential for physical evidence, artifacts, to still be present or not and, if they were there, were they likely to be undisturbed or significantly effected by radical landform changes. As it turned out, the geomorphological work determined that little soil buildup or loss had occurred along Sand Creek and that any physical evidence should still be there and *in situ*.

Formal and informal communication, speeded by email and telephone communications to the physically dispersed group, kept the team members abreast of the work and findings of their colleagues. Some work elements, such as gathering tribal oral histories, conducting geomorphological studies, and reassessing historical documents and maps, proceeded concurrently. Feedback from the team members was not only useful and valuable but also a critical element in the success of the project.

The team assembled at various points to share the results of their research to date and to share thoughts and ideas as the project developed and matured. This level of communication allowed concepts to be discussed, challenged, and accepted or rejected. The different disciplines' ideas bore careful consideration in the discussions and were valuable in formulating the next series of tasks or research work to be undertaken.

Upon completion of the documentary reassessments, elements of the oral-histories study, the aerial remote-sensing analysis, and the geomorphological study, the archeologists and geophysical remote-sensing specialists took the assembled data and tested the hypotheses with ground-truthing methods. Most of the team members, especially the tribal consultants, were present in the field during this phase of the investigation. When the 1864-era camp and munitions and ordnance artifacts began to be found very near the predicted location, there was a true feeling of elation among the team members. Excitement ran high, but underneath there was the recognition that the physical data still had to analyzed and verified and that we were, in fact, viewing for the first time in nearly 140 years the detritus of a tragic event. During the archeological-analytical phase of the project, questions were asked and reasked of every element: Did each data set agree or not? If not, where did it diverge? In the end the historical documentation, map analysis, aerial-photographic interpretation, geomorphology, archeology, geophysical remote sensing, and all but a few tribal oral traditions on the location of the massacre converged. The final team assessment developed a statement, based on the preponderance of evidence, that the Sand Creek Massacre site was located and defined within a reasonable scientific certainty. The team approach also allowed for a minority opinion to be voiced by those tribal members who accept the traditional South Bend site as the true village location.

The value of an integrated multidisciplinary team approach to this study and others like it cannot be understated. The important aspect of this approach is not that different disciplines studied different details of the project, reporting back to the team leaders; it was the constant interplay, exchange of ideas, and development of new concepts that added a scope, depth, and richness to the effort that led to its success. All too often, study teams are assembled, given their tasks, and told to report back. The disciplines do their work independently and in a piecemeal fashion, following the assumption that the team leaders are skilled enough to put together the diversity of research that results from the task assignments. The difference with the integrated multidisciplinary approach was and is the integrated nature of all elements. Team managers, leaders, and members exchanged ideas in a near constant round-robin dialogue. No idea was considered inappropriate for consideration. Many were dropped or rejected in the course of the effort, but none was ever considered inconsequential for discussion purposes.

Although by no means a new or wholly innovative concept, the integrated multidisciplinary team effort is one that deserves more use in studies of the past. We hope the lessons and successes of the Sand Creek effort can be a practical model for resolving questions about our shared cultural heritage.

Appendix A

ARCHEOLOGICAL ARTIFACT
DESCRIPTION AND ANALYSIS

A total of fifteen artifacts were collected during the 1997 field investigations, while 386 field numbers were assigned during the 1999 fieldwork. The 1999 investigation approach required a judgmental artifact collection. There were a great many finds of baling wire, barbed wire, farm-machine parts, nuts, bolts, and screws discovered during the metal detector sweeps. The obviously recent and clearly postbattle items were not recorded. For the most part, these were removed and discarded at the request of the landowners. Artifacts of questionable identification or temporal span were collected for further identification and analysis; they are described and identified, where possible. The emphasis on the analysis is to identify the object and determine its datable range for the purpose of determining if the materials recovered could be associated with the Sand Creek Massacre of 1864. As each artifact was collected in the field, it was given a unique field-specimen number in one of three numerical series—1000, 2000, or 3000—for the 1999 investigations, depending on whose land it was found. The 1997 investigation artifacts are also included and are labeled with a designator of DFS or RFS and an ordinal. The artifact or specimen numbers referred to in the analysis utilize these field numbers.

Firearms Munitions

.30-Caliber

Three .30-caliber balls or lead shot were found during the field investigations. Field specimen (FS) 1106 was intermixed with a cache or cluster of larger balls (see ".58-Caliber"). FS2036b and FS2036c were recovered with an unfired .36-caliber conical bullet. These balls or shot are consistent with the 1864 event.

.32-Caliber

Three .32-caliber conical bullets were recovered in 1999. FS1002 is very deformed and has teeth marks on the bullet body indicating that someone held the bullet in his mouth and chewed on it before it was placed in a weapon and fired. This bullet is probably period. The other two .32-caliber bullets (FS1061, FS3009) both have knurled canelures (lubricating grooves). Knurling was patented in the 1870s, and thus these bullets postdate the 1864 timeframe.

A broken and oxidized unfired .32-caliber Long cartridge (FS1075) was also recovered. The .32-caliber Long was introduced in 1861 for the Smith and Wesson Model No. 2 revolver.[1] Thus the cartridge could date to the 1864 event.

.36-Caliber

Three unfired .36-caliber conical bullets (FS1068, FS2036, FS2139) were found during the inventory. These bullets are of

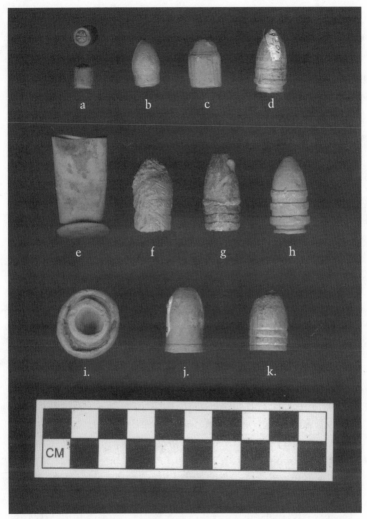

Fig. 22. Small-arms ammunition found in the village site: a. patent
variety percussion caps; b. .36-caliber bullet; c. .44-caliber bullet fired
in a Colt revolver; d. .44-caliber Sharps bullet; e. .50-caliber Maynard
carbine cartridge; f. .52-caliber Sharps two-ring variety bullet; g. .50-
caliber possible Maynard bullet; h. .52-caliber tie-base-variety Sharps
bullet; i. .58-caliber mushroomed Minié-style bullet; j. .54-caliber
Starr bullet; k. .54-caliber bullet.

the type used in various Civil War–era revolvers such as Colt, Remington, and Whitney, and possibly manufactured at one of the federal arsenals.[2] FS2139 exhibits teeth marks around its base.

.38-Caliber

A single .38-caliber conical bullet (FS3014) was recovered. It is deformed, making land and groove identification impossible. The .38-caliber was developed in the 1860s and was definitely commercially available by 1865–66 for several different firearms.[3] Although it is possible this bullet dates to 1864, it is more likely that its deposition postdates the massacre.

.44-Caliber

Five .44-caliber bullets were recovered. Three (FS1025, FS3018, FS3020) were fired in Colt revolvers, probably the Model 1860 Army, and the other two (FS1013, FS1076) in Sharps firearms. The Colt Model 1860 Army revolver was a standard-issue pistol for Civil War officers and cavalrymen.

The Sharps firearm was patented in 1852 and was a very popular military and commercial firearm for the next fifty years. It was produced in both percussion and cartridge styles. Its popularity was due to its accuracy and its reputation for having effective stopping power. Particularly in the larger calibers, it was the favored gun of big-game hunters on the plains and in the West generally.[4]

A single, distinctive .44- or .45-caliber Sharps bullet (DFS8), which was originally round nosed, smooth bodied, and paper patched, was found on the Dawson property during the 1997 investigations. A similar smooth-bodied paper-patched–type bullet (FS1013), which was deformed on impact, was found in 1999. It is either a .44-caliber or a .45-caliber round. In either case this bullet type was not introduced by Sharps until 1874 with the advent of their self-contained metallic cartridges, thus postdating the 1864 event.[5]

The second Sharps .44-caliber bullet is a tie-base type, which was produced for the .44-caliber Sharps.[6] This bullet is consistent with an 1864 date.

Henry .44-Caliber

The .44-caliber Henry rimfire cartridge was developed in the late 1850s by B. Tyler Henry, the plant superintendent for Oliver Winchester at the New Haven Arms Company; the company's name was changed to Winchester Repeating Arms Company in the mid-1860s. Henry also developed the first successful repeating rifle that would fire this cartridge by improving Smith and Wesson's Volcanic repeating arms. Henry's conception of a flexible, claw-shaped extractor was probably the most important single improvement leading to the success of the Henry rifle and its .44-caliber rimfire cartridge.[7] This extractor principle is still in use today, being used in the Ingram submachinegun.[8]

Henry designed a double firing pin for his repeating rifle that would strike the rim of the cartridge at two points on opposite sides. The firing pins were wedge-shaped, each being located on one side of the breech-pin collar. The collar was threaded into the breech pin that was designed to move a fraction of an inch forward and rearward during firing. Both the Henry rifle and its improved version, the Model 1866 Winchester, had firing pins that were exactly alike in shape and dimensions.[9] The firing pins were less pointed on some Model 1866s between serial numbers 24,000 and 26,000 but were changed back to their original shape due to misfire problems.[10]

A cartridge case (RFS4) was recovered on the Rhoades property in 1997, one (FS1112) on the Dawson property in 1999, and one (FS3022) on the Bowen property in 1999. All three are the long-case variety, two (RFS4, FS1112) with a raised-H headstamp in a recessed depression; this headstamp was used from about 1860 until the late 1880s.[11] The Dawson Henry case has two sets of firing-pin impressions, indicating the round did not fire the first time it was chambered. The Bowen case has a raised-US headstamp identifying it with the United States Cartridge Company. That headstamp was used from 1869 to 1875 and thus postdates the 1864 event.[12]

.44-Caliber Cartridge Case and Bullet

A single .44-caliber center-fire cartridge case (DFS1) of .44-40-caliber and a .44-caliber bullet (DFS2) were collected on the Dawson property in 1997. The lead bullet bears the rifling marks clear enough to identify it as having been fired from either a Henry rifle or Winchester Models 1866 and 1873; these weapons having five-groove, right-hand-twist rifling. The brass case is centerfire and is primed with a Boxer-type primer. The .44-40 cartridge was first introduced in 1873 along with the lever-action Model 1873 Winchester repeating rifle, thus this cartridge postdates the battle by at least nine years.[13]

.50-Caliber Bullets and Cartridge Case

One .50-caliber round ball (FS1176), a .50-caliber conical bullet (FS1179), and a .50-caliber brass cartridge case (FS2069) were collected in 1999. The .50-caliber round ball is deformed from impact. It is consistent with many calibers of muzzleloading firearms, including trade guns known to have been used by various Indians during the mid–nineteenth century.

The .50-caliber brass cartridge case (FS2069) is for a Maynard carbine. Dr. Edward Maynard patented a tipping-barrel, breechloading carbine in 1851. During the Civil War, Maynard applied himself to developing a brass cartridge for use in his weapons. He produced several types but patented one in 1859 that used a brass tube soldered to a large steel flange or base plate. The flange had a hole in the center to allow the flame from a percussion cap ignition to fire the cartridge.[14] The steel flange was later replaced by brass, as in the specimen recovered.

A single three-ring, flat-nosed bullet (FS1179) recovered as a surface find in a cow path may be a Maynard-variant-type bullet. It too is consistent with a Civil War use date.

.52-Caliber Bullets

As noted previously, the Sharps firearm was patented in 1852 and was a very popular military and commercial firearm; the .52-caliber rifle and carbine especially so with soldiers during the Civil War. Three .52-caliber Sharps bullets (FS1004, FS1009, FS1145) were collected in 1999. They represent two Sharps bullet styles of the two-ring and tie-base types. Both are Civil War–era production items.[15]

.54-Caliber Bullets

A single .54-caliber conical, hollow-based, Minié-type lead bullet (DFS10) was recovered on the Dawson property in 1997. Two additional bullets (FS2135, FS3032) were collected in 1999. All are standard U.S. arsenal–type hollow-based bullets; one (FS2135) has visible rifling marks, while the other (FS3032) was severely deformed on impact. The bullet diameter is consistent with the .54-caliber bullet used in the Model 1841 Mississippi rifle.[16]

Fifteen other .54-caliber bullets were also found. These have a single raised ring around the base and are for the Starr carbine. The Starr was patented in 1858, and approximately twenty thousand were purchased by the U.S. government for use during the Civil War.[17] The bullets recovered are of two types, one with a .205-inch hole in the base (FS1001, FS2127, FS2128, FS2134) and the other with a solid base (FS1008, FS1023, FS1071, FS1072, FS1080, FS1090, FS1171, FS2008a, FS2998b, FS2035, FS2039).

Only FS1001, FS1008, FS1071, and FS1090 exhibit rifling marks, indicating they were fired. The others were not fired and were probably dropped or otherwise lost.

.56-56-Caliber Spencer Cartridge Case

A single Spencer .56-56-caliber cartridge case (FS1178) is present in the collection. This seven-shot repeater was a military firearm used during the Civil War and the early Indian wars. It was also made in civilian models, was widely available, and was a popular weapon. There were several calibers offered for both the military and the commercial market during its production years.[18] The Spencer carbine was introduced in 1863 for use by Union cavalry. The earlier rifled musket had proven very popular with Michigan cavalry units, though the length was unwieldy for cavalrymen. Nearly ninety-five thousand Spencer carbines were purchased by the U.S. government prior to the end of the war, and they proved very popular with mounted troops.[19] The Spencer repeating rifle and carbine were originally chambered for the reliable Spencer .56-56-caliber rimfire cartridge.

Unlike most cartridge designations, where caliber is listed first and black powder load second (for example, .45-70), the Spencer designation is based on other nomenclature. The "56" in the .56-56 cartridge refers to a designation for the ammunition of No. 56 Spencer. The recovered specimen (FS1178) has no headstamp or other markings. This is consistent with U.S. Frankford Arsenal–produced Spencer ammunition. The cartridge case was fired in a Spencer-manufactured gun.

The only person known to have used a Spencer during the Sand Creek Massacre was none other than Col. John Chivington.[20] But since other Spencer cartridge cases were found by the Bowens on their property and at least two different gun types are represented by those cases, it is inappropriate to place too much emphasis on the presence of this cartridge case in the 1999 archeological collection.

.58-Caliber Bullets and Centerfire Cartridge Case

The Rhoades property revealed six .58-caliber centerfire cartridge cases. Two (RFS1 and RFS3) were collected as samples in 1997. The .58-caliber cartridge was introduced about 1869 for use in the Berdan breechloading conversion of the standard Civil War .58-caliber musket.[21] This cartridge was never manufactured or adopted by the U.S. Army but was used experimentally for a very short period. The guns and their cartridges were readily available on the civilian market during the last quarter of the nineteenth century. These artifacts postdate 1864 by at least five years.

One lead .58-caliber conical bullet (RFS2) was recovered on the Rhoades property in 1997, and three other conical bullets were found during the 1999 field investigations on the Kern and Bowen properties. The bullets are standard U.S. compressed-three-ring, hollow-base .58-caliber conical rounds.[22] The Rhoades bullet is flattened from impact and probably associated with the .58-caliber cartridge cases found on the property. Although a Civil War–style bullet, the probable association with the cartridge case suggests the likely deposition was postbattle.

The other three bullets (FS2184, FS3019, FS3033) are more likely associated with the massacre. FS2184 is mushroomed by impact, and FS3019 is deformed by impact, while FS3033 is unaltered.

Also found during the 1999 field investigations was a cache or cluster group of .58-caliber round balls (FS1106) buried about eight inches below the ground surface. They were clustered in a group measuring about four inches in diameter and were tightly packed together. They lay on an old soil horizon and were covered by wind- and water-laid sand and soil deposits.

The balls were probably in a bag at one time, which has since disintegrated.

There are 174 balls of .58-caliber in the group and one of .30-caliber. The .58-caliber balls are all hand cast, probably in the same mold, with clear evidence of the mold seam and cut sprue on the majority. The balls show random surface dimpling where they have been in contact with one another during movement at some time in the past, which further supports the idea that they were in some type of bag or pouch before their deposition on the site.

CANNON-RELATED CASE-SHOT FRAGMENTS

A variety of historical accounts document the use of four 12-pounder mountain howitzers during the attack.[23] The Model 1835 mountain howitzer was a light fieldpiece intended for use in rough terrain.[24] The bronze barrel of 4.62-inch bore diameter was just short of 33 inches long and weighed about 220 pounds. It was mounted on a lightweight two-wheeled mountain or prairie carriage. The gun could be towed by a single horse, with additional horses packing two ammunition chests each, or it could be dismounted and packed on horses or mules.

Federal ordnance tables allowed a six-gun battery thirty-six ammunition chests, each one containing eight rounds of fixed ammunition (six shell, one spherical case, and one canister), twelve friction primers, eighteen inches of slow match, and a single portfire (a paper tube to be used as an alternative ignition system in case the friction primers failed). The mountain howitzer was not intended to fire solid shot, and none were included in the ordnance table allocations for the guns.[25]

The mountain-howitzer shell is a 4.52-inch diameter, hollow gray cast-iron sphere. The shell was filled with a bursting charge of black powder, which was activated by a lead-alloy time-delay Bormann fuse screwed into an opening in the round. Spherical case shot is also a hollow gray cast-iron shell, but it was filled with about seventy-eight lead balls of approximately .65- to .69-caliber and set in sulfur matrix, with a bursting charge of powder in the center. The case shot was also activated by a Bormann time fuse.

Shell and case-shot fragments can readily be determined by the thickness of the sphere wall. Shell had a nominal thickness of .7 inch, and case shot a thickness of .36 inch.

A mountain-howitzer shell fired by a charge of a half pound of blackpowder had a maximum range of 1005 yards, while a case shot had a maximum range of 800 yards before bursting and scattering its lethal fragments.[26]

The Dawson property yielded four shell fragments (FS1003, FS1007, FS1011, FS1111). These are body fragments of the sphere and are .4 inch thick. As this thickness is larger than

Fig. 23. A 12-pounder spherical shot with Bormann fuse of the type fired at Sand Creek. This example was recovered from the steamboat *Bertrand*, which sank in the Missouri river in 1865.

Fig. 24. A cross-section of the 12-pounder spherical case shot, show-ing the fuse, powder chamber, and .69-caliber round balls in a matrix.

that prescribed in army regulations, measurements were made on another archeological specimen for comparative purposes. The Missouri River steamboat *Bertrand* sank near DeSoto Bend in April 1865, was salvaged in the late 1960s, and the cargo is now on display at the U.S. Fish and Wildlife Service's museum at DeSoto Wildlife Refugee, near Missouri Valley, Iowa.[27] Among the cargo bound for Deer Lodge, Montana, were several dozen spherical case shot for the 12-pounder mountain howitzer (Switzer 1972b). One example (catalog number 4115) has been sectioned for display purposes and was made available for study. This case shot ranges in wall thickness from .43 to .53 inch. The case-shot balls, visible in the sectioned example, range in diameter from .68 to .69 inch.

The fragments found on the Dawson property are .4 inch thick, which appears to be close to the range of variance for Civil War–era case shot.

The Bowen property has yielded fragments of at least four 12-pounder shell or case shot. It also yielded a single .69-caliber ball (FS3031) during the field work, and the Bowens have collected hundreds of .65- to .69-inch-diameter case-shot balls. The archeological specimen is impact deformed, but enough surface remains to determine it was not fired in a rifled weapon, and there are random dimples in the lead consistent with the ball touching other balls for some time. This is also consistent with either being carried in a sack or pouch or being a shrapnel round packed in a case shot.

LEAD

Four lumps of melted lead (FS2010, FS2018, FS3016, FS3017) were found during the 1999 field investigations. The first three lumps are fairly soft lead and may be spills of metal from bullet casting. The last lump (FS3017) is very hard and is an alloyed lead. This piece may be twentieth century in origin and may be spill from the pouring of babit metal to replace a bearing in an early motor vehicle.

PERCUSSION CAPS AND CAP TINS

Percussion caps were the most common form of firearm ignition during the mid–nineteenth century, though they were rapidly supplanted by self-contained metallic cartridges beginning with the Civil War. Three brass percussion caps of unusual style were found in 1999. They (FS2012a, FS2012b, FS2200) are known as patent caps and are about .187 inch in diameter and .25 inch long.[28] They have a bird design, possibly an eagle with a crown, on the top of the cap, which is probably a manufacturer's trademark, as yet unidentified. Two caps (FS2012a,

FS2012b) are unfired. The third (FS2200) is fired and the body
has split due to the ignition process.

Two tinned-iron pieces (FS2001, FS2135) are probably ends
to percussion-cap tins or containers. Each is about 1.25 inches
in diameter. Stylistically, they compare favorably with other
known examples.[29]

GUN PART

A single gun part, a lock bridle (FS1085), was recovered. The
bridle held the tumbler and sear in place on a gunlock. It is a
large size for either a musket or trade gunlock and is of the type
that would have been issued as an annuity item or was readily available at a trading post.[30] Similar bridles were found during archeological investigations at Bent's Old Fort National
Historic Site.[31]

ARROWHEADS

A brass arrowhead (DFS3) was found on the Dawson property.
Metal arrowheads, primarily iron, were common trade items
from the early 1600s to the early twentieth century and had
almost completely supplanted chipped-stone projectiles by the
mid–nineteenth century.[32] The brass arrowhead appears to be
handmade and is a stemmed, or tanged, point made from brass
stock. It is 1.12 inches long, and its maximum width is .42
inch. The tang is about .5 inch long. One side is flat and clean,
while the other bears a single scratch mark roughly along its
center axis, which may have originated with the maker, for it
appears to be a guide line for determining the center of the
point's axis. The 1999 investigations recovered six iron arrowheads. One (FS1012) is broken and only the base remains. It is a
tanged variety and is .68 inch across the base; the tang is serrated
with three notches and is .312 inch long and .25 inch wide. One
complete arrowhead (FS2055) is also tanged and is 2.5 inches

long and .625 inch across the base; the tang is also serrated with three notches and is .25 inch long and wide. This point appears to be commercially made and probably a stamped variety. The remaining arrowheads (FS2067, FS2068a, FS2068b, FS2084) are all unfinished. Each is in a different state of preparation, with tangs incomplete and edges blunt. Each appears to be cut from a piece of heavy strap iron or barrel hoop. One edge is smooth and blunt, while the other is ragged from the cutting-out process; the tip of each is flat. As a group the arrow points represent the various manufacturing steps undertaken by one or more arrowmakers in the village. FS2060a is 3.375 inches long with a blunt tip and .75 inch wide, with the asymmetrical tang .312 inch long and wide. FS2060b is 3.563 inches long, blunt tipped, and .75 inch wide at the base, with the tang .312 inch long and .375 inch wide. FS2084 is 3.875 inches long, with a blunt tip, and is .75 inch wide across the base; the unfinished tang is .312 inch long and .75 inch wide. (Chuck and Sheri Bowen have collected several iron arrowheads on their property, as noted earlier.)

The arrowhead styles found are typical of those available to Indians during the latter part of the nineteenth century. Metal arrowheads were neither endemic to the plains nor to the Cheyenne. Use of these types is documented by the surgeon general and are reported to have been found in the wounds of soldiers and civilians from Texas and Arizona to the northern plains.[33]

Military Equipment

Military Shoulder Scale

The crescent end of an enlisted man's brass shoulder scale (FS1079) was found in 1999. A mounting tongue for a similar shoulder scale was found by Mr. Dawson in the South Bend of Sand Creek in 1997. The brass shoulder scale was introduced

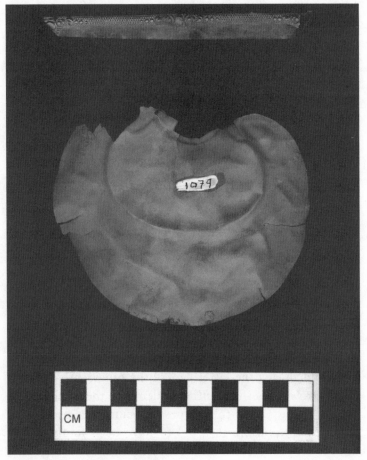

Fig. 25. A brass photograph preserver and a fragment of an enlisted man's brass dress shoulder scale found in the village site.

as a dress item for enlisted men in 1854 and went out of general use in 1872.[34]

Canteen Stopper Ring

A Model 1858 canteen stopper ring (FS1051) was found in 1999. The ring and shaft are complete, including a tin washer for the now-missing cork and iron retaining chain. It conforms to the Models 1858 stopper type used on the oblate-spheroid canteen of the Civil War and early Indian wars.[35] A canteen stopper chain was collected by the Bowens on their property.

Picket Pin

A Model 1859 army-issue picket pin (DFS4) was recovered on the Dawson property in 1997. It is typical of those commonly issued to cavalry units during the Civil War and well into the 1870s.[36] This specimen retains its figure-eight loop for attaching a snaphook. The head is battered and the tip is bent and slightly deformed, demonstrating use in hard or rocky ground prior to its deposition on the Dawson property.

PERSONAL ITEMS

Suspender Grip

A fragment of a stamped-brass suspender grip (FS1139) was recovered. The grip is a private purchase style and could have been used by anyone during the period. The military did not have a standard-issue suspender during the Civil War and did not adopt issue suspenders until 1883.[37]

Buttons

Twelve buttons were found during the 1999 investigations. The most distinctive are the three military general-service buttons. These brass line eagle buttons (FS1168, FS2100, FS2195) are approximately .5 inch in diameter and were commonly used on military blouse cuffs and on forage-cap chinstraps. One (FS1168) is backmarked "Extra Quality." In addition to the 1999 finds, Bill Dawson discovered two other military buttons along Sand Creek at the South Bend in 1997.

Both are the small size. One is a general-service type and the second is a staff-eagle type. Another military-type button (FS2007) was found on the August Kern property. It is the front only of a New York State Militia button. The front carries the New York State seal and motto "Excelsior." This button variety was authorized for the state militia in 1855, according to Warren Tice.[38] These three military-button types date to the Civil War era.[39]

There are three buttons (FS1093, FS1094, FS2034) that can be associated with trousers and are commonly found on soldiers' clothing. They are iron two-piece four-hole buttons in three diameter sizes (.625 inch, .68 inch, and .5 inch respectively). The larger was used to support suspenders and to close the trouser fly; the smaller buttons were commonly used to close the trouser fly. All three are common Civil War–era buttons. Five others found are civilian types. One (FS2078) is a .75-inch-diameter flat brass button with a loop shank. This is a common clothing button of the early nineteenth century and was popular in the Indian trade for many years. This button type is known to have a manufacturing date ranging from 1800 to 1865.[40] The other four buttons (FS1084, FS2054, FS2078, FS2198) are .25-inch-diameter brass ball, or "bullet," shaped buttons with a loop shank.[41] Two (FS1084, FS2198) have links of a lightweight brass chain attached to the shank. Such buttons were commonly used on ladies' clothing in the mid–nineteenth century but may have been an Indian trade item as well.

Boot Nails

Three boot nails (FS1086) about .75 inch long are of the type used to nail leather boot soles to the uppers.[42] This boot-nail type was commonly used throughout the nineteenth century.

Fig 26. Buttons recovered in 1999: a. brass ball button with chain links; b. U.S. general-service brass cuff or forage-cap button; c. face of a brass New York State Militia button; d. brass flat loop shank button.

Photograph Preserver

A three-inch-long ornate brass fragment (FS1046) represents one side of a photograph preserver or frame. The sheet-brass preserver is of the type commonly found on daguerreotype, ambrotype, and early ferrotype (tintypes) photographs. The preserver was used to hold the mat, glass, and photograph together for placement in a frame and dates to the mid–nineteenth century.

Trade-Silver Fragment and Ornament

A fragment of sheet silver (DFS6) found in 1997 is roughly square with rounded corners. It is .94 inch wide and .96 inch long. Under magnification, one finds that there are linear marks inscribed on one side. These may have formed part of a design element of a large piece from which this was cut. The item appears to be a scrap of sheet silver cut from another item.

A second sheet-silver ornament (FS1039) is a surface find. It is in the shape of a naja, a nearly closed crescent shape that originated with the Spanish entrada in the Southwest. The ornament form found wide acceptance among various Indian groups.[43] It is commonly seen as an appendage on crosses and pectoral ornaments.[44] When discovered, Luke Brady identified the item as a Cheyenne man's breast ornament.[45]

Bells

Three bells were recovered during the 1999 field investigations. Two (FS1037, FS2047) are so-called hawk bells, also known as Saturn bells.[46] These approximately .75-inch-diameter sheet-brass bells were common trade items throughout North America from the sixteenth through the nineteenth century. The third bell is a heavy-cast brass bell (FS1182). It is approximately 1.5 inches in diameter and is of the style known as the Circarch bell.[47] The Circarch bell is known to have been produced in England for the North American trade as early as the late seventeenth century and was still a popular trade item well into the nineteenth century.[48]

Thimble

A sewing thimble (FS2003a) is present in the collection. It has an open top and is identified as a nineteenth-century tailor's

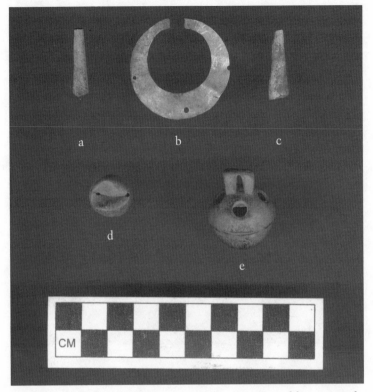

Fig. 27. Indian ornaments found in 1999: a., c. iron tinkling cones; b. silver naja or Cheyenne man's ornament; d. brass "hawk" bell; e. cast brass Circarch bell.

sewing thimble.[49] It was found in association with a 1-inch lightweight-brass, D-shaped buckle (FS2003b).

Tinkling Cones

Tinkling cones, or tinklers, were common ornamental items on Indian dress throughout the eighteenth and nineteenth centuries. Some were manufactured for distribution and others were camp made from tin cans or waste sheet metal. Both brass and iron tinklers are common finds. Three iron tinkling

Fig. 28. A tailor's thimble and a New York Militia button as recovered in 1999.

cones were found relatively close to one another during the field investigations. Two (FS2129, 2136) are 1 inch long and the other (FS2072) is .75 inch long.

Camp Equipage and Utensils

Tin Cups, Pans, Plates, Bowls, Boilers, and Buckets

A number of tinned-iron items were recovered. Among the artifacts are five tin cups, fragments of a coffee boiler, part of a tin plate, a tin bowl, several tin strap handles, a possible grater, and a number of fragments of sheet-iron pans or boilers. Two crushed and flattened tin cups (FS1014, FS1077) are identifiable as Civil War–era army-style cups.[50] These appear to be standard-issue tin cups with the rolled-wire reinforced rim. The body and bottom are soldered and the handle is riveted and soldered in place. Another group of tin-cup fragments and the wire-rim reinforcement (FS2088) may also represent a deteriorated army-style tin cup. Tinned-iron strap-handle fragments (FS1036, FS2009) are probably parts of cup handles. A fourth but smaller crushed and flattened tin cup (FS2186) is 3 inches tall and 2.5 inches in diameter; the strap handle is missing. This cup style was also common during the Civil War era.[51] The fifth cup (FS1006), intact except for its handle, is much more modern in construction, with lapped side seams and machine soldering that date it to post-1876 and more likely very late nineteenth or early twentieth century.

A crushed and mangled tin plate (FS1174) and three other fragments of a second plate (FS2049) are comparable with Civil War–era mess plates.[52] The plate is dished and has a wide rim; plates of this type were common in the second and third quarters of the nineteenth century. A crushed and deteriorated tin bowl is represented by FS2052. Again, this style was common in the nineteenth century.

A number of tinned-iron and sheet-iron fragments may be the remains of tin kettles, pans, and pots (usually called boilers in the nineteenth century). A coffee boiler or pot is represented by a crushed lid (FS1043) and the bottom (FS1042). The coffee boiler bottom has a .5-inch-by-.375-inch hole in its center. The hole size and configuration is consistent with it being struck with a pointed instrument, such as a pickaxe. A second coffee boiler may be represented by a long tinned-iron strap handle. Such handles are found on Civil War–era camp coffee boilers.[53] Other sheet-iron pots and pans are represented by various fragments: FS1113, a piece of sheet iron that has a later cut along one edge; FS1138, a wire reinforcement from a rim and some attached sheet-iron fragment that probably formed part of a large kettle;[54] FS1160, FS2075, and FS2194, bits of sheet iron that appear to have been part of larger pan- or kettle-like objects;

and FS2114, part of a large baking pan or possibly a kettle with a 3-inch-long wire-loop handle. The fragmented nature of these items prevents their positive identification and dating, though they appear consistent in form and manufacturing technique to known nineteenth-century vessel types.

There are four other sheet-iron fragments (FS1050a, FS1050b, FS1156, FS1159) that may represent parts of food graters. They are all container body pieces, and each are perforated with numerous small holes. The edges of the holes are raised to give a sharp edge. The fragments are probably parts of one or more small "radish" graters that could be found in many kitchens during the nineteenth century.

Parts of three buckets were discovered during the 1999 field investigations. FS1145 is a bucket bale with a brass attachment ear still present. The bale and ear are likely from an American-made, mid-nineteenth-century brass bucket.[55] Sheet-iron buckets are represented by some body and wire-reinforcement fragments (FS2044), an 8-inch-diameter iron bucket bottom (FS2089), and an iron-bucket bale ear with attaching rivet (FS2113). All are consistent with nineteenth-century bucket types.

Coffee Grinder/Mill

The handle and grinding gears (FS1177) of a nineteenth-century-style coffee grinder or mill were recovered. The handle, gears, and gear shaft were made of iron. The handle was detachable and held in place with a fancy brass nut. Additional parts of this mill or possibly a second are represented by three iron fragments to a flange or collar that held the beans during grinding. Two fragments (FS2106a, FS2106b) crossmend and are part of the collar's upper rim. The third fragment (FS2107) is flared and probably represents the lower part of the collar, where it joined with the box that held the ground coffee.

Utensils

Everyday utensils, including knives, forks, spoons, and possible meat skewers, are among the items collected in 1999. Common tablespoons are represented by three spoon bowls (FS1053, FS1107, FS1125) and two handle fragments (FS2081, FS2098). A larger, basting-size spoon bowl (FS2028) is also present. The spoons and handle fragments are all stamped tinned iron. The handles are spatula or fiddle shaped. These spoons are common utensils on mid-nineteenth-century and Civil War–era sites.[56]

There is one fork fragment (FS1144), consisting of the tine end and three tines (two broken but present). A second fork may be represented by an iron handle (FS1044). The handle has two iron attaching pins present, indicating the handle once had bone or wood slabs. Again, this is a common nineteenth-century-style utensil.

A common round-point table knife is represented by FS1047. It is iron with integral iron bolsters, and it once had bone or wooden slabs overlaying the handle. One butcher knife (FS2196) is iron, and the blade is extensively worn. The handle retains two brass pins for holding wood or bone slabs in place. The knife is too worn to determine its original style, though the shape suggests a common butcher knife. No impressed manufacturer's name could be found on the blade. The butcher knife was a common Indian trade item and settlers tool for generations.[57]

FS1117 is a nearly twelve-inch long rod, probably a pitchfork tine, that has been sharpened on both ends. The tine was made with a squared shank typical of pre-twentieth-century pitchforks. Its function is unknown, but it is possible it was used as a meat skewer. Another possible meat skewer (FS2062) is an eighteen-inch-long iron rod, sharpened on one end and with the other end turned over to make a small loop. These identifications are not considered conclusive, however.

The final utensil is a fragment of a scissors or cutting-shears blade (FS2140). The blade is broken just above the screw hole used to join the two blades together. Scissors and shears are common items of the nineteenth-century frontier on both Indian- and white-related sites.[58]

Cast Iron Kettles, Pots, and Pans

The 1999 collection contains thirty-six pieces of cast iron from several container types. A Dutch oven is represented by FS1038, FS1136, and FS1170. The three crossmend and are the bottom and three legs of an eight-inch-diameter Dutch oven. A second Dutch oven may be represented by another cast-iron fragment (FS2199), possibly a lid. It has four partial letters ("C," "C," "I," and a possible "I" or "H") visible on one surface, probably representing a manufacturer's name or logo; the manufacturer is unidentified.

Fig. 29. The base of a Dutch oven found in the village site. Note the broken pieces that have been refitted (crossmended).

A frying pan, about nine or ten inches in diameter, is represented by eight pieces (FS2191, FS2192a, FS2192b, FS2192c, FS2192d, FS2192e, FS2192f, FS2192g). Seven fragments crossmend to give the shape and identification. A single bottom fragment (FS2094) may be to another frying pan. It is about the same thickness as the crossmended pan, but its identification is not certain.

A cast-iron tea-type kettle is represented by two crossmended pieces of the rim and body (FS2188, FS2189). The two fragments have a straight rim and sharply angled body, typical of a nineteenth-century tea kettle.

The remaining fragments are from rounded-body cast-iron kettles. At least one kettle is represented by a series of crossmended fragments (FS2045a, FS2045b, FS2045c, FS2045d, FS2060). These include portions of the rim and body. FS2045 actually includes three additional body fragments found with the two rims and two body fragments that crossmended. Four other kettle rim and body fragments (FS2058, FS2059a, FS2059b, FS2060) are the same type and thickness as the crossmended pieces and may be part of this same kettle.

Three other kettles are represented by four other artifacts (FS1073a, FS1073b, FS2017, FS2147a, FS2147b). Each has a rim that is a different configuration from the others, thus suggesting that they represent three more individual kettles. The last artifact (FS1129) is a kettle-body fragment that cannot be associated with any other group.

The collection thus includes at least one Dutch oven, one frying pan, and four kettles among the thirty-six cast-iron artifacts. The body styles of the containers are typical of nineteenth-century origin.

Cast-Iron Stove

Three cast-iron fragments are parts to a stove. Two lids are present as fragments (FS2093, FS2120). An ash-shaker (FS2118) fragment still has clinkers adhering to its surface. The context of discovery and proximity of the pieces suggest that they are part of one stove. The discovery context and adjacent artifacts, such as fence wire (FS2119) and a zinc press-on can lid (FS2121), post-1880 items, suggest this area of the site may have had a later occupation. It is possible that ranching activities or the construction of the irrigation canal may be responsible for the presence of this later debris.

A highly ornamented cast-brass decorative device (FS3028) was found near some concrete-building foundations on the Bowen property. This piece is probably an ornament for a late-nineteenth- or early-twentieth-century heating stove. Similar examples can be found in the 1895 Montgomery Ward catalog and the 1897 and 1902 Sears and Roebuck catalogs.

Tin Cans

Tin cans, like nails, have a tale to tell to the archeologist. Can-manufacturing technology changed through time, and those changes are fairly well documented and dated. The various tin-can manufacturing methods have established date ranges. This allows archeologists to date a can to the period of manufacture. The can and can fragments from the investigations were analyzed based on the criteria provided by Jim Rock.[59]

Cans manufactured during 1864 would be hole-in-cap types, with stamped ends and simple side-seam overlap. The side seams were hand soldered; machine soldering was developed in 1876, and cans with machine-soldered seams would not have been present in 1864.

Among the collected artifacts are eleven crushed tin cans of the hole-in-cap type, one hole-in-cap top, one friction lid, and one sanitary can lid; forty field-specimen numbers were assigned to fragments of tin cans (the total number of fragments or cans is not possible to detail due to their fragile and oxidized nature). Little can be said about the artifacts (FS1018,

FS1026, FS1031, FS1040, FS1041, FS1060, FS1063, FS1074, FS1095, FS1096, FS1104, FS1114, FS1120, FS1123, FS1137, FS1149, FS1151, FS1161, FS1162, FS2013, FS2015, FS2023, FS2024, FS2026, FS2027, FS2031, FS2064, FS2090, FS2092, FS2095, FS2097, FS2104, FS2105, FS2130, FS2131, FS2132, FS2133, FS2203) other than they are consistent in thickness with can fragments. Many of the can fragments were found in proximity with one another, suggesting they were once associated, but the natural process of oxidation has taken its toll.

The friction lid (FS1032) may be a baking powder can lid. This type of lid can date to the 1864 period. The sanitary can lid (FS2204) definitely postdates the 1864 period and probably represents later use of the site by ranch hands, irrigation canal workers, or other late-nineteenth- or early-twentieth-century land users.

The hole-in-cap cans were all found crushed flat. The following measurements are approximate given their condition. There are three large cans (FS1110, FS1116, FS1131) that are about 5 inches tall and 3 inches in diameter. Another (FS1083) is 3.5 inches in diameter, but its height could not be determined due to oxidation and the effect of crushing. FS1172 is a 4.25-inch-tall, 3.25-inch-diameter can, and FS2112 is a 3-inch-tall, 2.5-inch-diameter can. A single hole-in-cap top (FS1082) was also found.

A sardine can (FS2086) measuring 4 inches long (the width could not be determined) has the top panel removed for opening. This opening type is consistent with a mid-nineteenth-century sardine can.

A rectangular can (FS2089) is so badly crushed that no reliable measurements could be obtained. It may be a can for potted meats, but its diagnostic features are so distorted by crushing that the identification is uncertain.

Three small cans were also found. One (FS2102) is 2.5 inches high and 2.25 inches in diameter. It is crushed, but the top was cut open with crosscuts, suggesting that its contents were solid or semisolid and not a liquid. The other two small cans (FS2109, FS2110) are 2.25 inches high and 2.25 inches in diameter condensed-milk cans.

The majority of the cans recovered are consistent with a mid-nineteenth-century date of manufacture and could easily be from the 1864 event. The cans' contents could have ranged from fruits to vegetables, and they could have been used by either the Cheyenne and Arapaho people, by members of the Colorado cavalry, or both. It is also possible that some cans may have been deposited later in time by other land users.

TOOLS

Ax

A broken ax head (DFS5) was recovered on the Dawson property in 1997. The forged-iron ax is missing its poll, apparently breaking due to its misuse as a wedge. The head is wrought iron with a steel edge or bit insert. The ax form is a style from 1750 to 1850 or slightly later.[60] A second ax of the same type was found by Mr. Dawson after the 1997 crew left the site. A third ax head (FS2201) was found during the 1999 field investigations. This latter is of a slightly different form than the 1997 finds but stylistically dates to the mid–nineteenth century.[61] The poll is battered, suggesting hard usage. At one time before its deposition, the ax handle was wedged in place with cut nails. The handle may have been loose since six cut nails of different sizes were inserted to secure the handle.

Awls

Three handmade awls were found during the investigations. Two (FS2071, FS2116) are made from wire. They are both about 3 inches long and about .187 inch in diameter. Both have their ends sharpened. The other handmade awl (FS2099) was crafted

Fig. 30. A farrier's hammer and ax found in the village site. Note the cut nails in the ax helve, suggesting repeated repairs to a loose handle.

from a worn-out butcher knife. The knife handle with mounting holes is present; the blade was filed or cut to form an awl point about 3 inches long. Hanson illustrates a similar example from the Pine Ridge area.[62] All are consistent with other awls dating to the nineteenth century.

Files

Five files were recovered. Four (FS1153, FS2011, FS2040, FS2050) are small triangular files with square shanks. They are 3.25, 3.5, and two are 4 inches long respectively. The fifth file (FS2180) is a 6-inch-long flat bastard file. The triangular types are typical nineteenth-century styles, while the flat file may date much later based on the hardness of the iron, which appears to be a low-carbon steel of more recent age.[63]

Hammer

A heavily oxidized iron cross-pien hammer (FS1165) was found during the investigations. Stylistically, it is nearly impossible to narrow the date range for its manufacture to any more than mid-nineteenth to early twentieth century.

Scrapers

Nine iron items can be categorized as scraping tools. Two artifacts (FS1140, FS1166) are fleshing irons. These are curved iron bits that were meant to be mounted in a wood or bone handle and used to deflesh animal hides. Hanson illustrates an identical specimen that is mounted on a bone handle, and he attributes it to a Southern Cheyenne origin.[64] FS1078 is a wide piece of flat iron that has a curved cutting edge. It is too heavily oxidized to determine if it was meant to be handheld or mounted to a handle. There are similar specimens from other Indian villages of the mid–nineteenth century as comparable examples.[65]

Two strap-iron fragments (FS1045, FS2030) were altered by filing in a series of small notches, creating a serrated edge. These modified pieces could be used for cutting or scraping, and similar examples exist in other archeological contexts.[66]

Four other artifacts have been modified with the addition of deeply filed W-shaped notches. FS2063 is the broken tip of a butcher knife that has a W-shaped notch. Two pieces of strap iron (FS2074, FS2108) have one or more W-shaped filed notches. FS2074 has two notches. It is a heavy piece of strap iron, and several letters were stamped into the metal before it was modified; the lettering is nearly illegible. FS2108 did triple duty. This piece of strap iron was modified by shaping one end into an awl, by creating serrations in one edge by filing shallow notches, and cutting a W-shaped notch. Finally, a scissors blade fragment (FS2181) has a W-shaped notch filed into its cutting edge. These notches are all about .375-to-.5-inch deep and across, varying from item to item. The outer edges of the W were not sharpened, but at least one inner angle is beveled by filing to create a cutting edge. The purposes of these notches are not obvious. They may have been intended either as a multipurpose cutting tool or for specific purposes. Among the several possible functions for the notch is cutting or splitting sinews, or as volunteer Dennis Gahagen demonstrated by replication, to groove an arrowshaft. The tool may also have been used to cut leather fringe.[67]

Wedge

FS2022 is an iron tool wedge. It shows heavy use on its upper surface. Its date of use spans a very broad range.

Horse Tack, Harness, and Related Horse Equipage

Spur

A nineteenth-century-style iron spur was recovered. The spur (FS1121) has the iron rowel and one arm with a strap-attachment stud present. The other arm is broken and missing.

Saddle and Tack Parts

Several saddle and tack items are among the artifacts collected. A fragment of a brass girth D-ring (DFS11) was found on the Dawson property in 1997. The remaining fragment is 1.77 inches long and 1.05 inches wide. The girth D-ring was used to attach various straps and the girth to a saddle. This style is consistent with the type used on the principal military saddles of the Civil War–era, the McClellan saddle.[68] Seven iron rings of the type used in girthing were recovered in 1999. Two rings (FS1069, FS1088) 1.5 inches in diameter, one ring (FS1035) 1.75 inches in diameter, and three rings (FS2020, FS2145, FS3021) 2 inches in diameter are nonmilitary types that probably represent a civilian or Indian saddles. FS1056 is a 2.5-inch-diameter girth ring, which could be either military or civilian in origin. The types are not readily amenable to dating since they are ubiquitous to the horse-transportation era. One military-type iron skirt ring (FS2004) was recovered, however. This item meets the specifications for the Civil War–era McClellan saddle.[69]

Three other tack-related artifacts (FS1141, FS2079, FS2123) are bridle curb chains. Two chains (FS1141, FS2079) are Civil War–era style. The other chain fragment (FS2123) is a civilian style of undetermined age. A halter, of undetermined affiliation, is represented by a single halter piece (FS2145). It is 1.5 inches square and is probably a post-1864 loss. A large rivet (FS1119), .187 inch in diameter and 1.5 inches long, is probably a halter rivet. One bridle item (FS3023) is a hand-forged-iron decorative device commonly found on Spanish- or Mexican-style bridles of the nineteenth century.[70]

Tack Buckles

Tack buckles are another difficult-to-date item from the horse era, and twenty-six were recovered in 1999. Sixteen are iron roller buckles (FS1049, FS1105, FS1126, FS1135, FS2032, FS2033,

FS2037, FS2043, FS2046, FS2053, FS2056, FS2077, FS2096, FS2125, FS3027, FS3030), eight are D-buckles in both brass and iron (FS1143, FS1158, FS2002, FS2003b, FS2076, FS2083, FS2182, FS2185), and one is a center-bar brass buckle (FS2057). The buckles range in width from .75 inch to 1.75 inches and have many potential uses. They may have been used on cinch straps, pack saddles, on the horse nose (feed) bag, or a number of other leather straps. FS3027 was found with remnants of the leather strap and two solid-copper rivets. One additional buckle is a hand-forged iron specimen (FS1059) measuring 4 inches long and 2.5 inches wide. Its function is unknown, but it may be a large belt or strap slide buckle, perhaps used on a pack saddle.

Horseshoes and Horseshoe Nails

There were eight horseshoes or horseshoe fragments recovered during the archeological project. It is difficult to ascertain, except for one instance, if the shoes could have been made around 1864. Horses were used for many years in the area, and the method of construction and attachment of shoes varies little through time. Nevertheless, manufacturing techniques are clues to their origin. All shoe identification and nomenclature follow Rick Morris.[71]

The shoes include two Burden pattern (FS1005, FS3001), a pony-sized horseshoe (FS1021), two draft-weight shoes (FS1024, FS2101), one shoe with a toe caulk (FS1034), a possible mule shoe (FS1142), and one shoe fragment (FS1070). The only style that can be reasonably dated is the Burden-type shoes. The Burden shoe was developed prior to the Civil War and used extensively through the remainder of the nineteenth century.

Horseshoe nails were a more common find during the investigations, with sixty-eight nails (FS1015, FS1016, FS1017a, FS1017b, FS1057, FS1058 [8 in one cache], FS1087, FS1127, FS2051, FS2073, FS2103) and five nail fragments (FS1020, FS1025, FS1033, FS1048, FS1134) recovered. FS1016 was a cache or group of horseshoe nails numbering fifty-one in total. Three other nails (FS1015, FS1017a, FS1017b) were found in the immediate vicinity of the FS1016 group and are probably associated. The nails in this assemblage are both used and unused. The purpose of the cache or group is unknown, but it was purposely assembled. It may represent an intentional collection of nails from various sources that were contained in a now-disintegrated bag or pouch and may have been intended for any number of functions.

Wagon Hardware

A few pieces of horse-drawn-wagon hardware were also recovered. One item (FS1019) is a wheel-hub band, which is 3.5 inches in diameter. Other artifacts include a wagon-box staple (FS1028), a possible wagon bracket fragment (FS2080, an eye to an end rod (FS1122), and a single tree fitting (FS1109). These items are also difficult to date and can fall anywhere in the era of horse-drawn transportation.

FASTENERS

Cut Nails, Wire Nails, and a Brass Tack

A single cut nail (DFS7) was collected from the Dawson property in 1997. It is a common cut nail of the 12d size. Sixteen other cut nails, six fragments, two wire nails, and a railroad spike were recovered in 1999. The cut nails are in nine sizes—2d (FS2137), 3d (FS1016a, FS1167, FS3002), 4d (FS1146), 6d (FS1016b, FS1124, FS3005), 7d (FS1101, FS3010), 8d (FS1132, FS1169), 20d (FS1102, FS3003), a hand-forged 8-inch spike (FS2075), and a 4.5-inch spike (FS1163). Cut-nail fragments include FS1130, FS1133, FS1150, FS1157, and FS3011. The wire nails are FS2115a and FS2115b, and the railroad spike is FS2117.

The cut nails are all common commercially manufactured types, with the one exception noted above. These were readily available from the second quarter of the nineteenth century through the early twentieth century. The railroad spike is also a common nineteenth-century type, but the wire nails are definitely post-1890. The wire nails were found in association with some charred wood, suggesting that someone was burning construction materials in the area. The charcoal and wire nails were near the stock tank on the Kern property.

A single brass upholstery tack (FS1155) was also recovered. The cast tack is about .5 inch long with a square shank and rounded head. This type is consistent with a nineteenth-century manufacturing date.[72]

Bolts, Nuts, and Washers

Among the artifacts recovered are a variety of fasteners. These include a .375-inch washer (FS1089), a hand-forged .375-inch by 3-inch square-shanked bolt (FS1128), and an rectangular-shaped washer with a .25-inch hole (FS2021).

STRAP IRON

Twenty-five pieces of strap iron (FS1027, FS1029, FS1048, FS1052, FS1054, FS1055, FS1062, FS1064, FS1066, FS1067, FS1098, FS1099, FS1118, FS1164, FS1181, FS2038, FS2065, FS2111, FS2122, FS2141, FS2144, FS2145, FS2150, FS2197, FS2202) were found during the investigations. These strap-iron items vary in width from .5 inch to 1.75 inches; most are about .625 inch to 1 inch wide. Strap iron had many uses, such as strapping boxes to bundling lumber, and is a nearly ubiquitous artifact on any historic archeological site. Two pieces (FS2065, FS2197) have been modified by cold cutting. Some of the others may be remains of small barrel hoops. The strap iron is not datable to any specific period and is still used today for similar purposes. Several were found near one another, such as FS1062, FS1064, and FS1065. These pieces were refitted, indicating many of these straps were much longer than the small scraps they are today.

BARREL HOOPS

Three easily recognizable barrel hoops were recovered. FS1115 is a 1-inch wide iron barrel hoop for a small keg or cask. It is flattened. Two other possible barrel-hoop fragments are represented by a .75-inch-wide piece (FS2016) and a 1.5-inch-wide piece (FS2019).

MISCELLANEOUS ARTIFACTS

There are twenty-five artifacts that are either unidentifiable or do not fit into the above classes. These include a broken 1.75-inch-long and 1-inch-wide trunk lock (FS1030) and a brass gas jet and housing (FS1108), probably a wall-mounted fixture called a hall pendant.[73] The brass housing is cast with fancy leaves and tendrils. The piece appears to be stylistically high Victorian of the 1850–60s era. Another nineteenth-century lighting device is represented by a stamped-brass collar (FS2124) for a kerosene lamp. The origin of these items is uncertain. The trunk lock and kerosene-lamp collar were found among the concentration of items attributed to the Indian village. The gas jet was an isolated find, well north of the village artifact concentration. It may be associated with the settlement of New Chicago but could be an item carried from the village.

Other miscellaneous items for which no positive identification can be made nor a firm date range established include a deteriorated iron bar (FS1081); a possible iron wagon staple (FS1091); an iron mounting plate about 4 inches long and 2.5 inches wide, with four screw holes and a central shaft hole (FS1173); a square iron operating rod (FS1180) of unknown function about 10 inches long and .125 inch in cross section; a 3.5-inch-long and .5-inch-diameter iron ferrule (FS22014); a 3-inch-long iron finger lever (FS2029) for operating some type of catch; a .75-inch-diameter lightweight iron ring (FS2041); an iron ferrule 2 inches long by .25 inch diameter (FS2042); a 1-inch-wide crushed brass band (FS2048); a possible chain-link fragment (FS2066); four pieces of flat sheet iron (FS2082); a riveted strap and .125-inch-diameter wire handle (FS2126); a .062-inch-diameter piece of wire (FS2135); a piece of iron (FS2183) with cold cuts on two sides; a fragment of sheet brass (FS3004); three iron fragments (FS3008, FS3012, FS3015); and an iron shaft-housing fragment (FS3026).

Automobile Parts

Three automobile parts were found among the nineteenth-century cluster, denoting later use of the site. One is a hood latch (FS1097) for a Model T Ford. The other two items are an operating rod for the carburetor of a Model T (FS1103) and another unidentified operating rod (FS2070).

Lithic Items

Two lithic artifacts were recovered as surface finds. One (FS1010) is a two-hand grinding stone of granite. The ends are battered, suggesting it functioned not only as a grinding tool but also as a hammer. The other lithic artifact (FS3029) is a work flake of Alibates flint. Whether the two items represent prehistoric occupation of the Sand Creek drainage or use by later Indian occupants is not known, though the Alibates flint flake is likely to be prehistoric in origin.

Appendix B

J. H. Haynes Cheyenne Depredation Claim

In 1864 J. H. Haynes was a government contractor to the Upper Arkansas Agency. The terms of his agreement specified that he would construct buildings at the agency and related irrigation features. During November, he lost his working stock and tools to raids by Cheyennes and Arapahos. On December 17, 1865, he filed the first of many claims for reimbursement for his losses of a stated value of $18,864.62. It would be 1868 before his claim was settled, and then for only $2500.00.

Source: Letters Received, Office of Indian Affairs, Upper Arkansas Agency, 1865–67, Record Group 75, M234, Roll 879, National Archives and Records Administration.

J. H. Haynes

Claim for damages alleged to have been sustained by depredations committed by the Arapahoe and Cheyenne Indians viz:

112,933 lbs corn	@ .12$^1/_2$ per lb	14,116.62
1 lot Blacksmith tools		150.00
1 dozen Planters hoes	@ 3.00	36.00
3 dozen Shovels	@ 30.00 per dozen	90.00
$^1/_2$ dozen Axes	@ 3.00 per each	18.00
200 lbs Steel	@ .65 per lb	130.00
2 large Quarry Bars		10.00
3 Stone Hammers		15.00
3 Sledges		24.00
1 lot Carpenter Tools		40.00
17 team Mules	@ 150.00 each	2,550.00
1 large Iron Gray Carriage Mule		250.00
4 Head Horses	150.00 each	600.00
1 large Bay Horse		175.00
1 Brown Mare		150.00
1 large Iron Gray Carriage Mule		250.00
1 Gray Horse		200.00
1 Remington Revolver		25.00
1 Saddle and Bridle		15.00
1 Saddle and Bridle		20.00
		$18,864.62

Appendix C

CHEYENNE AND ARAPAHO ANNUITY REQUESTS, RECEIPTS, AND LISTS

1858 LIST

Source: U.S. Department of the Interior, Office of Indian Affairs, Letters Received by the Office of Indian Affairs (Washington), from Upper Arkansas Agency, 1855–64, Record Group 75, M234, Roll 878, National Archives (Record Center, Denver).

> North Pawnee Fork K.T.
> Near Santa Fe Road
> Aug. 21, 1858

Sir

I herewith enclose to you duplicate Bills lading signed by Wm. W. Bent at Kansas City Mo. and duly certified as having been preformed by me agreeable to contract. I found all Indians (five Tribes) belonging to the Upper Ark. Agency assembled at this point from whence they design starting upon their usual summer hunt. I did not therefore think it necessary to compel

the Cheyennes & Arrappohoes [*sic*] to return to Bents
Fort before receiving their goods— . . . .

> Very Respectfully Your Obt. Servant,
> R. C. Miller
> U.S. Ind. Agent

Col. A. M. Robinson
Supt Ind Affairs
St. Louis Mo.

Top of page contains wording related to packages of Indian
goods being delivered by William Bent to R. C. Miller, with
signatures of both at bottom of page. The list includes numbers written in words as well as in numerals, and the weight
is supplied for each item.

33 bales Dry Goods
19 Boxes Dry Goods
6 Bales Domestics
1 Box Beads
1 Cask Beads
20 Boxes Hardware
3 Casks Hardware
20 Boxes Guns
1 Box Powder Horns
26 Boxes Tobacco
175 bags Flour
72 Bags Rice
26 Bags Coffee
80 Bags Sugar
73 Boxes Pilot Bread
4 Kegs Bullets
6 Bundles Hoop Iron [weight = 500]
27 11/32 kegs Powder

1859 Claim

Source: U.S. Office of Indian Affairs, Letters Received by the Office of Indian Affairs (Washington), from Upper Arkansas Agency, 1855–64, Record Group 75, M234, Roll 878, National Archives and Record Center, Denver.

Deposition of witnesses taken to be used in the matter of the claim of John Huntington against the Cheyenne Indians for indemnification for losses sustained by said John Huntington at the hands of said Indians.

Deposition of John Huntington [Huntington describes his trip from Leavenworth City in Kansas Territory to Denver City on Cherry Creek in March 1859, following the Smoky Hill Trail. He was robbed by Cheyenne Indians.]:

. . . The property stolen as aforesaid near to the best of my recolection [*sic*] & belief as follows:
To wit:

> Flour 125 lbs
> Corn meal 200 lbs
> Meat 250 lbs
> Coffee 25 lbs
> Sugar 25 lbs
> Beans 25 lbs

The following property was also lost as a consequence of the theft:

> One Yoke of oxen
> One ox cart
> One Government Tent
> Five Sets Mining Tools
> Cooking Utensils and Dishes
> One Trunk
> One Set of Mason's Tools
> Six Flannel Shirts
> Six Cotton Flannel Shirts

Two Overcoats
One Rifle & Acoutrement
One Mattress
One Quilt (B——) [?]
Five tin buckles [buckets?]
Three Camp Kettles
Three Gold Washers
Two large tin pans

[The list also included prices which have not been transcribed here.]

1861 REQUEST FOR GOODS

Source: U.S. Department of the Interior, Office of Indian Affairs, Letters Received by the Office of Indian Affairs (Washington), from Colorado Superintendency, 1861–80, Record Group 75, M234, Roll 197, National Archives and Record Center, Denver.

Begins with a transmittal letter from Gov. William Gilpin of Colorado Territory to Honorable William P. Dole, commissioner of Indian affairs, dated August 3, 1861, submitting an estimate of goods for the Cheyennes and Arapaho Indians as requested. List is addressed to "His Excellency William Gilpin, Superintendent of Indian Affairs," dated August 1, 1861, from "A. G. Boone, U.S. Indian Agent Upper Arkansas," "in regard to estimate & schedule of goods showing the kind and quality required for the Cheyenne & Arapaho Tribes of Indians for the ensuing year." The estimate begins with long list of a variety of soft goods, such as blankets, cloth, hats, hose, gloves, and ribbons. Prices are also listed, which are not included in this transcript. Hard goods are listed below.

6 Doz Large Blk. Cotton Umbrellas
2 Doz. Women's Green Silk Umbrellas . . .
6 Doz Green Wire Goggles
2 Gross Assorted Pins

200 # No. 12 Brass Wire
200 # No. 9 Brass Wire
20 Doz Gutta Pacha Hair Pins
20 Doz Wire Hair Pins
200 Large Bore Percussion Rifles
100 Large Bore Flint Rifles
25 Doz. Powder Horns
1,000 Extra Cast Steel Nipples
50 Nipple Wrenches
100 Ely's Water Proof Caps
50 Doz. Basting Spoons
10 Gross Iron Table Spoons
200 Doz. Ames Butcher Knives
100 Nests [Nest's?], Japanned Tin Kettles
200 Doz Tin Cups
40 Doz 2 Qt. Pans
40 Doz 3 Qt. Pans
50 Doz. Fish Lines
10 Gross Fish Hooks
14,000 Sharp's Assorted Needles
100 Doz. Crambo [?] Combs
50 Doz S.S.S. Fine Combs
20 Doz 10 in. Mill Saw Files
50 Doz Hand Saw Files
80 Doz Metallic Himrd [?]
100 Doz Fire Steels
500 # Assorted Cold. [Colored] Monntam [?] Beads
25 Doz. 1/2 Axes "Collins"
20 Doz Drawing Knives
20 Doz Pocket Knives
8 Doz "Westernholme" Knives
20 Doz Assorted Frying Pans
1,000 W [?] Assorted Brass Kettles
12 Doz Fine Hunting Knives
50 Doz Small Shears

50 Doz Assorted Scissors

500 Round Steel Awls

500 # Skillets & Lids

20 Doz Corn Brooms

5,000 # Family Salt (in Small cks [?])

2,300 # Soda (in Papers)

4,000 # Com. Chewing Tobacco

500 # Hoop Iron

2,000 # Lard

10,000 # Bacon (Clis [?] Side)

60 Kegs F.F.F. [might be crossed out] Powder

50 Bags Bullets [in different handwriting:] Trade Balls

20 Doz. Stew Pans

20 Doz. Coffee Mills

1,000 # Soap (Family)

2 Cases Chinese Vermillion

40 M Blk Wampum

20 M Wht. Wampum

50 M lbs Super Fine Flour

4 M lbs Rice

5 M lbs Rio Coffee

20 M lbs N.O. Sugar

300 Pd. 2 inch Hair Pipe (600 ins.)

300 Pd. 1 1/2 inch Hair Pipe (450 ins)

2 Doz 1 Bay State Shawls

N.B.

In the excess of this estimate for the Cheyennes & Arapahoes I would respectfully recommend if there is any deduction, that it be made from gew gaws, and not from provisions or necessaries of life. . . .

Denver City August 1st, 1861

A. G. Boone US Ind Agt

Upper Arkansas

[Note: In the column to the left, a person with a different hand has written numbers, Xs, Os, and forward slashes (one, two, or three of these per line), possibly while filling the order.]

1862 REQUEST FOR GOODS

Source: U.S. Department of the Interior, Office of Indian Affairs, Letters Received by the Office of Indian Affairs (Washington), from Colorado Superintendency, 1861–80, Record Group 75, M234, Roll 197, National Archives and Record Center, Denver.

> Upper Arkansas Agency
> Fort Lyon Colorado
> September 25th, 1862

Sir,

Herewith I submit my estimates for goods and presents for the Arapahoes and Cheyenne Indians for the year ending July 1st, 1864.

> [Begins with long list of soft goods]
> 20 Doz Canadian Belts . . .
> 100 lbs Seed Beads asst Colors . . . 20 M Wampum
> 200 Prs [?] Hair Pipe
> 15 Sks Rio Coffee . . .
> 15 kegs Powder
> 25 sks Bullets
> 10 sks Shot No 3
> 250 lbs Bar Lead
> 50 North West Guns Flint Locks
> 10 Rifles Guns Flint Locks
> 1,500 Flints
> 20 Nests Jap. Kettles
> 100 Camp Kettles

20 Doz 2 qt. Tin Pans
20 Doz 4 qt. Tin Pans
10 Doz 6 qt Tin Pans
50 Doz Tin Cups
20 Doz Half Axes
15 Doz Squaw Hatchets
10 Doz Handled Axes
100 Doz Squaw Awls
100 Doz Fish Lines
400 Doz Fish Hooks
20 Doz Hand Saw Files
10 Doz Nipples
10 Doz Nipple Wrenches
100 M Water Proof Caps
20 Doz Basting Spoons
150 Gross Needles
24 Doz Course Tooth Combs
12 Doz Fine Tooth Combs
20 Doz Shears
20 Doz Mirrors
200 Fry Pans
100 Doz Table Spoons
50 Powder Flasks
50 Powder Horns

All of which is respectfully submitted.
Your obt. servt.
S. G. Colley U.S.
Indian Agent
Upper Arkansas
To Hon. Wm. P. Dole
Com. Ind. Affr
Washington
D.C.

1863 LETTER

Source: U.S. Office of Indian Affairs, Letters Received by the Office of Indian Affairs (Washington), from Upper Arkansas Agency, 1855–64,. Record Group 75, M234, Roll 878, National Archives and Record Center, Denver.

Cronin, Hurxthal & Sears,
Dry Goods Importers & Jobbers,
118 & 120 Duane Street
New York April 3rd, 1863

Sir,

We have the honor to acknowledge receipt your letter 31st ult. ordering sundry articles as presents for Indians from Upper Arkansas now in your city. We have selected packed & forwarded . . . the goods needed. . . .

The "Silver arm bands" ordered are not to be had in the market & it would require 10 days to manufacture them, we therefore sent you the nearest approach to the article, "Silver Brooches," much in use by bands of Arkansas Indians & trust they will answer the purpose. . . .

Cronin Hurxthal & Sears

To
Hon. Wm. P. Dole
Com. Indian Affairs

APRIL 3, 1863, RECEIPT

[A receipt for items delivered to the United States, Hon. Wm. P. Dole, Comm. of Indian Affairs, bought from Cronin Hurxthal & Sears]

Case
10 pair 3 point Indigo Blue Mackinac Blankets

20 [might have "z" after 20, for doz?] Indian, Silver
   Brooches
2 Long Shawls
2 Balmoral Skirts
6 yards Crimson Cotton Velvet
10 Fancy Shells
1 Suit Soldiers Clothes for Boy
Cap, Leggings & shoes
1 suit Mens Clothes
14 pair Gold Epaulettes

[The receipt also has prices, which are not included in this
transcription.]
Transmitted from S. G. Colley, U.S. Indian Agent, Upper
Arkansas to Hon. W. P. Dole, Commissioner of Indian Affairs,
Washington D.C., September 30, 1863

Estimate for goods for the Cheyenne and Arapahoe Indians of
the Upper Arkansas

   [soft goods listed first]
   10 Doz Canadian Bells
   100 Pounds Seed Beads
   50 Doz Ebony Handled Knives
   100 Beaver Traps
   20 Doz Fancy Mirrors with Chains [?]
   20 Shears
   20 Basting Spoons
   100 Coffee Mills
   50 Rifles
   20 Kegs Powder
   500 Pounds Balls
   30,000 W.P. Caps
   50 West [Vest?] Japaned [?] Kettles
   50 Doz Tin Cups

20 Doz Half Axes
20 Gross Squaw Awls
50 Gross Needles large size
20 Doz C. S. Comb
200 Fry Pans
[more soft and perishable goods listed last]

1863 GOODS REQUESTS

Source: U.S. Office of Indian Affairs, Letters Received by the Office of Indian Affairs (Washington), from Upper Arkansas Agency, 1855–64, Record Group 75, M234, Roll 878, National Archives and Record Center, Denver.

Washington D.C.
April 1st, 1863
Sir:
I have to request that you will furnish me for the Arapahoes and Cheyennes the following articles under the late treaty with those Indians, viz.—

200 pairs 3pt. Indigo Blue Mackinac Blankets
100 Blk. Felt hats with gilt cou [?]
20 doz. Plaid flannel shirts
10 doz. Blk silk handkerchiefs
800 yds Plain Linseys
2,000 yds Calico
400 yds Jared [?] list blue cloth
280 8/4 wool shawls
20 doz. Ebony handled Knives 6 & 7 inches
40 doz Half Axes
200 sacks Flour
50 sacks Sugar
10 sacks Coffee
2,000 lbs Bacon

Very respectfully
Your Obdt. Srvt.
S. G. Colley
U.S. Agent
Upper Arkansas

Wm. P. Dole Esq.
Com. Of Indian Affairs
   Washington D.C.
   April 2, 1863
Sir,

As a portion of the presents you propose to make to the Indian Chiefs under my charge, I would recommend that twenty dragoon saddles, and the same number of fancy bridles be purchased at Leavenworth and await my arrival there for distribution to the said chiefs.

Very respectfully
Your Obdt Srvt
S. G. Colley
U.S. Ind. Agt.
Upper Arkansas

Hon. Wm. P. Dole
Com. Of Indian Affairs

Appendix D

LISTS OF ABANDONED GOODS FOUND IN THE CAMPS AT PAWNEE FORK, KANSAS (1867); WASHITA RIVER, OKLAHOMA (1868); AND SUMMIT SPRINGS, COLORADO (1869)

PAWNEE FORK, KANSAS

List of articles abandoned in the Sioux and Cheyenne camp at Pawnee Fork, Kansas, April 1867.
Source: Outpost: Newsletter of the Fort Larned Old Guard, n.d., p. 7.

Item	Sioux	Cheyenne
Lodges	140	132
Buffalo robes	420	522
Travesters	197	238
Par(i)leches [*sic*]	169	144
Whetstones	12	18
Rubbing stones	32	9

Water kegs	63	35
Saddles	239	191
Hoes	34	22
Head ma(l)s[sic]	145	142
Axes	142	49
Crowbars	15	12
Fleshing irons	42	39
Brass kettles	54	19

Loose

Kettles	141	49
Tea kettles	3	12
Coffee pots	59	8
Tin pans	149	152
Iron spoons	25	65
Tin cups	216	134
Fry pans	43	34
Skillets		1
Horn spoons	94	55
Chains	51	78
Drawing knives	9	4
Bridles	8	11
Curry combs	4	11
Blacksmith tongs		1
Lariatts [sic]	280	212
Coffee mills	15	13
Sacks paint	70	142
Ovens	5	1
Hammers	11	6
Stew pans	4	4
Spades	2	5
Pitchforks	3	5
Knives	6	9
Pick axes	4	6
Wooden spoons	19	14

Door mats	140	111
Stone mallets	61	13
Meat stones		22
Files		8
Scythes		4
Meat skewers		7
Lances	1	
U.s. mail bag	1	
Swords	1	
Bayonets	1	

WASHITA RIVER, OKLAHOMA

Cheyenne village property captured at the Washita, Oklahoma, November 27, 1868.
Source: Report of Lt. Col. George A. Custer, n.d., Philip H. Sheridan Papers, Library of Congress; and Afton et al., *Cheyenne Dog Soldiers,* 317–18.

Horses and mules	875
Bufflao robes	573
Untanned robes	160
Hatchets	140
Rifles	47
Lead, lbs.	1,050
Lances	75
Bows	35
Bullets, lbs.	300
Buckskin saddlebags	940
Coats	93
Saddles	241
Lodge skins	390
Axes	210
Revolvers	35
Gunpowder, lbs.	555

Arrows	4,000
Bullet moulds	90
Shields	12
Lariats	775
Blankets	470
Tobacco	700

SUMMIT SPRINGS, COLORADO

Cheyenne property captured at Summit Springs, Colorado, July 11, 1869.

Source: Afton et al, *Cheyenne Dog Soldiers*, pp. 320–21.

Rifles	56
Revolvers	22
Bow and arrow sets	40
Tomahawks	20
Axes	47
Knives	150
Lariats	200
Strychnine, bottles	16
Lodges	84
Parfleches	125
Meat, lbs	9,300
Tin cups	160
Powder, lbs	50
Bullets, lbs.	20
Bullet moulds	14
Lead, bars	8
Percussion caps, boxes	25
Sabers	17
War shields	17
Lances	9
War bonnets	13
Buffalo robes	690

Panniers	552
Moccasins	152
Raw hides	319
Saddles	361
Mess pans	31
Water kegs	52
Tin plates	180
Dressing knives	200
Shovels	8
Lodge skins (new)	75
Saddle bags	40
Bridles	75
Dresses	28
Hammers	50
Coats	9
Tobacco, lbs.	100
Tin coffee pots	200
Brass/iron kettles	67
Horses/mules	443
Gold and notes	$1,500

Appendix E

LISTS OF KNOWN ARMS AND AMMUNITION USED BY THE COLORADO VOLUNTEER CAVALRY

ORDNANCE ISSUED AND RETURNED BY THE THIRD COLORADO VOLUNTEER CAVALRY

In the testimony given during the investigation into the Sand Creek Massacre and reported in *Report of the Secretary of War*, February 4, 1867 (pp. 34–37), First Lieutenant Charles C. Hawley, First Colorado Volunteer Cavalry and acting ordnance officer for the District of Colorado, reported the ordnance stores issued and returned by the Third Colorado Volunteer Cavalry during their one-hundred-day enlistment period. Since some of these items were in use at the time of the massacre, it is useful to record them, for some of these types may be represented archeologically.

Ordnance Stores Issued	Returned	Deficiencies
772 rifles; caliber .54	493	279
224 muskets; caliber .69	92	132

16 muskets; caliber .71	8	8
1,012 cartridge boxes, infantry	658	354
1,105 cap pouches and picks	455	650
1,019 waist-belts and plates	523	496
633 gun slings	358	275
620 cartridge-box belts	279	341
650 screw-drivers and cone wrenches	160	490
28 Sharp's carbines	17	11
58 Starr's carbines	169	—
29 Starr's revolvers	19	10
2 Colt's army revolvers	2	—
72 Whitney revolvers	12	60
82 carbine slings and swivels	114	—
63 carbine cartridge boxes	16	3
39 brush wipers and thongs	49	-
107 pistol-belt holsters	43	64
pistol cartridge pouches	5	66
Colt's repeating rifles	—	5
Cavalry sabers	13	—
122 saber-belts and plates	59	63
527 saddles complete, (pattern of 1859)	412	115
527 curb-bridles	382	145
376 watering bridles	275	101
500 halters and straps	225	275
624 saddle blankets	80	544
426 surcingles	239	187
515 spurs and straps	193	322
562 horse brushes	321	241
565 curry combs	342	223
354 lariats	50	304
354 picket pins	64	290
500 links	139	371
146 nose bags	—	146

245 wipers	22	223
14 spring vices	4	10
12,000 cartridges; caliber .71	10,000	2,000
9,000 cartridges; caliber .69	1,000	8,000
11,000 cartridges; caliber .58	-	11,000
66,000 cartridges; caliber .54	1,000	65,000
22,500 cartridges; caliber .44	11,000	11,500
15,700 cartridges; caliber .36	1,000	14,700
1,500 pounds of lead	700	800
20 kegs of powder	12	8
15 quires of cartridge paper	15	—

Ordnance Returns Submitted by the Colorado Volunteers

The Colorado Volunteers submitted the following ordnance returns after their campaign. No returns (or none that have survived) are available for December 1864, but those for September 1864 are extant. The records indicate that many of the companies were armed only with revolvers and sabers.

> 1st Regt.:   Co. E   6 Rifles, M1840 & 1855, cal. .58
>   Co. G same as above

It appears that all companies had .44-caliber Colt Army revolvers along with a few .36-caliber Navy revolvers.

> 3rd Regt.:   Co. C—91 rifles as above
>   Co. G—70 rifles as above
>   Co. F—27 .52 Sharps Carbines
>   57 .54 Starr Carbines
>   21 .45 Starr Revolvers
>   2 .36 Whitney   "

The remaining companies show no entries.

NOTES

PREFACE AND ACKNOWLEDGMENTS

1. National Park Service, *Sand Creek Massacre Project, Site Location Study*, 2 vols. (Denver, Colo.: National Park Service, 2000).

CHAPTER 1

1. Sand Creek's official name is Big Sandy Creek, which is how it appears on U.S. Geological Survey maps. The creek is commonly known as Sand Creek, however, and is referred to by that name in this study.

2. Utley, *Frontiersmen in Blue*, 281–83; Josephy, *Civil War in the American West*, 292–94; West, *Contested Plains*, 287. The most definitive presentation of the events leading to Sand Creek appears in Roberts, "Sand Creek," chaps. 2–8.

3. For Cheyenne history and culture, see Powell, *Sweet Medicine*; Moore, *The Cheyenne*; Moore, *Cheyenne Nation*; Berthrong, *Southern Cheyennes*; Grinnell, *Cheyenne Indians*; Stands In Timber and Liberty, *Cheyenne Memories*; and Powell, *People of the Sacred*

Mountain. For the Arapahos, see Trenholm, *Arapahoes*; Swanton, *Indian Tribes of North America*, 384–86; and Fowler, *Arapahoe Politics*.

4. For the Solomon's Fork encounter, see Chalfant, *Cheyennes and Horse Soldiers*.

5. White Antelope (ca. 1789–1864) was a noted Cheyenne warrior and a leader of the Crooked Lance Society, when the Cheyennes engaged the Kiowas at Wolf Creek (in present Oklahoma) in 1838. Two years later he helped negotiate peace with the Kiowas, Comanches, and Kiowa-Apaches. He reportedly visited Washington, D.C., as part of a delegation of chiefs following the Horse Creek Treaty of 1851. He later signed the Treaty of Fort Wise of 1861 but later disavowed the accord. White Antelope aligned with Black Kettle and other peace chiefs in the events leading to Sand Creek. Thrapp, *Encyclopedia of Frontier Biography*, 3:1554. The Southern Arapaho Little Raven (ca. 1810–89) had gained a reputation by helping restore amity between the Cheyennes and the Kiowas, Comanches, and Kiowa-Apaches during the 1840s. He became a chief in approximately 1855. Like others, Little Raven signed the Treaty of Fort Wise in 1861 but later became disillusioned by it, refusing to join the tribal delegation to Washington, D.C., two years later. He avoided the Sand Creek Massacre by leading his people south to the Arkansas. He later signed the Medicine Lodge Treaty in 1867, acknowledging reservation status for his people. Ibid., 2:860.

6. Berthrong, *Southern Cheyennes*, 148–52; Utley, *Frontiersmen in Blue*, 283–84; Grinnell, *The Fighting Cheyennes*, 120; Hoig, *Sand Creek Massacre*, 12–17; Halaas, "'All the Camp Was Weeping,'" 7.

7. An Ohio native, John Evans (1814–97) received a Quaker education and earned a medical degree in 1838. Evans practiced medicine in Ohio, Illinois, and Indiana before moving to Chicago to teach and to edit a medical journal. He became involved in real estate in Chicago, where he served on the city council and helped establish Methodist schools. He ran for Congress in 1854 but lost. President Abraham Lincoln appointed Evans territorial governor of Colorado in 1862. Discredited following the Sand Creek Massacre, he resigned and entered business, becoming a prominent figure in railroad enterprises, and later helped found the University of Denver. Evanston, Illinois, is named for him. Lamar, *New Encyclopedia of the American West*, 352.

8. Roberts, "Sand Creek," 76–108; Utley, *Frontiersmen in Blue,* 284; Grinnell, *The Fighting Cheyennes,* 121–29; Josephy, *Civil War in the American West,* 295, 297–98; Berthrong, *Southern Cheyennes,* 155, 158–61, 166–69.

9. Born in Ohio, John M. Chivington (1821–94) was a lay minister in Ohio, Illinois, Missouri, Nebraska, and Kansas before becoming presiding elder in the First Methodist Episcopal Church in Denver in 1860. At the outbreak of the Civil War, he accepted a commission in the First Colorado Infantry and performed admirably in defeating invading Confederate troops in New Mexico. As commander of the District of Colorado, Chivington led the troops of the First and Third Colorado in perpetrating the massacre at Sand Creek, then resigned his commission to avoid the reach of military justice in its aftermath. He lived thereafter with the controversy and stigma of his actions, dying in Denver thirty years later. Lamar, *New Encyclopedia of the American West,* 209–10.

10. Samuel R. Curtis (1805–66), from New York, graduated from West Point in 1831. He served in the Seventh Infantry, resigning his commission in 1832 to pursue the practice of law and engineering. During the war with Mexico, Curtis served as colonel of an Ohio infantry regiment, then returned to his civilian engineering pursuits. Elected to Congress from Iowa, he served three terms and promoted the concept of a transcontinental railroad. During the Civil War, Curtis served as colonel of the Second Iowa Infantry. He rose to brigadier general and, following his important victory at Pea Ridge, to major general of volunteers. He variously commanded the Department of Missouri, the Department of Kansas (during which the Sand Creek Massacre occurred), and the Department of the Northwest. After the war he served as a peace commissioner to the Indians and as commissioner for the Union Pacific Railroad. Curtis died in Council Bluffs, Iowa. Patricia L. Faust, ed., *Historical Times Illustrated Encyclopedia of the Civil War* (New York: Harper and Row, 1986), 198–99; Thrapp, *Encyclopedia of Frontier Biography,* 1:360.

11. Utley, *Frontiersmen in Blue,* 284–85; Josephy, *Civil War in the American West,* 299.

12. Utley, *Frontiersmen in Blue,* 285–87; Halaas, "'All the Camp Was Weeping,'" 7; Berthrong, *Southern Cheyennes,* 176–91; Hoig, *Sand Creek Massacre,* 36–90; West, *Contested Plains,* 289–91; Grinnell, *The*

Fighting Cheyennes, 131–42. The quotes are cited in Josephy, *Civil War in the American West,* 300, 303.

13. Hoig, *Sand Creek Massacre,* 91–97; Utley, *Frontiersmen in Blue,* 287–89; Josephy, *Civil War in the American West,* 301–4; Berthrong, *Southern Cheyennes,* 193–208; Grinnell, *The Fighting Cheyennes,* 155–58. For a participant's view of these broad operations, see Ware, *Indian War of 1864.*

Scott Anthony (1830–1903), born in New York, moved to eastern Kansas in 1857 and to Colorado in 1860. He engaged in mining and commerce in Leadville, but in 1861, commissioned a captain in the First Colorado Infantry, he took part in the New Mexico operations, including the Battle of Glorieta Pass. Promoted to major in the First Colorado Cavalry, he campaigned against Indians on the plains and commanded Fort Larned, Kansas. Anthony succeeded Wynkoop as commander at Fort Lyon in early November 1864, assuming a more aggressive posture toward the tribes and directing Black Kettle to move to Sand Creek, where Chivington later struck his village with a force that included Anthony's troops. Mustered out of service in 1865, he later guided railroad surveyors, joined the gold rush to Dakota's Black Hills, and eventually opened a business in Denver, where he died. Thrapp, *Encyclopedia of Frontier Biography,* 1:27–28.

14. Black Kettle (1801–68) was a Suhtai, born near the Black Hills, and as a youth manifested traits of courage and leadership that attracted the notice of his people. He participated in horse-stealing expeditions against enemy tribes and in 1838 had joined Cheyenne and Arapaho warriors in combating the Kiowas, Comanches, and Kiowa-Apaches, with whom the Southern Cheyennes later allied in their wars against white invasion. Black Kettle married into the Wotapio band of Cheyennes and eventually rose to the position of chief. He urged a peaceful stance, however, and signed several accords with the U.S. government that cost him influence among the larger tribe, a matter that accelerated following Sand Creek. Unable to stem depredations by Cheyennes against whites in the summer of 1868, he moved his people south into the Indian Territory, where army troops attacked his village along the Washita River, during which Black Kettle and his wife were killed. Hyde, *Life of George Bent,* 322–24. See also Hoig, *Peace Chiefs of the Southern Cheyennes,* 104–21.

15. Edward W. Wynkoop (1836–91), a Pennsylvanian, played major roles in Indian-military affairs on the plains during the 1860s. He

helped found Denver in 1858 and promoted emigration there while serving as sheriff of Arapaho County. Commissioned in 1861 in the First Colorado Infantry, Wynkoop took part in the regiment's New Mexico operations and later commanded Fort Lyon. Transferring from the post before the Sand Creek Massacre, he formally investigated that affair and condemned Chivington's actions, for which he became almost universally hated in Colorado. Wynkoop left the military in 1866, becoming agent for the Cheyennes, Arapahos, and Kiowa-Apaches, who respected him, but frustrated over increased conflict between the army and the tribes, he resigned after three years and returned to Pennsylvania. During the 1880s, Wynkoop won appointments with the federal land office in Denver and Santa Fe and later served as adjutant general in New Mexico and as warden of the territorial penitentiary. Thrapp, *Encyclopedia of Frontier Biography*, 3:1605–6.

16. Left Hand (ca. 1823–64) was born on the Central Plains. He learned English as a youth from associations with traders. A brave warrior, he became a chief among the Southern Arapahos by the mid-1850s, a period that corresponded with increased white emigration through the plains. Left Hand reportedly tried farming in Nebraska and Iowa but returned west and perhaps embraced the notion of raising cattle as more conducive to his people's interests. He weathered the Colorado gold rush while trying to control his young men and maintain peace and later aligned with peace advocates Little Raven and Black Kettle. He and his small group of followers were camped near Black Kettle's people at Sand Creek when the massacre occurred, during which Left Hand was mortally wounded. Thrapp, *Encyclopedia of Frontier Biography*, 2:840.

17. Hoig, *Sand Creek Massacre*, 98–107; Utley, *Frontiersmen in Blue*, 290–91; Halaas, "'All the Camp Was Weeping,'" 7–9; Josephy, *Civil War in the American West*, 305–6; West, *Contested Plains*, 291; Grinnell, *The Fighting Cheyennes*, 152–53.

18. Berthrong, *Southern Cheyennes*, 210–13; Utley, *Frontiersmen in Blue*, 291; Hoig, *Sand Creek Massacre*, 110–28; Josephy, *Civil War in the American West*, 306–7 (quotes, 307); West, *Contested Plains*, 295; Grinnell, *The Fighting Cheyennes*, 153–54.

19. George L. Shoup (1836–1904), from Pennsylvania, arrived in Colorado Territory in 1859 via Illinois and became involved in mining and mercantile prospects. In 1862 he received a commission in

the Second Colorado Volunteer Infantry but the next year transferred to the First Colorado Cavalry. In 1864 Shoup helped formulate the constitution for the proposed state, then accepted the colonelcy of the Third Colorado Volunteer Cavalry, leading those troops against the Cheyennes at Sand Creek. Soon after, he moved to Montana, then to Idaho. In the latter place he rose politically to become territorial governor in 1889, then state governor in 1890. Shoup resigned the office to assume the role of U.S. senator from Idaho, serving in that position until 1901. *Biographical Directory of the American Congress*, 1694; Thrapp, *Encyclopedia of Frontier Biography*, 3:1302.

20. Utley, *Frontiersmen in Blue*, 292–93; Hoig, *Sand Creek Massacre*, 129–32; Berthrong, *Southern Cheyennes*, 214–15; West, *Contested Plains*, 297–98; Josephy, *Civil War in the American West*, 307–8.

21. Utley, *Frontiersmen in Blue*, 293–94 (quote, 294, cited from testimony of Lieutenant Joseph A. Cramer); Hoig, *Sand Creek Massacre*, 135–43; Grinnell, *The Fighting Cheyennes*, 159–62. For a discussion of the status of Black Kettle's people prior to Chivington's attack, see West, *Contested Plains*, 298–300.

22. One Eye, a Southern Cheyenne subchief, played an important role in the events leading to the Sand Creek Massacre. His daughter married white rancher John Prowers near Fort Lyon, and that relationship advanced One Eye's presence there and association with personnel at the post. During the summer of 1864, he carried a note from Black Kettle to Major Wynkoop at Fort Lyon that led to that officer's meeting with the tribesmen on the Smoky Hill, which in turn promoted the Camp Weld meeting with Governor Evans and Chivington. Thrapp, *Encyclopedia of Frontier Biography*, 2:1084. War Bonnet was head of the Oivimana clan of the Cheyennes and had joined a delegation to Washington, D.C., in 1863. During the visit, War Bonnet conversed with President Abraham Lincoln and later journeyed to New York City, where he met showman Phineas T. Barnum. Ibid., 3:1510.

23. The locations of the Cheyenne camp components are laid out according to George Bent in Hyde, *Life of George Bent*, 149. See also Powell, *People of the Sacred Mountain*, 1:299–300.

24. This account of Sand Creek is based upon information in Roberts, "Sand Creek," 421–41; Hoig, *Sand Creek Massacre*, 145–62; Utley, *Frontiersmen in Blue*, 295–96; Josephy, *Civil War in the*

American West, 308–11; Powell, *People of the Sacred Mountain,* 1:301–9; Hyde, *Life of George Bent,* 151–56; Grinnell, *The Fighting Cheyennes,* 163–73; and Berthrong, *Southern Cheyennes,* 217–22. Chivington's figure is in his report of Dec. 16, 1864, in *War of the Rebellion,* ser. 1, vol. 41(1):949.

25. Josephy, *Civil War in the American West,* 311–12 (including first quote); Utley, *Frontiersmen in Blue,* 297 (second quote), 309; Hoig, *Sand Creek Massacre,* 163–76 (including third quote, 166); Roberts, "Sand Creek," 479–521. The three published products of these investigations are U.S. Senate, *Report of the Joint Committee on the Conduct of the War;* idem., *Report of the Committee on Indian Affairs;* and idem., *Report of the Secretary of War.*

26. Berthrong, *Southern Cheyennes,* 240–44; Roberts, "Sand Creek," 510, 562–66.

27. The Cheyenne chief, Yellow Wolf (ca. 1779–1864), was leader of the Hevhaitano clan and as a young man had gained a reputation for his many successful raids against then-enemy Kiowas and Comanches. He helped William Bent select the site for Bent's Fort along the Arkansas and later promoted notions of farming and cattle raising among his people. Yellow Wolf went with a delegation of chiefs to Washington, D.C., in 1863, during which he met President Lincoln. George Bent indicated that, at the time of his death at Sand Creek, the chief was eighty-five years old. Thrapp, *Encyclopedia of Frontier Biography,* 3:1609. Bear Man, another Southern Cheyenne chief, had been wounded earlier that year during an engagement in Kansas. Ibid., 1:81.

28. Powell, *People of the Sacred Mountain,* 309–10; Roberts, "Sand Creek," 684–91.

29. For these events, see Utley, *Frontiersmen in Blue,* 300–40; and Roberts, "Sand Creek," 523–66, 686. The quote is from Indian Agent Jesse H. Leavenworth to Brevet Major General John B. Sanborn, Aug. 1, 1865, Record Group 393, Pt. 3, Entry 769, 2:171, National Archives, Washington, D.C.

30. Roberts, "Sand Creek," 568–69, 604.

31. Fatality figures for these encounters are from *Bear River Massacre Site,* 16; Greene, *Reconnaissance Survey of Indian–U.S. Army Battlefields,* 85; and Jensen, Paul, and Carter, *Eyewitness at Wounded Knee,* 20.

CHAPTER 2

1. This synopsis is based upon material cited in the notes to chapter 1, but see particularly Hoig, *Sand Creek Massacre*, 145–62; and Powell, *People of the Sacred Mountain*, 299–310.

2. See Douglas D. Scott, Anne Wainstein Bond, Richard Ellis, and William B. Lees, "Archeological Reconnaissance of Two Possible Sites of the Sand Creek Massacre of 1864," Apr. 1998 (unpublished report, Department of Southwest Studies, Fort Lewis State College, Durango, Colo.), Midwest Archeological Center, National Park Service, Lincoln, Neb., copy on file. See more on this project in chapter 3.

3. Colorado repositories that contributed to the effort were the Western History Department, Denver Public Library; Colorado Historical Society, Denver; University of Colorado Library, Boulder; National Park Service Library, Lakewood; University of Denver Library; Colorado College Library, Colorado Springs; Pioneer Museum, Colorado Springs; Kiowa County Museum, Eads; Big Timbers Museum, Lamar; Kit Carson Museum, Kit Carson; and the National Archives Denver Branch, Denver Federal Center. Other repositories visited or otherwise consulted during the course of the research were the National Archives, Washington, D.C.; Library of Congress, Washington, D.C.; U.S. Army Military History Institute, Carlisle, Pa.; Little Bighorn Battlefield National Monument, Crow Agency, Mont.; Oklahoma Historical Society, Oklahoma City; Brigham Young University Library and Archives, Provo, Utah; Newberry Library, Chicago; National Anthropological Archives, Smithsonian Institution, Washington, D.C.; Southwest Museum, Los Angeles; Huntington Library, San Marino, Calif.; Beineke Library, Yale University, Hartford, Conn.; Dr. John Woodenlegs Memorial Library, Dull Knife College, Lame Deer, Mont.; Missouri Historical Society, St. Louis; New York Public Library, New York City; Washita Battlefield National Historic Site, Cheyenne, Okla.; National Archives Great Lakes Branch, Chicago; and National Museum of Medicine and Health, Bethesda, Md. In addition, a number of individuals with knowledge bearing upon the location of the site were interviewed by the historians.

4. Lysa Wegman-French and Christine Whitacre, "Historical Research on the Location of the Sand Creek Massacre Site (Interim Report No. 1)," Sept. 11, 1998. National Park Service Intermountain

Support Office–Denver, 3–4; Douglas D. Scott, email to Jerome A. Greene, Dec. 21, 1998, subject, "Sand Creek geomorp."

5. This was "Old Fort Lyon," originally named Fort Wise, established in 1860 and abandoned by the army in 1867 because of flooding of the Arkansas. A "New Fort Lyon" was raised that year twenty miles to the west, not far from the modern community of Las Animas. A brief overview of the early post is in Boyd, *Fort Lyon*, 3–6. See also Frazer, *Forts of the West*, 41–42.

6. The first two locational references were given by Chivington in correspondence following the massacre. See Chivington to Major General Samuel R. Curtis, Nov. 29, 1864, in *War of the Rebellion*, ser. 1, 41(1):948; and Chivington to Charles Wheeler, Nov. 29, 1864, in Senate, Report of the Secretary of War, 48. The last appears in First Lieutenant Clark Dunn, Company E, First Colorado Cavalry, to Chivington, Nov. 30, 1864, in War of the Rebellion, ser. 1, 41(1):955; and in Second Lieutenant J. J. Kennedy, Company C, First Colorado Cavalry, to Chivington, Nov. 30, 1864, in ibid., 954–55. See also "Record of Events," Muster Rolls for Companies C and E, First Colorado Cavalry, Nov.–Dec. 1864, Compiled Records Showing Service of Military Units in Volunteer Union Organizations, Record Group [hereafter RG] 94, M594, Roll 4, National Archives [hereafter NA] and Record Center, Denver.

7. These figures are from Baker, *Aerial Archaeology at Sand Creek*, 32.

8. The distance figures of between twenty-five and forty-five miles from Fort Lyon to the village have been excerpted from a variety of original sources and are presented in Lysa Wegman-French and Christine Whitacre, "Historical Research on the Location of the Sand Creek Massacre Site (Interim Report No. 2)," Jan. 29, 1999, National Park Service Intermountain Support Office–Denver, 3–6; and Lysa Wegman-French and Christine Whitacre, "Historical Research on the Location of the Sand Creek Massacre Site (Interim Report No. 3)," Apr. 27, 1999, National Park Service Intermountain Support Office–Denver, 2–3.

9. Hyde, *Life of George Bent*, 151.

10. One of Bent's two diagrams of the village site, both prepared about 1905–14, is in Folder 1, George Bent–George E. Hyde Collection, Western History Collections, University of Colorado Library, Boulder. The other is in Cheyenne/Arapaho Agency File, "Warfare,"

1864–85, microfilm roll 24, Indian Archives Division, Oklahoma Historical Society, Oklahoma City.

11. Aerial photos AC298–31, 32, 48, 49, Records of the Soil Conservation Service, RG 114, NA.

12. John Lewis Dailey Diary, Western History Department, Denver Public Library, microfilm; George Wells, letter, *The (Central City, Colo.) Miner's Register*, Dec. 27, 1864.

13. Unidentified correspondent [George A. Wells?], letter, *The (Central City, Colo.) Miner's Register*, Jan. 4, 1865.

14. Morse H. Coffin, letters to the *(Greeley) Colorado Sun*, Dec. 1878–Feb. 1879, typed copies in Box 4, Raymond G. Carey Manuscript Collection, University of Denver; C. B. Horton, "Survivor Tells of the 'Chivington Massacre,'" *Chicago-Herald Record*, n.d., reprinted in *The Denver Times*, July 24, 1903, 8; Interview with Eugene Weston, Nov. 14, 1907, Cragin Notebook 10, p. 11, Starsmore Research Center, Pioneer Museum of Colorado Springs; Howbert, *Memories*, 122.

15. Baker, *Aerial Archaeology at Sand Creek*, 30–31.

16. Palmer testimony, in Senate, *Report of the Secretary of War*, 144; Henry Blake Diary, Boulder Historical Society Collections, Carnegie Branch Library for Local History (published in the *Boulder Daily Camera*, Aug. 2, 1941); Hal Sayre Diary, Dec. 1, 1864, Hal Sayre Papers, Western History Collections, University of Colorado Library, Boulder; John Lewis Dailey Diary, Dec. 1, 1864; Morse H. Coffin, letters to the *(Greeley) Colorado Sun*, Dec. 1878–Feb. 1879. Interpreter John Smith stated that he returned with Chivington "on his trail towards Fort Lyon from the camp where he made this raid. I went down with him to what is called the forks of the Sandy." Testimony of John S. Smith, Mar. 14, 1865, in Senate, *Report of the Joint Committee on the Conduct of the War*, 5–6.

17. The Bent/Hyde regional maps are in the George Bent–George Hyde Papers, Western History Collection, University of Colorado Library, Boulder (see also Wegman-French and Whitacre, "Sand Creek Massacre Site (Interim Report No. 2)," maps B, C.

18. Army regulations directed that

> commanding officers of troops marching through a country little known, will keep journals of their marches according to the form and directions hereto annexed. At the end of the march a copy of the journal will be retained at the station

where the troops arrive, and the original will be forwarded to the head-quarters of the Department, or *corps d'armee*. Thence, after a copy has been taken, it will be transmitted, through the head-quarters of the army, to the Adjutant-General, for the information of the War Department. . . . The object of the journal is to furnish data for maps, and information which may serve for future operations. Every point of practical importance should therefore be noted. . . . [The journal was to be kept in a pocket notebook.] The horizontal divisions in the column headed *"Route"* represent portions of a day's march. The distance, in miles, between each of the horizontal divisions, will be noted in the column headed *"Distance."* . . . The notes within each horizontal division are to show the general direction of the march, and every object of interest observed in its course. All remarkable features of the country, therefore, such as hills, streams, fords, springs, houses, villages, forests, marshes, &c., and the places of encampment, will be sketched in their relative positions, as well as noted by name. . . . The *"Remarks"* corresponding to each division will be upon the soil, productions, quantity and quality of timber, grass, water, fords, nature of the roads, &c., and important incidents. They should show where provisions, forage, fuel, and water can be obtained; whether the streams to be crossed are fordable, miry, have quicksands or steep banks, and whether they overflow their banks in wet seasons; also the quality of the water; and, in brief, every thing of practical importance. [*Revised United States Army Regulations of 1861*, 99–104.]

Pages 100–103 of the *Revised United States Army Regulations of 1861* contain the precise format of the journal exactly as followed by Lieutenant Bonsall. Although his product strictly complied with army regulations, its large format suggests that it might have been prepared from notes after completion of his march.

19. "Journal of the march of the men belonging to the Garrison of Fort Lyon, C.T., under the command of Lieut. S.W. Bonsall 3rd Infantry, from Old Fort Lyon C.T., to Cheyenne Wells, pursuant to S.O. No 66 Hdqrs Fort Lyon C.T. June 12, 1868," Records of the Office of the Chief of Engineers, RG 77, NA (Great Lakes Branch).

20. Heitman, *Historical Register*, 1:230; Appointment, Commission, and Personal File of Samuel W. Bonsall, B530 CB 1865, Records of the Adjutant General's Office, RG 94, M1064, Roll 144, NA.

21. Special Orders No. 66, Headquarters, Fort Lyon, C.T., June 15, 1868, Post Orders, 1868–1908, Entry 2634, Records of U.S. Army Continental Commands, RG 393, Pt. 1, NA.

22. Sherman to the Adjutant General, Edward D. Townsend, June 24, 1868, 793M1868, Letters Received, RG 94, M619, Roll 639, NA.

23. Sheridan to Lieutenant Colonel Alfred Sully, Third Infantry, June 16, 1868, Box 2, Letters Received, District of the Upper Arkansas, May 1867–69, RG 393, Pt. 3, 799, NA.

24. Luke Cahill, "Recollections of a Plainsman," ca. 1915, MSS 99, Manuscripts Division, Colorado Historical Society, Denver. Cahill's service is referenced in White, *Index to Indian Wars Pension Files*, 1:224.

25. *United States Army Medical Museum Anatomical Section*, 28, and appended documentation; Lenore Barbian, anatomical collections manager, to Gary L. Roberts, Nov. 20, 1998, in Gary L. Roberts, "The Sand Creek Massacre Site: A Report on Washington Sources," Jan. 1999 (unpublished report prepared for the National Park Service); and Memorandum, "Sand Creek Skeletal Remains," Museum Technician Scott Brown to Tom Killiam, case officer, Repatriation Office, Oct. 21, 1991, in ibid. An engraving of one of the Sand Creek skulls collected by Bonsall appears in War Department, Surgeon-General's Office, *Circular No. 3*, 15–16.

26. Based on LORAN (Long Range Aid to Navigation) used in aerial readings that compute distance from latitude/longitude fixes on landmarks. Baker, *Aerial Archaeology at Sand Creek*, 6.

27. Army Map Service aerial photos, 1954, Western United States Project No. 133, Lot AU, Roll 29, frames 3978–80; Roll 30, frames 4253–63; Roll 34, frames 4585–96; and Roll 35, frames 4658–62, all at U.S. Geological Survey, Earth Science Information Center, Denver, Colo.

28. It is not clear from the documents whether Bonsall's party was mounted or traveled by riding in the wagons. The rate of march appears to have been more or less consistent with period regulations governing the use of infantry, i.e, roughly 3.3 miles per hour. See Farrow, *Farrow's Military Encyclopedia*, 2:270; and *Field Service*

Regulations, United States Army, 86. "Greenwood's Camp" was likely named for either Commissioner of Indian Affairs Alfred B. Greenwood, who negotiated the Treaty of Fort Wise with the Cheyennes and Arapahos in 1860, or Colonel William H. Greenwood, chief engineer of the Kansas Pacific Railroad, who supervised the line's surveys (which included a prospective route through the area north and east of Sand Creek); maintained headquarters at Sheridan, Kansas; and laid out the town of Kit Carson in November 1869. Colonel Greenwood later became chief engineer of the narrow-gauge Denver and Rio Grande Railway. For Alfred B. Greenwood, see *Biographical Directory of the American Congress,* 973; and Berthrong, *Southern Cheyennes,* 148–49. For William H. Greenwood, see Anderson, *Kansas West,* 32, 69; and *Poor's Manual of Railroads,* 1868–75 (annual issues).

29. There might be a slight discrepancy in Bonsall's distance-traveled column in that, although the two areas representing the eleven-mile segments of the march are identical in measurement, that addressing the 11:00 A.M.–6:00 P.M. portion ends perhaps a mile below the crossing of Sand Creek, making the actual estimated distance from "Greenwood's Camp" to "Camp No. 2" more like twelve miles.

30. Kiowa County, Colo., Plats 17-45, 17-46, Kiowa County Courthouse, Eads, Colo.

31. Soil Conservation Service aerial photos, Kiowa County, Colo., Roll AG 298, frames 31–33, 46–48; and Roll AG 299, frames 5–8, (all taken Oct. 17, 1936); Roll YO 56, frame 56; and Roll YO 55, frame 68 (both taken Oct. 27, 1937), Records of the Soil Conservation Service, RG 114, Cartographic Archives Division, NA.

32. See Testimony of John S. Smith, Mar. 14, 1865, in Senate, *Report of the Joint Committee on the Conduct of the War;* Testimony of Captain Silas S. Soule, Feb. 20, 1865, in Senate, *Report of the Secretary of War,* 23; Testimony of Second Lieutenant Joseph Cramer, Feb. 28, 1865, in ibid., 63; Morse H. Coffin, letters to the *(Greeley) Colorado Sun,* Dec. 1878–Feb. 1879; and Testimony of Private Alexander F. Safely, May 19, 1865, in Senate, *Report of the Secretary of War,* 221–22.

33. A variant of the Bent village diagram in Folder 1, Bent-Hyde Papers, Western History Collection, now circulating is a second-generation tracing that shows the presence of a spring north of the village site. Yet the notation "spring" and a designating "x" on this diagram is incorrect and were added by a scholar studying the site to

his personal-research photocopy of Bent's sketch along with annotations respecting area soil valences, etc. In the circulating copy, however, all annotations but the word "spring" and the "x" have been removed, making it appear that this notation might be George Bent's, which it is not. John H. Moore, telephone communication with Jerome A. Greene, Mar. 11, 30, 1999. The original tracing of the Bent diagram is in Moore, *Cheyenne Nation*, 160. The subsequent tracing appears in Baker, *Aerial Archaeology at Sand Creek*, 36 (and in its second printing, 36, 48).

34. Hyde, *Life of George Bent*, 153–54.

35. Ibid., 151.

36. Testimony of Private Alexander F. Safely, May 19, 1865, in Senate, *Report of the Secretary of War*, 222; Testimony of Sergeant Lucian Palmer, Company C, First Colorado Cavalry, Apr. 1, 1865, in ibid., 143.

37. See testimony of Private David H. Louderback, First Colorado Cavalry, Mar. 31, 1865, in ibid., 138; Interview with Eugene Weston, Nov. 14, 1907, Cragin Notebook 10, p. 11.

38. Coffin, *Geology and Ground-Water Resources*, 30, 32.

39. Baker, *Aerial Archaeology at Sand Creek*, 47–48; "North of Chivington, CO," U.S. Geological Survey (hereafter USGS) Quadrangle, 7.5 Minute Series, 1982.

40. See Wegman-French and Whitacre, "Sand Creek Massacre Site (Interim Report No. 2)," map A; and George Bent, untitled diagram of the Cheyenne village and Sand Creek Massacre, Cheyenne/ Arapaho Agency File, "Warfare," 1864–85, Indian Archives Division, Oklahoma Historical Society, microfilm roll 24.

41. Wegman-French and Whitacre, "Sand Creek Massacre Site (Interim Report No. 2)," 10, 12, 13, 14, 15–16, 18–21. The figure of three hundred yards was advanced by John S. Smith, an interpreter who had been in the village when attacked. Testimony of John S. Smith, Mar. 8, 1865, in Senate, *Report of the Committee on Indian Affairs*, 41. Within a week, Smith had revised his figure to "about a mile above the village." Testimony of John S. Smith, Mar. 14, 1865, in Senate, *Report of the Joint Committee on the Conduct of the War*, 6. Participant Cornelius J. Ballou stated that the Indians "broke and ran for their fortifications 200 or 300 yards further up the creek [from the village]." *National Tribune*, Nov. 23, 1905. The quarter-mile- to one-mile-distance estimates are from Testimony of Corporal James J.

Adams, Company C, First Colorado Cavalry, Apr. 4, 1865, in Senate, *Report of the Secretary of War*, 149; Report of Colonel John M. Chivington, Dec. 16, 1864, in *Massacre of Cheyenne Indians*, 49; Morse H. Coffin, letters to the *(Greeley) Colorado Sun*, Dec. 1878–Feb. 1879; and Testimony of Stephen Decatur, Company C, Third Colorado, May 8, 1865, in Senate, *Report of the Secretary of War*, 199. The two- or over-two-mile figure was given by George Bent and Little Bear, both of whom were in the village and ran upstream to the sand-pit area. See Bent to George Hyde, Mar. 15, 1905, George Bent Letters, Coe Collection, Yale University Library, New Haven, Conn.; Bent to Hyde, Apr. 14, 1906 [containing Little Bear's account according to Bent], in ibid.; Bent to Hyde, Apr. 30, 1913, in ibid.; and Hyde, *Life of George Bent*, 152–54.

42. Senate, *Report of the Joint Committee on the Conduct of the War*, 102.

43. See, for example, the testimony of Second Lieutenant Joseph A. Cramer, First Colorado Cavalry, Feb. 28, 1865, who to the question "How far did you move *from the position first assumed by you during the fight*, and in what direction [italics added]?" responded, "Up the creek perhaps three or four miles." Senate, *Report of the Secretary of War*, 64. See also Chivington's statement that "the Indians . . . fell back from one position to another for five miles, and finally abandoned resistance and dispersed in all directions and were pursued by my troops until nightfall." Senate, *Report of the Joint Committee on the Conduct of the War*, 49.

44. Howbert, *Memories*, 124; quote of Cornelius J. Ballou in "The Sand Creek Affair," *National Tribune*, Nov. 23, 1905. Major Anthony recalled that the bed of the creek was "from 200 to 500 yards wide." Testimony of Major Scott Anthony, First Colorado Cavalry, Mar. 14, 1865, in Senate, *Report of the Joint Committee on the Conduct of the War*, 22. A reminiscent account by C. B. Horton states that "the creek at that point was nearly a quarter of a mile wide." "Survivor Tells of the 'Chivington Massacre,'" *Chicago-Herald Record*, n.d., reprinted in *The Denver Times*, July 24, 1903, 8.

45. See Morse H. Coffin, letters to the *(Greeley) Colorado Sun*, Dec. 1878–Feb. 1879; Ballou, "Sand Creek Affair"; Horton, "Survivor Tells of the 'Chivington Massacre'"; and Howbert, *Memories*, 124. Anthony stated that "the banks upon the side of the creek were two or three feet high, in some places as high as ten feet." Testimony of

Major Scott Anthony, First Colorado Cavalry, Mar. 14, 1865, in Senate, *Report of the Joint Committee on the Conduct of the War*, 22.

46. Coffin wrote, "it was along the banks of the creek, but more especially the west bank, that most of the fighting took place. . . . There was a general scattering . . . up the creek and to the banks, especially to the west bank." Morse H. Coffin, letters to the *(Greeley) Colorado Sun*, Dec. 1878–Feb. 1879. Participant Charles E. Clark described the features as "lines of rifle pits in the bed of Sand Creek, along the base of the bank." *St. Louis Globe-Democrat*, Sept. 15, 1876. For references to the action occurring along both banks, see Wegman-French and Whitacre, "Sand Creek Massacre Site (Interim Report No. 2)," 19–22.

47. In 1887 the community of New Chicago, or Upper Water Valley, a prospective railroad boomtown, stood briefly in this area. Land Records, Kiowa County Abstract Company, Eads, Colo.; *(Eads) Kiowa County Press*, Jan. 26, 1917.

48. For references regarding the dispersal and use of the artillery pieces, which is somewhat murky as to how many of the four were actually employed, see the statements compiled in Wegman-French and Whitacre, "Sand Creek Massacre Site (Interim Report No. 2)," 12–15.

49. Bent, untitled diagram of the Cheyenne village and Sand Creek Massacre, Oklahoma Historical Society.

50. For this concern, see Testimony of Second Lieutenant Joseph A. Cramer, First Colorado Cavalry, Feb. 28, 1865, in Senate, *Report of the Secretary of War*, 49–50. One of Bent's diagrams indicates that the troops effectively formed a total cordon around the area, to include the streambed above and below the pits, as they directed small-arms fire against the tribesmen refuged there. Bent, untitled diagram of the Cheyenne village and Sand Creek Massacre, Oklahoma Historical Society. The small arms used by the troops at Sand Creek reflected a wide range of weapons. Ordnance issues to the Third Colorado Cavalry in the weeks preceding the massacre consisted of the following types: Austrian rifles, Harpers Ferry muskets, Harpers Ferry rifles [Model 1841 Mississippi rifles], Model 1840 U.S. rifles [?], Whitney revolvers, and Springfield rifles. Among the weapons of the First Colorado Cavalry were Harpers Ferry muskets, Austrian rifles, and "citizen rifles." Ammunition consisted of cartridges for these weapons as well as for Colt Navy pistols and Sharps rifles, with ball and conical-

bullet calibers of .36, .44, .52, .54, .58, and .69. Data provided by Melinda Ellswick as compiled from various special orders, Headquarters, District of Colorado, Aug.–Oct. 1864, Records of the Colorado Adjutant General's Office, Denver. On November 9 the Third Colorado was directed to receive seventy-four thousand rounds of ammunition for carbines, muskets, and Colt Army pistols. Assistant Adjutant General Joseph S. Maynard to First Lieutenant Charles H. Hawley, Nov. 9, 1864, Entry 3254, vol. 2, RG 393, Pt. 3, NA. In addition, on the day before the massacre, troops of the First Colorado Cavalry received issues of "Three thousand Carbine Cartridges, One thousand ball Army Pistol Cartridges, [and] One Remingtons Army Pistol . . . [as well as] One thousand Carbine (Starr) Cartridges." Special Orders No. 252, Headquarters, Fort Lyon, Nov. 28, 1864, Entry 2632, vol. 459 (Fort Lyon Special Orders), RG 393, Pt. 1, NA. The spherical case was discharged by the 12-pounder howitzer using a friction primer. Each round contained a pewter five-second-limit Bormann fuse. The shell wall's thickness measured .475 inch, and each shell contained about eighty .69-caliber lead balls. Farrow, *Farrow's Military Encyclopedia*, 3:155; Ripley, *Artillery and Ammunition of the Civil War*, 268–69. Some of the howitzer ammunition likely used at Sand Creek apparently had been transferred from Fort Garland to Fort Lyon in July 1864. Special Orders No. 11, Headquarters, District of Colorado, June 29, 1864, Entry 3254, vol. 2, RG 393, Pt. 3, NA.

51. Testimony of Stephen Decatur, Company C, Third Colorado, May 8, 1865, in Senate, *Report of the Secretary of War*, 199. Decatur believed that the Indians had dug the pits previously. "They were dug under the banks, and in the bed of the creek, and, in fact, all over, where there was a little mound or bunch of grass or weeds favorable for concealment. They were dug . . . from three to four feet wide, some six feet long and longer." Ibid., 196.

52. Chivington in ibid., 102.

53. Cornelius J. Ballou, "Sand Creek Affair," *National Tribune*, Nov. 23, 1905.

54. See Testimony of Captain Preston Talbot, Company M, Third Colorado, in Senate, *Report of the Joint Committee on the Conduct of the War*, 207; and Testimony of First Lieutenant James Dean Cannon, Company K, First Colorado, in Senate, *Report of the Secretary of War*, 111.

55. Record of Events, Company K, First Colorado Cavalry, Muster Roll, Nov.–Dec. 1864, RG 94, M594, Roll 4, NA; Testimony of Private David H. Louderback, First Colorado Cavalry, Mar. 31, 1865, in Senate, *Report of the Secretary of War*, 138; Interview with Eugene Weston, Nov. 14, 1907, Cragin Notebook 10, p. 11. Weston identified the camp as belonging to the Arapahos. But George Bent wrote George Hyde fifty-one years later that One Eye's Arapaho camp stood *up* the creek and *north* of the main village. Bent to Hyde, Jan. 20, 1915, George Bent Letters, Coe Collection, Yale University Library. Furthermore, one of Bent's diagrams depicting the relative position of Indian camps at Sand Creek, as well as subsequent statements made by Bent, indicate that the Arapahos were camped either within the village or at its northern edge and that the smaller downstream camp may have been Cheyenne. Bent's drawing shows the "Arapaho Camp" as being part of the larger group and situated between "One-Eye's Camp" and "Black Kettle's Camp." He offered addition explanation of this diagram in a 1913 letter in which he stated: "I have made a map . . . [on which] I mark camps of One Eye, White Antelope, War Bonnet, Black Kettle, Sand Hill, Left Hand, Arapaho camp of 7 lodges." In a 1914 letter Bent further attested to the accuracy of this drawing: "I did not change the map because it is correct. Several Cheyennes helped me to mark the different camps as they stood when Chivington attacked it." As previously stated, Bent offered further information on the placement of the Arapaho lodges in a 1915 letter in which he reported, "Left Hand, Arapaho chief, had only a few lodges at Sand Creek and were camped with One Eye or Lone Bear up the creek and north of main village." This description corresponds with Bent's diagram showing the "Arapaho Camp" adjacent to "One Eye's Camp." Moreover, his 1915 correspondence indicates that it may have been Sand Hill's Cheyenne camp that was "camped further down Sand Creek, away from other bands." Testimony of Private David H. Louderback, First Colorado Cavalry, Mar. 31, 1865, in Senate, *Report of the Secretary of War*, 138; Interview with Eugene Weston, Nov. 14, 1907, Cragin Notebook 10, p. 11; Record of Events, Company K, First Colorado Cavalry, Muster Roll, Nov.–Dec. 1864; Bent to Hyde, Apr. 30, 1913, Oct. 23, 1914, and Jan. 20, 1915, Coe Collection; Bent to Joseph Thoburn, Mar. 13, 1914, Thoburn Collection, Oklahoma Historical Society, as cited in Memorandum, Thomas Meier to Eugene Ridgely Sr. and Gail Ridgely, Mar. 2, 2000.

56. Bent diagram, ca. 1905–14 [Wegman-French and Whitacre, "Sand Creek Massacre Site (Interim Report No. 2)," map A], Folder 1, George Bent–George Hyde Collection, Western History Collections, University of Colorado Library, Boulder; Report of Major Scott Anthony, First Colorado Cavalry, Dec. 1, 1864, in Senate, *Report of the Joint Committee on the Conduct of the War*, 53–54; Testimony of Second Lieutenant Joseph A. Cramer, First Colorado Cavalry, Feb. 28, 1865, in Senate, *Report of the Secretary of War*, 48; Testimony of Corporal James J. Adams, Company C, First Colorado Cavalry, Apr. 4, 1865, in ibid., 149; Bent to Hyde, Jan. 20, 1915, George Bent Letters, Coe Collection, Yale University Library; Howbert, *Memories*, 122–24; Report of Colonel Chivington, Nov. 29, 1864, in *War of the Rebellion*, ser. 1, 41(1):948. A group of twenty ponies was apparently sighted about four miles "to the right," or north, of the village. Captain T. G. Cree to Colonel George L. Shoup, Third Colorado Cavalry, Dec. 6, 1864, in Senate, *Report of the Joint Committee on the Conduct of the War*, 53. Bent recalled that some of the escaping Indians managed to get to herds three or four miles upstream. Bent to Hyde, Jan. 20, 1915, Bent Letters, Coe Collection. The quote is from Coffin, *Battle of Sand Creek*, 29. This book is composed of Coffin's letters to the Sun.

57. Unidentified correspondent's [George A. Wells?] letter, *The (Central City, Colo.) Miner's Register*, Jan. 4, 1865.

58. Testimony of Second Lieutenant Clark Dunn, Company E, First Colorado Cavalry, in *Massacre of Cheyenne Indians*, 55; Howbert, *Memories*, 122–24. Howbert notes that, from the point at which the soldiers marched "northward down the slope to Sand Creek," the Indian village stood "a mile or more to the westward."

59. Testimony of Stephen Decatur, Company C, Third Colorado, May 8, 1865, in Senate, *Report of the Secretary of War*, 194–95; Morse H. Coffin, letters to the *(Greeley) Colorado Sun*, Dec. 1878–Feb. 1879; Interview, Theo. Chubbuck, Aug. 30, 1886, Hubert H. Bancroft Collection, Western History Collections, University of Colorado Library, Boulder; Horton, "Survivor Tells of the 'Chivington Massacre.'" See also Coffin, *Battle of Sand Creek*, 19.

60. Testimony of Captain Silas S. Soule, Feb. 20, 1865, in Senate, *Report of the Secretary of War*, 11, 13; Testimony of Second Lieutenant Joseph A. Cramer, First Colorado Cavalry, Feb. 28, 1865, in ibid., 48, 64.

61. Testimony of Second Lieutenant Joseph A. Cramer, First Colorado Cavalry, Feb. 28, 1865, in ibid., 64; Testimony of First Lieutenant James Dean Cannon, Company K, First Colorado, in ibid., 114; Testimony of John S. Smith, Mar. 14, 1865 in Senate, *Report of the Joint Committee on the Conduct of the War*, 5–6.

62. Testimony of Sergeant Lucian Palmer, Company C, First Colorado Cavalry, Apr. 1, 1865, in Senate, *Report of the Secretary of War*, 143; Testimony of Second Lieutenant Joseph A. Cramer, First Colorado Cavalry, Feb. 28, 1865, in ibid., 40–50. Quote is from Testimony of John W. Prowers, Mar. 27, 1865, in ibid., 194–95. Jacob Downing recalled years later that "a Howitzer was planted on the side of the hill to shell the camp." *The Denver Post*, Dec. 31, 1903.

63. Testimony of Stephen Decatur, Company C, Third Colorado, May 8, 1865, in Senate, *Report of the Secretary of War*, 194–95; Testimony of Second Lieutenant Joseph A. Cramer, First Colorado Cavalry, Feb. 28, 1865, in ibid., 63; Interview, Theo. Chubbuck, Aug. 30, 1886, Bancroft Collection; David C. Mansell, Company A, Third Colorado Cavalry, in *Winners of the West*, Dec. 15, 1925. One account states that Chivington "ordered us to go to a high hill and turn our artillery fire loose on the village. We went to the place ordered, but . . . we refused to unlimber our guns, and so we sat there and watched the massacre." Isaac Clarke, First Colorado Cavalry, *American Pioneer*, 39, 41.

64. These howitzer ranges appear in the "Table of Fire," ca. 1860, glued on the inside of the lids of period limber chests that accompanied the pieces. Information provided by Norman Hughes, Denver, Colo. The eight-hundred-yard effective range, though at elevation of four degrees, thirty seconds, appears in *Ordnance Manual for the Use of Officers of the United States Army*, 386.

65. Captain T. G. Cree to Colonel George L. Shoup, Third Colorado Cavalry, Dec. 6, 1864, in Senate, *Report of the Joint Committee on the Conduct of the War*, 53; Report of Colonel George L Shoup, Third Colorado Cavalry, Dec. 7, 1864, in ibid., 51; Testimony of Corporal James J. Adams, Company C, First Colorado Cavalry, Apr. 4, 1865, in ibid., 149; Testimony of John S. Smith, Mar. 14, 1865, in ibid., 5–6, 8; Report of Colonel John M. Chivington, Dec. 16, 1864, in ibid., 49; account of Little Bear, in Hyde, *Life of George Bent*, 153–54.

66. Report of Major Anthony, Dec. 2, 1864, in *War of the Rebellion*, ser. 1, 41(1):952.

67. Breakenridge, *Helldorado*, 32–33. Morse Coffin also reported that tipis were used to house the wounded. *Battle of Sand Creek*, 31, 32.

68. Report of Colonel John M. Chivington, Dec. 16, 1864, in Senate, *Report of the Joint Committee on the Conduct of the War*, 49; Testimony of Corporal James J. Adams, Company C, First Colorado Cavalry, Apr. 4, 1865, in ibid., 150; Morse H. Coffin, letters to the *(Greeley) Colorado Sun*, Dec. 1878–Feb. 1879. One official document states that the troops "returned to the battlefield & encamped." Record of Events, Company E, First Colorado Cavalry, Muster Roll, Nov.–Dec. 1864, RG 94, M594, Roll 4, NA. Sergeant Lucian Palmer, Company C, First Colorado Cavalry, testified on Apr. 1, 1865, that the bivouac stood "on the ground that the Indian had their lodges on." Senate, *Report of the Secretary of War*, 144. See also Testimony of Stephen Decatur, May 8, 1865, in ibid., 195.

69. Testimony of Captain Silas S. Soule, Feb. 20, 1865, in Senate, *Report of the Secretary of War*, 22.

70. During the research phase of this study, the historians sought information regarding relic collecting that had taken place in the area evidently since shortly after the turn of the century. Also, interviews conducted with area residents or past residents acquainted with such activity determined that many people used to hunt arrowheads and other artifacts there. *Kiowa County Press*, Sept. 21, 1906; *Pueblo Chieftain*, Mar. 22, 1998; Herzog, "History of Kiowa County," 186–88. While most references to relic collecting at the site are nonspecific as to its location, at least one by a longtime collector includes the notation that "the battle field [sic] is located some two miles north of where the stone marker would indicate." *The Lamar Tri-State Daily News*, Feb. 23, 1963. For other information about artifact collecting in the vicinity, see Wegman-French and Whitacre, "Sand Creek Massacre Site (Interim Report No. 3)," 9–10. Another indicator from local sources consists of references to the location of the headgates of the Chivington Canal, an irrigation facility built around 1910, as being on the massacre site. The headgates of the structure stood in the SE 1/4 of Section 24. Roleta Teal Papers, ca. 1960s–70s (M76–1387), Western History Department, Denver Public Library; Colorado State Engineer's Office, Division of Water Resources, various records, notably Water Filing No. 4101 (Chivington Canal).

CHAPTER 3

1. Douglas D. Scott, Anne Wainstein Bond, Richard Ellis, and William B. Lees, "Archeological Reconnaissance of Two Possible Sites of the Sand Creek Massacre of 1864," Apr. 1998 (unpublished report, Department of Southwest Studies, Fort Lewis State College, Durango, Colo.), copy on file, Midwest Archeological Center, National Park Service, Lincoln, Neb.

2. Amy Holmes and Michael McFaul, "Geomorphological and Geoarcheological Assessment of the Possible Sand Creek Massacre Site, Kiowa County, Colorado," 1999, manuscript on file, Intermountain Regional Office, National Park Service, Lakewood, Colo.

3. Scott et al., "Archeological Reconnaissance."

4. The Colorado Magazine 9 (Feb. 1932): 120; Tom Meier, FAX to Christine Whitacre, Oct. 15, 1999, National Park Service, Denver.

5. Luke Cahill, "Recollections of a Plainsman," ca. 1915, MSS 99, Manuscripts Division, Colorado Historical Society, Denver, 16.

6. Lysa Wegman-French and Christine Whitacre, "Historical Research on the Location of the Sand Creek Massacre Site (Interim Report No. 2)," Jan. 29, 1999, National Park Service Intermountain Support Office–Denver, 35; Stone, History of Colorado, 4:239–40.

7. Lisa Wegman-French and Christine Whitacre, "Historical Research on the Location of the Sand Creek Massacre Site (Interim Report No. 3)," Apr. 27, 1999, National Park Service Intermountain Support Office–Denver, 8–9.

8. Ibid, 9.

9. Werner, Sand Creek Fight, 159–85.

10. William Schneider, personal communication to Douglas D. Scott, Apr. 10, 1999.

11. Metal detecting is well established in the field of historical archeology. See Connor and Scott, "Metal Detector Use in Archaeology," 73–82; and Scott, Fox, Connor, and Harmon, Archaeological Perspectives on the Battle of the Little Bighorn.

12. The weapons and equipment carried by the Colorado volunteers are well documented. See Testimony of First Lieutenant Charles C. Hawley, First Colorado Volunteer Cavalry and acting ordnance officer for the District of Colorado, Feb. 4, 1867, in Senate, Report of the Secretary of War, 34–37. Appendix E provides a complete transcription of Hawley's ordnance list.

13. Steven L. DeVore, "Geophysical Investigations at the Sand Creek Massacre Site, Colorado," 1999, Cultural Resources and National Register Program Services, Intermountain Support Office–Santa Fe, National Park Service.

14. Appendix C provides transcriptions of various annuity requests and lists taken from U.S. Department of the Interior, Office of Indian Affairs, Letters Received by the Office of Indian Affairs (Washington), from Upper Arkansas Agency, 1855–64, RG 75, M234, Roll 878, NA (Record Center, Denver).

15. J. H. Haynes, "Claim for damages alleged to have been sustained by depredations committed by the Arapahoe and Cheyenne Indians," Letters Received, Office of Indian Affairs, Upper Arkansas Agency, 1865–67, Record Group 75, M234, Roll 879, NA. See Appendix B for a transcription of this source.

16. Albright and Scott, *Historic Furnishing Study*, 179–88.

17. Chamberlain, "Historic Furnishings Report."

18. Morse H. Coffin, letters to the *(Greeley) Colorado Sun*, Dec. 1878–Feb. 1879, typed copies in Box 4, Raymond G. Carey Manuscript Collection, University of Denver.

19. Bruce A. Jones, "Archeological Investigations of the Hancock Village Site, Ness County, Kansas," 2002, Midwest Archeological Center, National Park Service, Lincoln, Neb.

20. Andrew E. Masich, "Russellville Archaeology Project: A Preliminary Report on Ammunition and Ammunition Components," n.d., Office of the State Archeologist, Colorado Historical Society, Denver, manuscript on file.

21. Ripley, *Artillery and Ammunition of the Civil War*.

CHAPTER 4

1. Among the differences: diagram 1 (University of Colorado Libraries) shows Chivington's trail crossing Sand Creek and running between Sand Hill's camp and White Antelope's and Black Kettle's camps, while diagram 2 (Oklahoma Historical Society) shows the trail crossing the creek and running between Bear Tongue's camp and War Bonnet's camp; diagram 1 places Sand Hill's camp closer to the other camps and slightly northeast of Black Kettle's camp, while diagram 2 shows Sand Hill's camp some distance east and south of Black Kettle's camp; diagram 1 places White Antelope's camp directly north of

Black Kettle's camp, while diagram 2 places it directly west of it; diagram 1 represents the stream bend of Sand Creek to be curvilinear, while diagram 2 shows the bend as being much more abruptly sharp; diagram 1 shows what appears to be a much shorter distance between the village and the first soldier position at the sand pits than does diagram 2; diagram 1 shows no guns positioned on the north side of Sand Creek opposite the sand pits, though diagram 2 locates two guns there; diagram 1 indicates the soldiers' approach splitting from the presumed Fort Lyon Trail and leading along the south side of Sand Creek to the sand pits, while diagram 2 shows no such division; diagram 1 shows the location in the bed of Sand Creek where the women and children were killed en route from the village to the sand pits, while diagram 2 omits this feature altogether.

2. See pertinent testimony of participants, as excerpted from appropriate historical documents, in Wegman-French and Whitacre, "Sand Creek Massacre Site (Interim Report No. 2)," 8, 9–10, 11, 14.

3. Ibid., 9–10; Arthur K. Ireland, "Analysis of Aerial Photography from 1936–37, 1954, and 1975," 1999, draft report, National Park Service, Santa Fe, figs. 6, 11.

4. Hyde, *Life of George Bent*, 152; Wegman-French and Whitacre, Sand Creek Massacre Site (Interim Report No. 2)," 22.

5. Wegman-French and Whitacre, Sand Creek Massacre Site (Interim Report No. 2)," 7, 13–16.

6. See "North of Chivington, CO," USGS Quadrangle, 1982.

7. Ibid.

8. C. Frost Liggett, "Pioneers," *Kiowa County Press*, Apr. 5, 1940 (typescript copy in Sand Creek, Copies of Various Papers Relating to the Incident, Big Timbers Museum, Lamar, Colo.).

9. Roleta Teal Papers, ca. 1960s–70s, M76-1387, Western History Department, Denver Public Library, which contain further mention of the juxtaposition of the headgates of the canal with the immediately adjacent place where at least part of the massacre took place (for which the canal received its name).

10. "Sand Creek Battlefield Area Map. Copy of blue print from old drawing made by John Baumbach, early settler of the area. From office of Co. Surveyor, Cheyenne Co., Colo., September 12, 1938," Office of County Surveyor, Cheyenne County, Colo., Colorado Historical Society, Denver.

11. *Lamar Tri-State Daily News*, Feb. 23, 1963; interviews cited in Wegman-French and Whitacre, "Sand Creek Massacre Site (Interim Report No. 3)," 9.

12. See Banks and Snortland, "Every Picture Tells a Story"; Brasser, "The Tipi as an Element in the Emergence of Historic Plains Indian Nomadism"; Kehoe, *Stone Tipi Rings in North-Central Montana and the Adjacent Portion of Alberta Canada*; and idem, "Retrospectus and Commentary."

13. See National Park Service, *Sand Creek Massacre Project*, 1:160–277.

14. Ibid., 278–81.

15. Ibid., 281–82.

16. Ibid., 222–31.

17. Interviews cited in Wegman-French and Whitacre, "Sand Creek Massacre Site (Interim Report No. 3)," 13–17.

Appendix A

1. Logan, *Cartridges*; Barnes, *Cartridges of the World*, 364.

2. Thomas and Thomas, *Civil War Bullets and Cartridges*, 2.

3. Barnes, *Cartridges of the World*, 365.

4. Gluckman, *Identifying Old U.S. Muskets, Rifles, and Carbines*, 230, 268; Barnes, *Cartridges of the World*, 139.

5. Sellers, *Sharps Firearms*.

6. Thomas and Thomas, *Civil War Bullets and Cartridges*, 25–26.

7. Harmon, "Henry .44-Caliber."

8. Kinzer, "Invention of the Extractor," 34–38.

9. Madis, *The Winchester Book*, 97.

10. Ibid., 79.

11. Barber, *Rimfire Cartridge*.

12. Ibid., 40.

13. Madis, *The Winchester Book*, 132, 214.

14. Logan, *Cartridges*, 31; Switzer, "Maynard Cartridges and Primers from the Steamboat Bertrand," 85–87.

15. Thomas and Thomas, *Civil War Bullets and Cartridges*, 26–28.

16. Logan, *Cartridges*; Thomas and Thomas, *Civil War Bullets and Cartridges*.

17. Flayderman, *Guide to Antique Firearms*.

18. Barnes, *Cartridges of the World*, 281; Gluckman, *Identifying Old U.S. Muskets, Rifles, and Carbines*, 388.

19. Coates and Thomas, *Civil War Small Arms*, 48.

20. George A. Wells, correspondence, *The (Central City, Colo.) Miner's Register*, Jan. 4, 1865; William F. Dawson, "Ordnance Artifacts at the Sand Creek Massacre Site: A Technical and Historical Report," Sept. 1999, report on file, Intermountain Regional Office, National Park Service, Denver.

21. Barnes, *Cartridges of the World*, 142.

22. Thomas and Thomas, *Civil War Bullets and Cartridges*, 39–40.

23. See Dawson, "Ordnance Artifacts at the Sand Creek Massacre Site."

24. Ripley, *Artillery and Ammunition of the Civil War*, 198–201.

25. Ibid., 199.

26. Gibbon, *Artillerist's Manual*, 42.

27. Petsche, *Steamboat* Bertrand.

28. Hunt, "Firearms and the Upper Missouri Fur Trade Frontier," 359–61.

29. Ibid, 359–61.

30. Ibid., 238–39.

31. Moore, *Bent's Old Fort*, 87–99.

32. Hanson, "Upper Missouri Arrow Points," 2–8; Russell, *Firearms, Traps, and Tools*.

33. War Department, Surgeon-General's Office, *Circular No. 3*.

34. Todd, *American Military Equipage*, 100–102.

35. Sylvia and O'Donnell, *Civil War Canteens*; Todd, *American Military Equipage*, 216.

36. Steffen, *Horse Soldier*.

37. Herskovitz, *Fort Bowie Material Culture*.

38. Tice, *Uniform Buttons*, 380–84.

39. Ibid.

40. William J. Hunt Jr., "Fort Union Trading Post National Historic Site, 32WI17, Material Culture Reports, Part V: Buttons as Closures, Buttons as Decorations: A Nineteenth Century Example from Fort Union," 1986, Midwest Archeological Center, National Park Service, Lincoln, Neb., 17–20.

41. Ibid., 23.

42. Anderson, "Mass-Produced Footwear," 56.

43. Woodward, *Denominators of the Fur Trade*, 66–68.

44. Hanson, *Metal Weapons*, 90–93; Afton et al., *Cheyenne Dog Soldiers*, xiv, 133.

45. Luke Brady, personal communication with Douglas D. Scott, May 21, 1999.

46. Brown, "Historic Trade Bells," 75–76.

47. Ibid., 73–76.

48. Ibid., Hanson, *Metal Weapons*, 80–82; G. Smith, *Like-A-Fishhook Village*.

49. Smith, *Like-A-Fishhook Village*, 76.

50. Hedren, "Army Tincups," 57–63.

51. Lord, *Civil War Collectors Encyclopedia*, 169.

52. Ibid., 167–71.

53. Ibid.

54. Hanson, "Upper Missouri Arrow Points."

55. Hanson, "Identifying Open Kettles," 2–13.

56. Lord, *Civil War Collectors Encyclopedia*, 166–69.

57. Hanson, "Scalping Knife," 8–12; idem, "Butcher Knives," 1–5; Switzer, "Butcher Knives as Historical Sources," 5–7.

58. Smith, *Like-A-Fishhook Village*.

59. Rock, *Commentary on Cans*.

60. Peterson, *American Indian Tomahawks*; Russell, *Firearms, Traps, and Tools*.

61. Smith, *Like-A-Fishhook Village*, 138.

62. Hanson, *Metal Weapons*, 62.

63. Lyle and Porter, "Report on the Manufacture and Issue of Files and Rasps," 320–85.

64. Hanson, *Metal Weapons*, 62.

65. Smith, *Like-A-Fishhook Village*, 74–75.

66. Ibid., 75.

67. James Hanson, personal communication with Douglas D. Scott, July 1, 1999.

68. Steffen, *United States Military Saddles*; idem, Horse Soldier.

69. Steffen, *Horse Soldier*.

70. Scott and Scott, *Analysis of the Historic Artifacts and Evidence from Pollen*; Metcalf, "Notes on Two Paiute Burials," 2–22.

71. Rick Morris, personal communication with Douglas D. Scott, Jan. 8, 1987; Spivey, *Guide to Wagon Hardware and Blacksmith Supplies*; Berge, *Springs Station Historical Archaeology*, 237–49.

72. Hanson, *Metal Weapons*, 90.

73. Myers, *Gaslighting in America*, 92–93.

Bibliography

Manuscript Material

Bloomington. Indiana University. Lilly Library. Walter M. Camp Collection.

Boulder, Colorado. Boulder History Museum. Boulder Historical Society Collections.

———. Carnegie Branch Library for Local History. Henry Blake Diary.

———. University of Colorado Library. Western History Collections.

David H. Nichols Papers.

George Bent–George Hyde Papers.

Hal Sayre Papers.

Harper A. Orahood Papers.

Hubert H. Bancroft Collection.

Colorado Springs. Colorado College. Tutt Library Special Collections and Archives.

Irving Howbert Manuscript Collection.

Frank Murray Wynkoop, "Data Concerning Col. Edward W. Wynkoop."

————. Pioneer Museum of Colorado Springs. Starsmore Research Center.

Andrew J. Templeton Collection.

Cragin Notebooks.

Howbert Family Collection.

John Wolfe Collection.

Denver. Bureau of Land Management.

    Colorado State Office. Field notes for surveys in Townships 16 and 17 South, Ranges 45, 46, and 47 West.

    U.S. Post Office Department. Applications for establishment of post offices.

————. Colorado Adjutant General's Office. Special Orders, Third Colorado Cavalry, 1864.

————. Colorado Historical Society.

Scott J. Anthony Papers.

George Baxter Collection.

Luke Cahill, "Recollections of a Plainsman," ca. 1915.

Thomas Dawson Scrapbooks.

James R. Doolittle Collection.

John Evans Papers.

Andrew E. Masich, "Russellville Archaeology Project: A Preliminary Report on Ammunition and Ammunition Components," n.d. Office of the State Archeologist, manuscript on file.

Samuel Forster Tappan Manuscript Collection.

————. Colorado State Archives. "A Collection of Documents Concerning the Battle of Sand Creek, November 29, 1864."

————. Colorado State Engineer's Office. State Engineer Records. Division of Water Resources.

————. Denver Public Library. Western History Department.

Arthur Ewing Stevens Letters, 1968.

Flora Ellice (Bishop) Stevens Reminiscences, 1903.

John Lewis Dailey Diary.

Silas Soule Papers, 1861–65.

Roleta Teal Papers, ca. 1960s–70s.

William B. Thom Letters.

William Dixon Manuscript Collection.

————. Intermountain Regional Office, National Park Service.

William F. Dawson, "Ordnance Artifacts at the Sand Creek Massacre Site: A Technical and Historical Report," 1999. Unpublished report on file.

National Park Service Intermountain Support Office–Denver.

    Lysa Wegman-French and Christine Whitacre, "Historical Research on the Location of the Sand Creek Massacre Site (Interim Report No. 1)," September 11, 1998.

    ——, "Historical Research on the Location of the Sand Creek Massacre Site (Interim Report No. 2)," January 29, 1999.

    ——, "Historical Research on the Location of the Sand Creek Massacre Site (Interim Report No. 3)," April 27, 1999.

——. University of Denver Archives. Raymond G. Carey Manuscript Collection.

Eads, Colorado. Kiowa County Abstract Company. Land Records.

Lakewood, Colorado. Intermountain Regional Office, National Park Service. Amy Holmes and Michael McFaul, "Geomorphological and Geoarcheological Assessment of the Possible Sand Creek Massacre Site, Kiowa County, Colorado," 1999. Unpublished manuscript on file.

Lamar, Colorado. Big Timbers Museum. "Sand Creek, Copies of Various Papers Relating to the Incident."

Lincoln, Nebraska. Midwest Archeological Center, National Park Service.

    William J. Hunt Jr., "Fort Union Trading Post National Historic Site, 32WI17, Material Culture Reports Part V: Buttons as Closures, Buttons as Decorations: A Nineteenth Century Example from Fort Union," 1986.

    Bruce A. Jones, "Archeological Investigations of the Hancock Village Site, Ness County, Kansas," 2002.

    Douglas D. Scott, Anne Wainstein Bond, Richard Ellis, and William B. Lees, "Archeological Reconnaissance of Two Possible Sites of the Sand Creek Massacre of 1864," April 1998. Unpublished report, Department of Southwest Studies, Fort Lewis State College, Durango, Colorado. Copy on file.

Santa Fe, New Mexico. Intermountain Support Office–Santa Fe, National Park Service.

    Cultural Anthropology Projects, PECO-01. Charles Haecker, "Archeological Remote Sensing Survey of the Civil War Site of Camp Lewis, Pecos National Historical Park, San Miguel County, New Mexico," 1998.

    Cultural Resources and National Register Program Services. Steven L. DeVore, "Geophysical Investigations at the Sand Creek Massacre Site, Colorado," 1999.

Washington, D.C. Library of Congress. William T. Sherman Papers.
————. National Archives.
Record Group 46. Records of the U.S. Senate.
Record Group 49. Records of the Bureau of Land Management.
Record Group 75. Records of the Bureau of Indian Affairs.
Record Group 77. Records of the Office of the Chief of Engineers.
Record Group 94. Records of the Office of the Adjutant General.
Record Group 108. Records of the Headquarters of the Army.
Record Group 112. Records of the Office of the Surgeon General.
Record Group 114. Records of the Soil Conservation Service.
Record Group 153. Records of the Office of the Judge Advocate.
Record Group 159. Records of the Inspector General.
Record Group 393. Records of U.S. Army Continental Commands.

GOVERNMENT PUBLICATIONS

Albright, John, and Douglas D. Scott. *Historic Furnishing Study: Historical and Archeological Data, Fort Larned National Historic Site, Kansas.* Denver: Denver Service Center, National Park Service, 1974.

Atlas to Accompany the Official Records of the Union and Confederate Armies. Washington, D.C.: Government Printing Office, 1891 (reprint entitled *The Official Military Atlas of the Civil War.* New York: Arno and Crown Publishers, 1978).

Bear River Massacre Site: Final Special Resource Study and Environmental Assessment. Denver: National Park Service, 1996.

Berge, Dale Simpson. *Springs Station Historical Archaeology in Western Utah.* Cultural Resource Series 6. Salt Lake City: Bureau of Land Management, 1980.

Biographical Directory of the American Congress, 1774–1961. Washington, D.C.: Government Printing Office, 1961.

Chamberlain, Andrew B. "Historic Furnishings Report: Indian Trade House and Storage Room, Fort Union Trading Post National Historic Site, Williston, North Dakota." Harpers Ferry, W.V.: Division of Historic Furnishings, Harpers Ferry Center, National Park Service, 1993.

Coffin, Donald L. *Geology and Ground-Water Resources of the Big Sandy Creek Valley, Lincoln, Cheyenne, and Kiowa Counties, Colorado.* Geological Survey Water-Supply Paper, 1843. Washington, D.C.: Government Printing Office, 1967.

Field Service Regulations, United States Army. Washington, D.C.: Government Printing Office, 1905.

Greene, Jerome A. *Reconnaissance Study of Indian–U.S. Army Battlefields of the Northern Plains*. Denver: National Park Service, 1998.

Haecker, Charles. *A Thunder of Cannon: Archeology of the Mexican-American War Battlefield of Palo Alto*. Southwest Cultural Resources Center Professional Papers No. 52. Santa Fe, N.M.: Division of Anthropology and History, Southwest Regional Office, National Park Service, 1994.

Heitman, Francis B., comp. *Historical Register and Dictionary of the United States Army, from Its Organization, September 29, 1789, to March 2, 1903*. 2 vols. Washington, D.C.: Government Printing Office, 1903.

Killion, Thomas W.; Scott Brown; and J. Stuart Speaker. "Naevahoo'ohsteme (We are going back home): Cheyenne Repatriation: The Human Remains." Washington, D.C.: Repatriation Office, National Museum of Natural History, Smithsonian Institution, May 10, 1992.

Lyle, D. A., and Samuel W. Porter. "Report on the Manufacture and Issue of Files and Rasps." In *Executive Documents of the House of Representatives, 47th Congress, Appendix 35 to Ordnance Reports No. 1, part 2, volume 3*, pp. 320–85. Washington, D.C.: Government Printing Office, 1882.

Myers, Denys Peter. *Gaslighting in America: A Guide for Historic Preservation*. Washington, D.C.: Technical Preservation Services Division, Office of Archeology and Historic Preservation, Heritage Conservation and Recreation Service, 1978.

The Ordnance Manual for the Use of Officers of the United States Army. Philadelphia: J. B. Lippincott, 1862.

Report of the Secretary of the Interior, 1864. Washington, D.C.: Government Printing Office, 1865.

Revised United States Army Regulations, of 1861. With an Appendix containing the Changes and Laws Affecting Army Regulations and Articles of War to June 25, 1863. Philadelphia: George W. Childs, 1864.

Scott, Douglas, and Linda Scott. *Analysis of the Historic Artifacts and Evidence from Pollen: A 19th Century Ute Burial from Northeastern Utah*. Cultural Resource Series 16. Salt Lake City: Bureau of Land Management, Utah, 1984.

Smith, G. Hubert. *Like-A-Fishhook Village and Fort Berthold, Garrison Reservoir, North Dakota*. Anthropological Papers 2. Washington, D.C.: National Park Service, 1972.

United States Army Medical Museum Anatomical Section: Records Relating to Specimens Transferred to the Smithsonian Institution. Washington, D.C.: National Anthropological Archives, Smithsonian Institution, 1990.

U.S. Congress. Senate. *Report of Lieutenant J. W. Abert of His Examination of New Mexico in the Years 1846–1847.* 30th Cong., 2d sess., 1847. S. Ex. Doc. 23.

———. *Report of the Joint Committee on the Conduct of the War, Massacre of the Cheyenne Indians.* 38th Cong., 2d sess., 1865. 3 vols. S. Rept. 142. Serial 1214.

———. *Report of the Committee on Indian Affairs: Report of the Joint Special Committee. Condition of the Indian Tribes with Appendix (The Chivington Massacre).* 39th Cong., 2d sess., 1867. S. Rept. 156. Serial 1279.

———. *Report of the Secretary of War, Communicating . . . a Copy of the Evidence Taken at Denver and Fort Lyon, Colorado Territory by a Military Commission Ordered to Inquire into the Sand Creek Massacre, November, 1864.* 39th Cong., 2d sess., 1867. S. Ex. Doc. 26. Serial 1277.

War Department, Surgeon-General's Office. Circular No. 3, August 17, 1871. *A Report of Surgical Cases Treated in the Army of the United States from 1865 to 1871,* by George A. Otis, assistant surgeon. Washington, D.C.: Government Printing Office, 1871.

———. *The War of the Rebellion: A Compilation of the Official Records of the Union and Confederate Armies.* 73 vols. in 128 pts. Washington, D.C.: Government Printing Office, 1880–1901.

BOOKS AND PAMPHLETS

Afton, Jean; David Fridtjof Halaas; and Andrew W. Masich (with Richard N. Ellis). *Cheyenne Dog Soldiers: A Ledgerbook History of Coups and Combat.* Niwot: Colorado State Historical Society and University of Colorado Press, 1997.

Anderson, George L. *Kansas West.* San Marino, Calif.: Golden West, 1963.

Baker, James H., and LeRoy R. Hafen, eds. *History of Colorado*. 3 vols. Denver: Linderman, 1927.

Baker, Thomas. *Aerial Archaeology at Sand Creek: An Attempt to Locate the Site of the Sand Creek Massacre of 1864 in Southeastern Colorado from the Air*. Tijeras, N.M.: Aerial Archaeology, 1998.

Barber, John L. *The Rimfire Cartridge in the United States and Canada, 1857–1984*. Tacoma, Wash.: Armory, 1987.

Barnes, Frank C. *Cartridges of the World*. 6th ed. Northbrook, Ill.: DBI, 1989.

Bent County (Colorado) History. Las Animas: Holly, 1987.

Berthrong, Donald J. *The Southern Cheyennes*. Norman: University of Oklahoma Press, 1963.

Betz, Ava. *A Prowers County History*. Lamar, Colo.: Big Timbers Museum, 1986.

Bowles, Samuel. *Across the Continent: A Summer's Journey to the Rocky Mountains, the Mormans, and the Pacific States with Speaker Colfax*. Springfield, Mass.: Samuel Bowles, 1865.

Boyd, LeRoy. *Fort Lyon, Colorado: One Hundred Years of Service*. Fort Lyon, Colo.: VA Medical Center, 1967.

Breakenridge, William M. *Helldorado: Bringing the Law to the Mesquite*. New York: Houghton Mifflin, 1928.

Carroll, John M., comp. *The Sand Creek Massacre: A Documentary History*. New York: Sol Lewis, 1973.

Chalfant, William Y. *Cheyennes and Horse Soldiers: The 1857 Expedition and the Battle of Solomon's Fork*. Norman: University of Oklahoma Press, 1989.

Chapman, Arthur. *The Story of Colorado: Out Where the West Begins*. Chicago: Rand McNally, 1924.

Coates, Earl, and Dean S. Thomas. *An Introduction to Civil War Small Arms*. Gettysburg, Pa.: Thomas, 1990.

Coffin, Morse H. *The Battle of Sand Creek*. Edited by Alan W. Farley. Waco, Tex.: W. M. Morrison, 1965.

Conner, Daniel Ellis. *A Confederate in the Colorado Gold Fields*. Edited by Donald J. Berthrong. Norman: University of Oklahoma Press, 1970.

Craig, Reginald S. *The Fighting Parson: The Biography of Colonel John M. Chivington*. Los Angeles: Westernlore, 1959.

Dickey, Thomas S., and Peter C. George. *Field Artillery Projectiles of the American Civil War*. Mechanicsville, Va.: Arsenal Publications II, 1993.

Farrow, Edward S., comp. *Farrow's Military Encyclopedia*. 3 vols. New York: Military-Naval, 1895.

Flayderman, Norm. *Flayderman's Guide to Antique Firearms and Their Values*. Northfield, Minn.: DBI, 1990.

Fowler, Loretta. *Arapahoe Politics, 1851–1978*. Lincoln: University of Nebraska Press, 1982.

Frazer, Robert W. *Forts of the West*. Norman: University of Oklahoma Press, 1965.

Gibbon, John. *The Artillerist's Manual, Compiled from Various Sources and Adapted to the Service of the United States*. 1860. Reprint, Glendale, N.Y.: Benchmark, 1970.

Gluckman, Arcadi. *Identifying Old U.S. Muskets, Rifles, and Carbines*. New York: Bonanza, 1965.

Grinnell, George Bird. *The Cheyenne Indians*. 2 vols. New York: Cooper Square, 1923.

———. *The Fighting Cheyennes*. New York: Charles Scribner's Sons, 1915. Reprint, Norman: University of Oklahoma Press, 1956.

Haecker, Charles M., and Jeffery G. Mauck. *On the Prairie of Palo Alto*. College Station: Texas A&M University Press, 1997.

Hanson, James. *Metal Weapons, Tools, and Ornaments of the Teton Dakota Indians*. Lincoln: University of Nebraska Press, 1975.

Hazlett, James C.; Edwin Olmstead; and M. Hume Parks. *Field Artillery Weapons of the Civil War*. Newark: University of Delaware Press, 1983.

Herskovitz, Robert M. *Fort Bowie Material Culture*. Anthropological Papers of the University of Arizona 31. Tucson: University of Arizona, 1978.

History of the Arkansas Valley, Colorado. Chicago: O. L. Baskin, 1881.

Hogan, Marion A., et al. *Kit Carson, Colorado: Home of the Famous Scout, Friendly People and Land of Prime Beef Cattle*. Kit Carson, Colo.: Kit Carson Historical Society, 1974.

Hogarth, Andrew, and Kim Vaughan. *Battlefields, Monuments, and Markers: A Guide to Native American & United States Army Engagements from 1854–1890*. Sydney, Australia: Andrew Hogarth, 1993.

Hoig, Stan. *Peace Chiefs of the Southern Cheyennes*. Norman: University of Oklahoma Press, 1980.

———. *The Sand Creek Massacre*. Norman: University of Oklahoma Press, 1961.

Howbert, Irving. *Memories of a Lifetime in the Pike's Peak Region*. New York: G. P. Putnam's Sons, 1925.

Hyde, George E. *Life of George Bent, Written from His Letters*. Edited by Savoie Lottinville. Norman: University of Oklahoma Press, 1968.

Jackson, Helen Hunt. *A Century of Dishonor: The Early Crusade for Indian Reform*. New York: Harper and Brothers, 1881. Reprint, New York: Harper and Row, 1965.

Josephy, Alvin M., Jr. *The Civil War in the American West*. New York: Random House, 1991.

Jensen, Richard E.; R. Eli Paul; and John E. Carter. *Eyewitness at Wounded Knee*. Lincoln: University of Nebraska Press, 1991.

Kehoe, Thomas F. *Stone Tipi Rings in North-Central Montana and the Adjacent Portion of Alberta Canada: Their Historical, Ethnological, and Archeological Aspects*. Anthropological Papers 62, Bureau of American Ethnology Bulletin 173. Washington, D.C.: Smithsonian Institution, 1960.

Lamar, Howard R., ed. *New Encyclopedia of the American West*. New Haven: Yale University Press, 1998.

Linville, Leslie. *Visiting Historic Sites on the Central Hi-Plains*. Osborne, Kans.: Osborne County Farmer, 1979.

Logan, Herschel. *Cartridges: A Pictorial Digest of Small Arms Ammunition*. New York: Bonanza, 1959.

Lord, Francis A. *Civil War Collectors Encyclopedia, Volumes I and II*. Edison, N.J.: Blue and Grey, 1995.

Lowe, Percival G. *Five Years a Dragoon ('49 to '54): And Other Adventures on the Great Plains*. Norman: University of Oklahoma Press, 1965.

Madis, George. *The Winchester Book*. Brownsboro, Tex.: Art and Reference House, 1959.

McChristian, Douglas. *The U.S. Army in the West, 1870–1880*. Norman: University of Oklahoma Press, 1995.

Melton, Jack W., Jr.; and Lawrence E. Prawl. *Introduction to Field Artillery Ordnance, 1861–1865*. Kennesaw, Ga.: Kennesaw Mountain, 1994.

Moore, Jackson W., Jr. *Bent's Old Fort: An Archeological Study*. Boulder: State Historical Society of Colorado and Pruett, 1973.

Moore, John H. *The Cheyenne*. Cambridge, Mass.: Blackwell, 1996.

———. *The Cheyenne Nation: A Social and Demographic History*. Lincoln: University of Nebraska Press, 1987.

Nankivell, John H. *History of the Military Organizations of the State of Colorado, 1860–1935*. Denver: W. H. Kistler, 1935.

Otero, Miguel Antonio. *My Life on the Frontier, 1864–1882*. New York: Press of the Pioneers, 1935.

Petersen, Philip L. *Arkansas Valley Railway: Branch of the Kansas Pacific Railroad*. N.p.: Philip L. Petersen, 1993.

Peterson, Harold. *American Indian Tomahawks*. New York: Museum of the American Indian, Heye Foundation, 1965.

Petsche, Jerome E. *The Steamboat* Bertrand: *History, Excavation, and Architecture*. Washington, D.C.: National Park Service, 1974.

Pitzer, Henry Littleton. *Three Frontiers: Memories, and a Portrait of Henry Littleton Pitzer*. Muscatine, Iowa.: Prairie, 1938.

Powell, John Peter. *People of the Sacred Mountain: A History of the Northern Cheyenne Chiefs and Warrior Societies, 1830–1879, with an Epilogue, 1969–1974*. San Francisco: Harper and Row, 1981.

———. *Sweet Medicine: The Continuing Role of the Sacred Arrows, the Sun Dance, and the Sacred Buffalo Hat in Northern Cheyenne History*. 2 vols. Norman: University of Oklahoma Press, 1969.

Reish, E. C. *Lamar, Colorado: Its First Hundred Years, 1886–1986*. N.p., n.d.

Ripley, Warren. *Artillery and Ammunition of the Civil War*. New York: Van Nostrand-Reinhold, 1970.

Rock, Jim *A Brief Commentary on Cans*. Salinas, Calif.: Coyote, 1987.

Russell, Carl P. *Firearms, Traps, and Tools of the Mountain Men*. New York: Alfred A. Knopf, 1967.

Sand Creek Papers: "Testimonies and Statements Reflecting Facts Concerning the Killing of Cheyenne and Arapaho Indians on November 29, 1864 by the Third Colorado Volunteers. Black Forest, Colo.: Black Forest Bookman, 1959.

Sanford, Mollie Dorsey. *Mollie: The Journal of Mollie Dorsey Sanford in Nebraska and Colorado Territories, 1857–1866*. Lincoln: University of Nebraska Press, 1959.

Scott, Douglas D. *A Sharp Little Affair: The Archeology of the Big Hole Battlefield.* Reprints in Anthropology 45. Lincoln, Neb.: J and L Reprint, 1994.

Scott, Douglas D., and Richard A. Fox Jr. *Archaeological Insights into the Custer Battle: A Preliminary Assessment.* Norman: University of Oklahoma Press, 1987.

Scott, Douglas D.; Richard A. Fox Jr.; Melissa A. Connor; and Dick Harmon. *Archaeological Perspectives on the Battle of the Little Bighorn.* Norman: University of Oklahoma Press, 1989.

Sellers, Frank. *Sharps Firearms.* North Hollywood, Calif.: Beinfield, 1982.

Shaw, Luella. *True History of Some of the Pioneers of Colorado.* Hotchkiss, Colo.: W. S. Coburn, John Patterson, and A. K. Shaw, 1909.

Spivey, Towana, ed. *A Historical Guide to Wagon Hardware and Blacksmith Supplies.* Contributions of the Museum of the Great Plains 9. Lawton, Okla.: Museum of the Great Plains, 1979.

Stands In Timber, John, and Margot Liberty. *Cheyenne Memories.* New Haven: Yale University Press, 1967.

Steffen, Randy. *The Horse Soldier, 1776–1943: Volume II, The Frontier, The Mexican War, The Civil War, The Indian Wars, 1851–1880.* Norman: University of Oklahoma Press, 1978.

———. *United States Military Saddles, 1812–1943.* Norman: University of Oklahoma Press, 1973.

Steinel, Alvin. *History of Agriculture in Colorado, 1858–1926.* Fort Collins, Colo.: State Agricultural College, 1926.

Stone, Wilbur Fiske. *History of Colorado.* 4 vols. Chicago: S. J. Clarke, 1918–19.

Swanton, John R. *The Indian Tribes of North America.* Washington, D.C.: Smithsonian Institution Press, 1971.

Sylvia, Stephen W., and Michael O'Donnell. *Civil War Canteens.* Orange, Va.: Moss, 1983.

Taylor, Ralph C. *Colorado: South of the Border.* Denver: Sage, 1963.

Thomas, James E., and Dean S. Thomas. *A Handbook of Civil War Bullets and Cartridges.* Gettysburg, Pa.: Thomas, 1996.

Thrapp, Dan L. *Encyclopedia of Frontier Biography.* 3 vols. Glendale, Calif.: Arthur H. Clark, 1988.

Tice, Warren K. *Uniform Buttons of the United States, 1776–1865.* Gettysburg, Pa.: Thomas, 1997.

Todd, Frederick P. *American Military Equipage, 1851–1872, Volume I*. Providence, R.I.: Company of Military Historians, 1974.

Trenholm, Virginia Cole. *The Arapahoes, Our People*. Norman: University of Oklahoma Press, 1970.

Utley, Robert M. *Frontiersmen in Blue: The United States Army and the Indian, 1848–1865*. New York: Macmillan, 1967.

Ware, Eugene. *The Indian War of 1864*. Topeka, Kans.: Crane, 1911. Reprint, New York: St. Martin's, 1960.

Werner, Fred H. *The Sand Creek Fight, November 29, 1864*. Greeley, Colo.: Kendall, 1993.

West, Elliott. *The Contested Plains: Indians, Goldseekers, and the Rush to Colorado*. Lawrence: University Press of Kansas, 1998.

White, Virgil D., comp. and ed. *Index to Indian Wars Pension Files, 1892–1926*. 2 vols. Waynesboro, Tenn.: National Historical Publishing, 1987.

Williams, Scott C., comp. *Colorado History through the News (A Context of the Times):The Indian Wars of 1864 through the Sand Creek Massacre*. Aurora, Colo.: Picket of Ware, 1997.

White, Lonnie J., ed. *Chronicle of a Congressional Journey: The Doolittle Committee in the Southwest, 1865*. Boulder, Colo.: Pruett, 1975.

Woodward, Arthur. *The Denominators of the Fur Trade*. Pasadena, Calif.: Westernlore, 1970.

Wynkoop, Edward W. *The Tall Chief: The Unfinished Autobiography of Edward W. Wynkoop, 1856–1866*. Edited by Christopher B. Gerboth. Mongraph 9. Denver: Colorado Historical Society, 1993.

ARTICLES

Anderson, Adrienne. "The Archeology of Massed-Produced Footwear." *Historical Archaeology* 2 (1968): 56.

Ashley, Susan Riley. "Reminiscences of Colorado in the Early 'Sixties.'" *The Colorado Magazine* 13 (1936): 219–30.

Banks, Kimball M., and J. Signe Snortland. "Every Picture Tells a Story: Historic Images, Tipi Camps, and Archaeology." *Plains Anthropologist* 40, no. 152 (1995): 125–44.

Bloc, Augusta Hauck. "Lower Boulder and St. Vrain Valley Home Guards and Fort Junction." *The Colorado Magazine* 15 (1939): 186–91.

Brasser, Ted J. "The Tipi as an Element in the Emergence of Historic Plains Indian Nomadism." *Plains Anthropologist* 27, no. 98, pt. 1 (1982): 323–26.

Brown, Ian. "Historic Trade Bells." *The Conference on Historic Site Archaeology Papers 1975*, pt. 1, vol. 10 (1977): 69–82.

Burkey, Elmer R. "The Site of the Murder of the Hungate Family by Indians in 1864." *The Colorado Magazine* 12 (1935): 135–42.

Carey, Raymond G. "Colonel Chivington, Brigadier General Connor, and Sand Creek." *Denver Westerners Brand Book* 16 (1960): 105–35.

———. "The 'Bloodless Third' Regiment, Colorado Volunteer Cavalry." *The Colorado Magazine* 38 (1961): 275–300.

"Chivington in Colorado." *Masonic News-Digest*, n.d. [ca. 1950s].

Chivington, John M. "The Pet Lambs." *Masonic News-Digest*, n.d.

———. "Reminiscences." *Field and Farm*, February 25, 1888.

———. "To the People of Colorado: Synopsis of the Sand Creek Investigation." Denver: N.p., 1865.

"Colorado's Territorial Days." *The Trail* 1 (March 1909): 2–3.

Dormois, John T. "Chivington, Sand Creek." *Masonic News-Digest*, n.d.

———. "The Chivingtons." *Masonic News-Digest*, n.d.

———. "Chivington's Address on Sand Creek." *Masonic News-Digest*, n.d.

———. "'Friendly' (?) Indians." *Masonic News-Digest*, n.d.

Connor, Melissa, and Douglas D. Scott. "Metal Detector Use in Archaeology: An Introduction." *Historical Archaeology* 32, no. 4 (1998): 73–82.

Ellis, Elmer. "Colorado's First Fight for Statehood, 1865–1868." *The Colorado Magazine* 8 (January 1931): 23–30.

Fay, George E., ed. "Military Engagements between United States Troops and Plains Indians: Documentary Inquiry by the U.S. Congress." In *Occasional Publications in Anthropology: Ethnology Series* no. 26, pts. 1a–1b. Greeley: University of Northern Colorado, 1972.

Goodykoontz, Colin B. "Colorado as Seen by a Home Missionary, 1863–1868." *The Colorado Magazine* 12 (1935): 60–69.

Hafen, LeRoy. "Map of Early Trails, Forts, and Battlefields of Colorado." *Municipal Facts Magazine* 3 (March–April 1925): 17–18.

Halaas, David F. "'All the Camp Was Weeping': George Bent and the Sand Creek Massacre," *Colorado Heritage* (summer 1995): 2–17.

Hall, J. N. "Colorado's Early Indian Troubles as I View Them." *The Colorado Magazine* 15 (1938): 126–30.

Hanson, James. "Butcher Knives." *Museum of the Fur Trade Quarterly* 23, no. 3 (1987): 1–5.

———. "Identifying Open Kettles of Copper and Brass." *Museum of the Fur Trade Quarterly* 33, no. 2 (1997): 2–13.

———. "The Scalping Knife." *Museum of the Fur Trade Quarterly* 23, no. 1 (1987): 8–12.

———. "Sheet Iron Kettles." *Museum of the Fur Trade Quarterly* 28, no. 1, (1992): 2–6.

———. "Upper Missouri Arrow Points." *Museum of the Fur Trade Quarterly* 8, no. 4 (1972): 2–8.

Harmon, Dick. "Henry .44-Caliber." In *Archaeological Insights to the Custer Battle*, by Douglas D. Scott and Richard A. Fox Jr., 69–74. Norman: University of Oklahoma Press, 1987.

Hedren, Paul L. "Army Tincups on the Western Frontier." *Military Collector and Historian* 44, no. 2 (1992): 57–63.

Herzog, Lillie A. "History of Kiowa County." In *The Historical Encyclopedia of Colorado*, edited by Thomas S. Chamblin, 186–88. Denver: Colorado Historical Association, 1957.

Hewet, Edgar L. "Tom Tobin." *The Colorado Magazine* 23 (1946): 210–11.

Hurd, C. W. "The Chivington Massacre (Sand Creek Battle)." In *The Historical Encyclopedia of Colorado*, edited by Thomas S. Chamblin, 88–90. Denver: Colorado Historical Association, 1957.

Isern, Thomas D. "The Controversial Career of Edward W. Wynkoop." *The Colorado Magazine* 40 (1979): 1–18.

Kelsey, Harry. "Background to Sand Creek." *The Colorado Magazine* 45 (1968): 279–300.

Kehoe, Thomas F. "A Retrospectus and Commentary." In "From Microcosm to Macrocosms: Advances in Tipi Ring Investigation and Interpretation," edited by Leslie B. Davis. *Plains Anthropologist Memoir* 19 28, no. 102, pt. 2 (1983): 327–42.

Kinzer, James B. "The Invention of the Extractor: The Successful Winchester Repeating Rifle." *Gun Report* 28, no. 8 (1983): 13–16.

LeCompte, Janet. "Charles Autobees." *The Colorado Magazine* 35 (1958): 303.

Lees, William B. "When the Shooting Stopped the War Began." In *Look to the Earth: Historical Archaeology and the American Civil War*, edited by Clarence R. Geier Jr. and Susan E. Winter, 39–59. Knoxville: University of Tennessee Press, 1994.

Livermore, Marlin. "The Era of Fictitious Surveys: Part I." "Following in the Footsteps of a Fraudulent Survey: Part II." Canton, Mich.: P.O.B., 1991.

Lubers, H. L. "William Bent's Family and the Indians of the Plains." *The Colorado Magazine* 13 (1936): 19–22.

Metcalf, George "Notes on Two Paiute Burials and Associated Artifacts." *Museum of the Fur Trade Quarterly* 10, nos. 1–2 (1974): 2–22.

Mumey, Nolie. "John Milton Chivington: The Misunderstood Man." In *Denver Westerners Brand Book*, edited by Charles S. Ryland, 127–48. Denver: Westerners, 1956.

Myers, J. Jay. "The Notorious Fight at Sand Creek." *Wild West*, December 1988, 42–47.

Nankivell, John H. "Fort Garland, Colorado." *The Colorado Magazine* 16 (1939): 13–28.

Perrigo, Lynn I., ed. "Major Hal Sayr's Diary of the Sand Creek Campaign." *The Colorado Magazine* 15 (1938): 41–57.

Prentice, C. A. "Captain Silas S. Soule, a Pioneer Martyr." *The Colorado Magazine* 12 (1935): 224–28.

Sanford, Albert B., ed. "Life at Camp Weld and Fort Lyon in 1861–1862: An Extract from the Diary of Mrs. Byron N. Sanford." *The Colorado Magazine* 7 (July 1930): 132–39.

Sayre, Hal. "Early Central City Theatrical and Other Reminiscences." *The Colorado Magazine* 6 (1929): 47–53.

Shields, Lillian B. "Relations with the Cheyennes and Arapahoes in Colorado in 1861." *The Colorado Magazine* 4 (August 1927): 145–48.

Switzer, Ronald R. "Butcher Knives as Historical Sources." *Museum of the Fur Trade Quarterly* 8, no. 1 (1972): 5–7.

———. "Maynard Cartridges and Primers from the Steamboat *Bertrand*." *Military Collector and Historian* 24, no. 3 (1972): 85–87.

———. "Munitions on the Bertrand." *Archaeology* 25, no. 4 (1972): 250–55.

"That Chivington TV Program." *Masonic News-Digest*, n.d. [ca. 1950s].

Thompson, George W. "Experiences in the West." *The Colorado Magazine* 4 (1925): 175–79.

Tobin, Thomas J. "The Capture of the Espinosas." *The Colorado Magazine* 9 (1932): 59–66.

The Trail. Vol. 1 (nos. 5, 6, 12); vol. 2 (nos. 10, 12); vol. 3 (nos. 4, 12); vol. 4 (no. 1); vol. 8 (nos. 4, 12); vol. 15 (no. 3); vol. 20 (no. 5).

Whitacre, Christine. "The Search for the Site of the Sand Creek Massacre." *Prologue* 33, no. 2 (2001): 96–107.

"Why the Chivingtons?" *Masonic News-Digest*, n.d., [ca. 1950s].

Willard, James F. "The Tyler Rangers: The Black Hawk Company and the Indian Uprising of 1864." *The Colorado Magazine* 7 (1930): 147–52.

Wright, Arthur A. "Colonel John P. Slough and the New Mexico Campaign." *The Colorado Magazine* 39 (1962): 89–105.

Wroten, William M., Jr. "Colorado and the Advent of the Civil War." *The Colorado Magazine* 36 (1959): 174–86.

PERIODICALS

American Pioneer, n.d.

Army and Navy Journal, 1867

Colorado Prospector, 1969

Colorado Springs Gazette, 1904, 1906, 1908, 1921, 1923, 1924, 1932

Colorado Springs Telegraph/Gazette, 1884, 1886

The Denver Post, 1903, 1908, 1921, 1968

The Denver Republican, 1883

The Denver Times, 1883, 1905

(Colorado Springs) Gazette Telegraph, 1975

(Eads) Kiowa County Press, 1906, 1917, 1927, 1929, 1940, 1941

Lamar Daily News, 1950, 1994

Lamar Tri-State Daily News, 1963

Leadville Daily Chronicle, 1879

The (Central City, Colo.) Miner's Register, 1864, 1865

Montrose Press, 1937

The (Manhatten, Kans.) Nationalist, 1890

National Tribune, 1905

Poor's Manual of Railroads, 1868–75 (annual issues)

Pueblo Star Journal and Sunday Chieftain, 1968, 1994

Rocky Mountain News, 1867, 1868, 1876, 1893, 1904, 1923, 1947, 1963, 1967
(Pueblo, Colo.) Star Journal, 1948
St. Louis Globe-Democrat, 1876
(Denver) Westword, 1998
Winners of the West, 1925, 1926

MAPS AND PLATS

"Asher and Adams's Colorado." 1875. Denver Public Library, Western History Department.

Bent, George. Untitled diagram of the Cheyenne village and Sand Creek Massacre. Cheyenne/Arapaho Agency File, "Warfare," 1864–85, Indian Archives Division, Oklahoma Historical Society, Oklahoma City. Microfilm Roll 24.

Bent, George, and George Hyde. "Arapahoe [Cheyenne] Positions at Sand Creek." ca. 1905–14. Folder 1, George Bent–George Hyde Papers, Western History Collections, University of Colorado Library, Boulder.

———. "Arkansas River Area." ca. 1905–14. Folder 2, George Bent–George Hyde Papers, Western History Collections, University of Colorado Library, Boulder.

———. "Camp after Sand Creek & Trail." ca. 1905–14. Folder 4, George Bent–George Hyde Papers, Western History Collections, University of Colorado Library, Boulder.

———. "Map of Arkansas River Valley." ca. 1905–14. George Bent–George Hyde Papers, Western History Collections, University of Colorado Library, Boulder.

———. "Map of Arkansas River, Sand Creek, and Western Kansas." ca. 1905–14. George Bent–George Hyde Papers, Western History Collections, University of Colorado Library, Boulder.

———. "Sand Creek Area." ca. 1905–14. Folder 10, George Bent–George Hyde Papers, Western History Collections, University of Colorado Library, Boulder.

Bonsall, Samuel W. Map accompanying "Journal of the March of a Detachment of the Men Belonging to the Garrison of Fort Lyon, C.T., under the Command of Lieut. S. W. Bonsall, 3rd Infantry, from Old Fort Lyon C.T., to Cheyenne Wells, Pursuant to S.O.

No. 66 Hdqrs., Fort Lyon C.T., June 12, 1868." Record Group 177, National Archives, Chicago Branch Office.

"Center Line Survey." Union Pacific Railroad, ca. 1870. Bureau of Land Management, Colorado State Office, Denver.

"Cheyenne Wells" and "Kit Carson." Topographical maps. U.S. Geological Survey, 1890–91.

"Colton's Sectional & Topographical Map of Colorado." New York, 1872. Denver Public Library, Western History Department.

Ebert, Frederick J. "Map of Colorado Territory, Showing the System of Parks." Philadelphia, Jacob Monk, 1865. Annotated copy in Raymond G. Carey Collection, University of Denver.

"Hotchkiss Historical Railroad Map of Colorado." Rocky Mountain Railroad Club, 1913. Map No. 1178. Bureau of Land Management, Colorado State Office, Denver.

"Map of Colorado Territory, Compiled from Government Maps and Actual Surveys." Francis M. Case, Surveyor General of Colorado Territory. 37th Cong., 2d sess., 1861. S. Ex. Doc. 1.

"Map of Colorado Territory to Accompany Hollister's 'Mines of Colorado,' Corrected from the Public Surveys of 1866." Denver Public Library, Western History Department.

"Map of Utah and Colorado." Compiled under the direction of Brevet Colonel William E. Merrill. St. Louis, H. DeWerthern, 1869. Denver Public Library, Western History Department.

"North of Chivington, CO." U.S. Geological Survey Quadrangle, 7.5 Minute Series, 1982.

Ranching Settlement of East Central Colorado. Sheet 1, ca. 1898. Accession no. EP-74, M-92. Colorado Springs Pioneers Museum.

"Sand Creek Battlefield Area Map. Copy of blue print from old drawing made by John Baumbach, early settler of the area. From office of Co. Surveyor, Cheyenne Co., Colo., September 12, 1938." Office of County Surveyor, Cheyenne County, Colorado. Colorado Historical Society, Denver.

"State of Colorado." Compiled under the direction of Harry King, General Land Office, 1897. Bureau of Land Management, Colorado State Office, Denver.

"State of Colorado." Compiled under the direction of I. P. Berthrong, General Land Office, 1910. Bureau of Land Management, Colorado State Office, Denver.

Survey maps, Townships 16 and 17 South, Ranges 45, 46, 47 West.

General Land Office, 1880–81. Bureau of Land Management, Colorado State Office, Denver.

"Thayer's Sectional Map of Colorado Compiled from the Plats and Records of the Surveyor General's Office." Denver, 1871. Denver Public Library, Western History Department.

MISCELLANEOUS

Balster, Carolyn. "William Bent of Bent's Fort and the Sand Creek Massacre: An Oral Re-Creation." Transcript of an audio cassette, 1981. Las Animas Public Library.

Cheyenne Dog Soldiers: A Courageous Warrior Society. CD-ROM based on the work of Andrew E. Masich, David F. Halaas, and the Colorado Historical Society. Denver: Metaphor, n.d.

"Documents on the Sand Creek Massacre." *Archives of the West* <www.pb.org/weta/thewest/wpges640/sandcrk.htm>.

Hunt, William J., Jr. "Firearms and the Upper Missouri Fur Trade Frontier: Weapons and Related Materials from Fort Union Trading Post National Historic Site (23WI17), North Dakota." Ph.D. diss., University of Pennsylvania, 1989.

Roberts, Gary L. "An Address on the 'Sand Creek Massacre.'" Paper presented to the Colorado Historical Society, November 17, 1992. Transcribed from a recording by Clark Harbach, March 1993. Big Timbers Museum, Lamar, Colorado.

———. "Sand Creek: Tragedy and Symbol." Ph.D. diss., University of Oklahoma, 1984.

———. "The Sand Creek Massacre Site: A Report on Washington Sources," January 1999. Unpublished report prepared for the National Park Service. Ann Arbor, Mich.: University Microfilms.

INDEX

Adams, James J., 200–201n.41
Anthony, Scott, 12, 15, 16, 17, 20, 35, 56, 59, 201n.44; background of, 190n.13
Apache Canyon, New Mex. Terr., 8
Arapaho County, Colo. Terr., 191n.15
Arapaho Indians. *See* Southern Arapaho Indians
Archeology: artifact analysis, 82–98; artifact descriptions, 123–61; artifact types recovered, 71, 73, 80, 83–86; investigation methods, 71–73
Arkansas River, 6, 7, 11, 12, 15, 16, 20, 27, 28, 32, 33, 39, 49, 188n.5, 193n.27, 195n.5

Arkansas River Valley, 7, 8, 9, 23
Army Medical Museum, 46
Artillery deployment at Sand Creek, 27, 54–55, 58, 202n.48, 203n.50, 206nn.62–64

Ballou, Cornelius J., 200n.41
Barnum, Phineas T., 192n.22
Baumbach, John, 105
Bear River Massacre, Idaho Terr., 5, 24
Bear Robe, 22
Bear Tongue, 17
Bent, Charles, 33
Bent, George, 52, 53, 193n.27, 201n.41, 205n.56; background of, 33; and Sand Creek

Massacre account of, 33; site diagrams drawn by, 33–35, 41, 52, 54, 56, 60, 101–103, 195–96n.10, 199–200n.33, 202n.50, 204n.55; regional maps of, 40–41, 102, 196n.17

Bent, William, 33, 193n.27

Bent's Fort, Colo. Terr., 33, 39, 193n.27

Bertrand, steamboat munitions, 134

Big Man, 22

Bijou Basin, 16

Black Hills, 5, 190nn.13,14

Black Kettle, 7, 12, 14, 16, 17, 18, 27, 35, 40, 51, 86–87, 96–98, 99, 188n.5, 190n.13, 191n.16, 192n.22; background of, 190n.14; moves to Sand Creek, 15; seeks peace at Camp Weld, 14–15

Blake, Henry, 39

Bloomington, Ind., 45

Blunt, James G., 11–12

Bonsall, Samuel W., 60, 99, 197nn.18,19, 198n.28; background of, 45; strip map prepared by, 41–51, 68, 101, 103, 199n.29

Boulder History Museum, 30

Bowen, Chuck and Sherri, artifact collection activities of, 70–71, 86, 93, 95

Box Elder Creek, 11

Bozeman Trail, 23

Butterfield Stage Road, 50

Cahill, Luke, 46, 47, 50–51

California, 5, 8

Camp Fillmore, Colo. Terr., 16

Camp Weld, Colo. Terr., council at, 14–15, 192n.22

Cheyenne and Arapaho Tribes of Oklahoma (political entity), 26

Cheyenne Indians. *See* Southern Cheyenne Indians

Cheyenne Wells, Colo. Terr., 41, 45, 46, 47, 49, 50

Chicago Branch Center of the National Archives, 41

Chicago, Ill., 188n.7

Chivington, Colo., 32

Chivington, John M., 3, 31, 33, 35, 39, 53, 55, 56, 102, 105, 130, 190n.13, 191n.15, 192n.22, 196n.16, 201n.43, 206n.63; background of, 8–9, 189n.9; and dealings of, with Indians, 9–15; exaggerated casualty claims of, 20; movement of, from Fort Lyon, 17–18, 47; post-Sand Creek Massacre discrediting of, 21; preparations of, for attacking Cheyennes, 15–17; at Sand Creek Massacre, 17–20, 27–28, 58, 59

Chivington Irrigation Canal, 105–106, 207n.70

Civil War, 4, 45, 189nn.9,10

Coffin, Morse, 39, 89

Colorado, 27, 30

Colorado Historical Society, 30, 71

Colorado Terr., 3, 4, 6, 7, 8, 9, 11, 14, 23, 190n.13, 191nn.15,16,19

Comanche Indians, 5, 6, 7, 188n.5, 190n.14, 193n.27
Confederate Army, 4, 8, 9, 12, 189n.9
Connor, Patrick E., 5
Council Bluffs, Iowa, 189n.10
Council of Forty-Four, 22
Cramer, Joseph, 201n.43
Crooked Lance Society, 188n.5
Crow Indians, 6
Curtis, Samuel R., 9, 11, 12, 14, 15, 16, 17, 21; background of, 189n.10
Custer, George Armstrong, 89

Dailey, John Lewis, 39
Dakota (Sioux) uprising (Minnesota), 4, 7
Dawson, William F., 64; collecting activities of, 84, 137, 139
Denver, Colo. Terr., 8, 9, 11, 14, 15, 16, 20, 49, 189n.9, 190n.13, 191n.15
Department of Kansas, 9, 189n.10
Department of the Missouri, 8–9, 46, 189n.10
Department of the Northwest, 189n.10
District of Colorado, 8, 189n.9
District of the Upper Arkansas, 11
Dog Soldiers, 7, 9, 22
Doolittle, James R., 21
Downing, Jacob, 206n.62

Ellis, Richard, 64
Evans, John, 192n.22;
background of, 188n.7; dealings of, with Cheyennes and Arapahos, 7–15; post-Sand Creek dismissal of, as governor, 21; proclamations of, 12, 14

First Colorado Cavalry, 9, 12, 15, 16, 21, 39, 58, 192n.19; in Sand Creek Massacre, 18–20, 27–28, 56, 60, 105, 189n.9, 190n.13; weapons of, 202–203n.50
First Colorado Infantry, 189n.9, 191n.15
First Methodist Episcopal Church (Denver), 189n.9
Fort Laramie, Dak. Terr., 5
Fort Larned, Kans., 8, 9, 11, 12, 64, 190n.13
Fort Leavenworth, Kans., 46
Fort Lewis State College, 28
Fort Lyon, 12, 14, 15, 16, 20, 27, 31, 32, 33, 35, 39, 41, 45, 46, 47, 48, 50, 104, 190n.13, 191n.15, 192n.22, 195nn.5,8, 196n.16
Fort Riley, Kans., 9, 15
Fort Union, Dakota Terr., 88
Fort Union, New Mex. Terr., 45
Fort Wallace, Kans., 12, 45, 46
Fort Wise, Colo. Terr., 195n.5
Fremont's Orchard, Colo. Terr., 9

General Land Office, 30, 32
Geomorphology, 66–68
Geophysics, techniques and investigation, 81–82, 209n.13

Glorieta Pass, New Mex. Terr., 8, 190n.13
Grant, Ulysses S., 45
Great Lakes, 5
Great Plains, 25
Great Sioux War, 23
Greenwood, Alfred B., 199n.28
Greenwood, William H., 199n.28

Hancock, Winfield Scott, 89
Haynes, J. H., depredation claim of, 87, 163–64
Hughes, Norman, 206n.64
Hungate family, 11, 14
Hyde, George E., 40

Idaho, 192n.19
Idaho Terr., 192n.19
Illinois, 188n.5, 189n.9, 191n.19
Indiana, 188n.7
Indian Terr., 4, 9, 190n.14
Ingram, A.J., 105
Iowa, 189n.10, 191n.16

Joint Committee on the Conduct of the War, 21

Kansas, 5, 6, 9, 11, 12, 27, 189n.9, 190n.13
Kansas Pacific Railroad, 46, 50, 199n.28
Kern, August, artifacts found, 140
Kiowa–Apache Indians, 5, 188n.5, 190n.14, 191n.15
Kiowa County, Colo., 27, 28
Kiowa Indians, 5, 6, 7, 11, 46, 188n.5, 190n.14, 193n.27

Lakota Indians, 5, 6, 11, 23, 24, 25
Lamar, Colorado, 12, 27, 32
Las Animas, Colo., 195n.5
Leadville, Colo. Terr., 190n.13
Left Hand, 12, 15; and Arapaho camp at Sand Creek, 17, 22, 204n.55; background of, 191n.16
Lester, Blanche Squires, gift of, 68
Limon, Colo., 32
Lincoln, Abraham, 9, 188n.7, 192n.22, 193n.27
Little Bear, 52, 53, 201n.41
Little Blue River, 11
Little Raven, 7, 15, 188n.5, 191n.16
Lone Bear, 204n.55

Marias River Massacre, 24
McFaul, Michael, 66
Metal detecting, as archeological technique, 208n.11
Minnesota, 4, 5
Missouri, 9, 12, 189n.9
Missouri River, 5, 6
Montana, 6
Montana Terr., 24, 192n.19

National Anthropological Archives (Smithsonian Institution), 46
National Park Service, 12, 26, 30
Nebraska, 6, 11, 189n.9, 191n.16
New Chicago, Colo., 202n.47

New Mexico Terr., 4, 189n.9, 190n.13, 191n.15
New York, 189n.10, 190n.13
New York City, N.Y., 192n.22
North Bend of Sand Creek, 32, 33
North Platte River Valley, 23
Northern Arapaho Tribe (political entity), 26
Northern Cheyenne Tribe (political entity), 26

Ohio, 188n.7, 189nn.9,10
One Eye, 17, 22, 204n.55; background of, 192n.22
Owl Woman, 33

Palmer, Lucian, 39
Pawnee Fork, Kans., camp destroyed, 89; camp goods destroyed, 90–91, 177–79
Pawnee Indians, 5
Pea Ridge, Ark., 189n.10
Pennsylvania, 190–91n.15, 191n.19
Peyton, Colo., 32
Piegan Indians, 24
Pine Ridge Reservation, S.Dak., 24
Platte River, 5, 6, 11
Platte River Valley, 7, 8, 9
Prowers, John, 192n.22
Public Law 105–243. See Sand Creek Massacre Site Study Act of 1998
Pueblo, Colo. Terr., 16

Relic collecting, on Sand Creek, 68–71

Republican River, 16, 23
Rocky Mountains, 5
Root, Preston, 69
Rush Creek, 32, 39, 40, 47, 48

Sand Creek, 15, 16, 17, 18, 19, 20, 27, 28, 31, 32, 33, 35, 39, 40, 46, 47, 48, 50, 52, 53, 54, 55, 57, 59, 60, 62, 99, 102, 103, 104, 105, 187n.1, 190n.13, 196n.16, 199nn.28,29, 205n.58
Sand Creek Massacre, 3–4, 17–20, 60, 99, 101, 188n.5, 189nn.9,10, 191n.15, 192n.22, 202n.50; aftermath of, 20–21, 59; casualties of, 19; evidence-based troop and Indian movement scenario, 56–59, 103–105; influence of, on military and Indian policy, 24; opening action of, 17–19, 54, 58; sand pits phase of, 19–20, 54–55; significance of, 22–25
Sand Creek Massacre site, 30, 31–62, 99–101; boundary of, 60–62; sand pits area of, 53–55, 103; village area of, 52–53, 101–105
Sand Creek Massacre Site Study Act of 1998 (Public Law 105–243), 26
Sand Hill, 17, 204n.55
Santa Fe, New Mex. Terr., 191n.15
Santa Fe Trail, 5
Sayre, Hal, 39
Schneider, William, 70

Second Colorado Volunteer Infantry, 191n.19

Second Iowa Infantry, 189n.10

Seventh Infantry, 189n.10

Sheridan, Kans., 199n.28

Sheridan, Philip H., 24, 46

Sherman, William T., 24, 41, 45, 46, 48, 50, 101

Shoshone Indians, 5, 24

Shoup, George L., 16, 17, 56; background of, 191–92n.19

Sixth U.S. Veteran Volunteers, 45

Smith, John, 196n.16, 200n.41

Smoky Hill Line of Kansas Pacific Railroad, 45

Smoky Hill River, 11, 12, 16, 20, 28, 33, 35, 59, 192n.22

Soil Conservation Service, 35, 50

Solomon's Fork, Kans., 6

Soule, Silas, 60

South Bend of Sand Creek, 32, 33, 39, 48, 56, 60, 101–105

South Dakota, 6

Southern Arapaho Indians, 3–4, 5, 11, 25, 27, 28, 30, 190n.14, 191n.15,16, 199n.28; annuity requests of, 165–77; and camp at Sand Creek, 17–20, 52, 55, 204n.55; early history of, 5–6; effects of Sand Creek among, 22; go to Fort Lyon, 15; relationship with Colorado territorial officials, 8–15; relationship of, with whites, 6–7

Southern Cheyenne Indians, 3–4, 24, 25, 27, 28, 30, 53, 102, 190n.14, 191n.15, 192n.22, 199n.28; annuity request of 165–77; casualties in Sand Creek Massacre, 17–20; consequences of Sand Creek Massacre among, 22–23; early history of, 5–6; early relationship of, with whites, 6–7; go to Sand Creek, 15; raiding activities of, 11; relationship with Arapahos, 6; relationship with Colorado territorial officials, 8–15; village at Sand Creek, 17, 204n.55

South Platte River, 9

South Platte River Valley, 23

Spotted Crow, 22

Squires, George, 68

Starving Bear, 9

State of Colorado (political entity), 26

St. Louis, Mo., 46

Summit Springs, battle of, 90; camp goods captured at, 90–91, 180–81

Texas, 4

Third Colorado Cavalry, 14, 16, 21, 56; organization of, 16; in Sand Creek Massacre, 18–20, 27–28, 105, 189n.9, 192n.19; weapons of, 183–85, 202–203n.50, 208n.12

Third U.S. Infantry, 45, 46

Three Forks, Colo. Terr., 48–50

Treaty of Fort Laramie, 6, 7, 188n.5

Treaty of Fort Wise, 7, 188n.5, 199n.28

Treaty of Medicine Lodge,
188n.5
Treaty of the Little Arkansas,
21
Trinidad, Colo. Terr., 45

Union Pacific Railroad,
189n.10
*United States Army
Regulations*, 41, 196–97n.18
United States Geological
Survey, 30
University of Denver, 188n.7
Upper Arkansas Reservation, 8
Upper Water Valley, Colo.,
202n.47
Ute Indians, 5

Walnut Creek, 12
War Bonnet, 17, 22;
background of, 192n.22
War Department, 11

War with Mexico, 189n.10
Washington, D.C., 9, 14, 15, 46,
188n.5, 192n.22, 193n.27
Washita River, 190n.14; battle
of, 89; camp goods destroyed
at, 89–91, 179–80
Werner, Fred, 69
West Point, N.Y., 189n.10
White Antelope, 7, 17, 18, 22,
188n.5
Wilson, Luther, 17, 56
Wounded Knee Massacre, 24,
25
Wynkoop, Edward W., 12, 14,
15, 17, 190n.13, 192n.22;
background of, 190–91n.15
Wyoming, 6

Yellowstone River, 5
Yellow Wolf, 22; background
of, 193n.27